MORNING & EVENING
DEVOTIONAL

Be
Still
AND
Know

BroadStreet
PUBLISHING

BroadStreet Publishing Group LLC
Savage, MN, USA
Broadstreetpublishing.com

Be Still and Know (Morning & Evening)

978-1-4245-5842-1 (faux)
978-1-4245-5843-8 (e-book)

Devotional entries compiled by Michelle Winger.

Design by Chris Garborg | garborgdesign.com
Edited by Michelle Winger | literallyprecise.com

Printed in China.

19 20 21 22 23 24 25   7 6 5 4 3 2 1

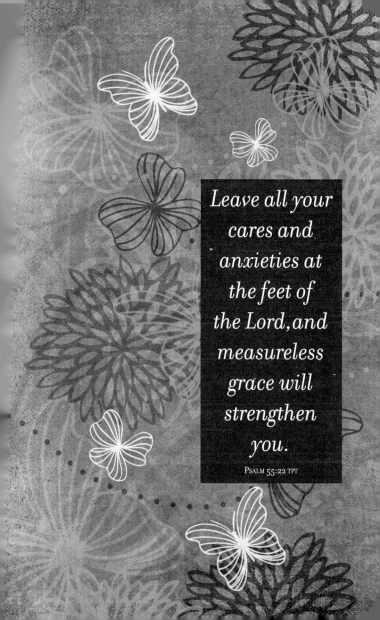

Leave all your cares and anxieties at the feet of the Lord, and measureless grace will strengthen you.

PSALM 55:22 TPT

Introduction

In the busyness of life, it's easy to forget that we need God in every moment.

Be still for a while today and find rest as you reflect on God's Word. Draw near to him confidently, boldly making your requests known. Be assured of his unwavering love for you. Unashamedly ask him for strength, joy, peace, and hope.

God loves to meet you wherever you are. Let him fill you with everything you need for each new day.

Something New

"I am about to do something new.
See, I have already begun! Do you not see it?
I will make a pathway through the wilderness.
I will create rivers in the dry wasteland."

ISAIAH 43:19 NLT

Whether you have generated a color-coded list of goals, dreams, and an execution plan for the next year, or you've banned resolutions and vowed to make this just another day on the calendar, the clean slate represented by the first day of a new year is filled with an undeniable air of expectation.

The excitement of new decor or the latest gadget pales in comparison to the promise of a new beginning. Deep down inside, there is a part of us which thinks, "This could be my year!"

Change that statement today to say in faith, "This *is* my year!"

Lord, thank you for letting me start new today and new this year.
I pray for faith to see what you have already begun.

"Behold, I will do something new,
Now it will spring forth;
Will you not be aware of it?
I will even make a roadway in the wilderness,
Rivers in the desert."

Isaiah 43:19 NASB

It might not feel like it today, but it is your year. This day, and every one that follows, is yours. It is yours to choose who and how to love, to serve, and even to be.

The choice you made in reading this page represents the choice to take this journey in the company of your heavenly Father. This is how you give him space to create pathways and rivers in those dry areas of your life. That is a beautiful place to start the year.

Lord, thank you for remaining faithful to me today. Help me to make space for you to create paths and rivers in areas that I feel tired and dry.

What new thing would you like to do this year? What pathways do you need God to clear?

Continual Praise

*From the rising of the sun to its going down
The LORD's name is to be praised.*

PSALM 113:3 NKJV

What would it look like to be a woman who praises God from the time she awakens each morning until the time she falls asleep each night? Not only would we be pleasing God as we worship him constantly, but we would also effect an incredible change in our personal outlook.

As we go about our day, we can look for reasons to praise God. Out of an overflow of a heart of thankfulness, we will share God's goodness with those around us and give them a reason to praise his name as well.

God, I praise you for your love for me. Help me to be a woman who praises you all day, every day. Cultivate in me an appreciation of your goodness and a longing to worship you constantly.

Everywhere—from east to west—praise the name of the LORD.

PSALM 113:3 NLT

Intentional, continual praise can only naturally result in intentional, continual joy. When we choose to look at each moment as a moment in which to be thankful and worshipful, then we will find in each moment beauty, joy, and satisfaction.

As we reflect on the day, let us do so with a heart of praise. Let us choose to remember how God's goodness echoed in everything around us.

God, I see your goodness all around me. Tonight I choose to remember all that I have to be thankful for. I choose to see your beauty and grace in all circumstances. You alone are worthy of my praise, and I direct my heart of thanksgiving toward you now. Be praised in my life, God!

Take a moment to reflect on the goodness of God shown to you today.

What He Says

Mary responded, "I am the Lord's servant.
May everything you have said about me come true."
And then the angel left her.

LUKE 1:38 NLT

In a memorable scene from a movie about teenage girls, a teacher asks a gymnasium full of young women to close their eyes and raise their hands if they've ever said anything bad about another girl. Virtually every hand is raised. Sadly, we are often even harder on ourselves.

In addition to the amazing news that Mary would bear God's Son, the angel who visits her in Luke 1 also tells Mary of her goodness, of her favor in God's eyes. Mary was a teenage girl. Chances are, she'd heard—and thought—something less than kind about herself on more than one occasion. Consider her brave, beautiful response. Mary chose to believe God's Word instead of her own.

God, I thank you that your words are truth. I begin boldly declaring that I am your servant. Help me to honor you today.

"I am the Lord's servant," Mary answered.
"May your word to me be fulfilled."
Then the angel left her.

LUKE 1:38 NIV

Mary understood the truth of God's Word and she had faith in his unfailing goodness. She also declared truth about who and what God had called her to be—his servant with a very special task.

Are you self-critical? If asked to describe yourself, what would you say? Now think of someone who loves you. What do they say about you? Decide today to let their words— and God's—be the truth. Join Mary in saying to God, "May everything you have said about me come true."

God, even though I may have let you down today, I know that your Word never fails. As I prepare for bed tonight, help me to dwell on the truth of who you have called me to be. I am here to serve you.

What truth about yourself do you need to declare this evening?

Something New

"I am about to do something new.
See, I have already begun! Do you not see it?
I will make a pathway through the wilderness.
I will create rivers in the dry wasteland."

ISAIAH 43:19 NLT

Whether you have generated a color-coded list of goals, dreams, and an execution plan for this year, or you've banned resolutions and vowed to make this just another year, the clean slate represented by a new year is filled with an undeniable air of expectation. Deep down inside, there is a part of us which thinks, "This could be my year!"

Guess what? It is your year. This day, and every one that follows, is yours. It is yours to choose who and how to love, to serve, and even to be. And the choice you made in spending time with God represents the choice to take this journey in his company. That is a beautiful place to start.

Heavenly Father, I give you this year. I ask that you would help me keep you in the forefront of my mind as I make decisions and plans. I want to seek your advice in everything I set my hand to.

"Behold, I am doing a new thing;
now it springs forth,
do you not perceive it?
I will make a way in the wilderness
and rivers in the desert."

ISAIAH 43:19 ESV

The excitement of a new bauble or gadget pales in comparison to the promise of a new beginning. What a blessing to know you can start over each year, each month, each day with a God who makes a way in your wilderness. He creates refreshing rivers in your desert.

Watch closely for the new things God is bringing into your life this year. Choose to spend time gleaning wisdom and encouragement from his Word each day.

God, you have new things for me this year, and I trust you to reveal them to me in your perfect time. As I go to sleep tonight, help me rest peacefully, knowing your plans for me are good.

What new things can you imagine God doing for you this year?

Stuck

The Sovereign Lord is my strength;
he makes my feet like the feet of a deer,
he enables me to tread on the heights.

HABAKKUK 3:19 NIV

"Local authorities are reporting blizzard conditions on the Interstate…" Did your pulse just quicken, your muscles tense? No one likes to feel stuck, and blinding snow and unmoving vehicles on every side can cause even the most rational, laid-back person to imagine leaping from the car and running over rooftops and across hoods, action hero style. What a fun way to test out the traction on your new winter boots. Or not. Anyway, stuck is stuck, right?

If you are feeling stuck this morning, wanting to move but not sure how, remember that God is your strength, able to move you to greater heights.

God, I feel a little stuck in certain areas of my life. I give these areas over to you this morning, and ask for your strength to guide me along the right path.

The Lord God is my strength.
He makes me like a deer that does not stumble
so I can walk on the steep mountains.

HABAKKUK 3:19 NCV

Have you been able to reflect on areas that you feel stuck in? A job that doesn't utilize our gifts, a relationship that is more take than give, a habit that is edging toward addiction. Unlike that snow-covered freeway-turned-parking-lot, there is a direction to turn when circumstances have you feeling boxed in. Turn your face toward God; let him fill you with the strength to move.

Where are you stuck right now? Professionally, personally, or perhaps in your prayer life, is there an area where you've simply stopped moving? Ask God for surefooted strength, and then go where he leads you.

Lord Jesus, help me to accept things in my life where I just need to persevere. Give me the strength to keep going. If there are things that I need to take action on, make me surefooted and courageous. Build my strength as I rest in you tonight.

In what areas do you need to rely on God's strength to keep going? What areas do you need to courageously move on from?

Fresh and New

*If anyone is in Christ, the new creation has come:
The old has gone, the new is here!*

2 CORINTHIANS 5:17 NIV

When we accept Christ as our Savior, we get to start over, as if from scratch. Our old, ugly lives and selfish ways are forgotten, and we are brand new. Oh goodness, aren't you thankful for it?

We all have plenty of days we could happily erase: memories of bad choices we made and poor decisions followed through. But we can give those regrets to God and start again—every day if we need to!

Lord, I'm once again in awe of the depth of your love for me. Thank you for the gift of forgiveness and for making me fresh and new. Help me to live today differently than I did yesterday.

Anyone who belongs to Christ has become a new person.
The old life is gone; a new life has begun!

2 Corinthians 5:17 NLT

Every day, we get to stand before our King and hold our heads up high, knowing we are forgiven and clean. There's no checklist of our sins and faults, no remembering the worst of our mistakes.

There is nothing in this world that can take away past regrets. Only the tender love of our Father's heart flowing down in abundance upon us, can make us new.

God, I receive your newness today. Thank you for washing me with your grace, filling me with your life, and giving me hope for an even better tomorrow. Watch over me as I rest tonight and fill me with your peace.

How do you feel when you think of God's love washing over you and making you new?

The Father's Love

> *"If a man has a hundred sheep but one of the sheep gets lost, he will leave the other ninety-nine on the hill and go to look for the lost sheep. I tell you the truth, if he finds it he is happier about that one sheep than about the ninety-nine that were never lost."*

MATTHEW 18:12-13 NCV

Regardless of how beautifully or how imperfectly your earthly father showed his love, your heavenly Father's love is utterly boundless. Rest in that thought a moment. There is nothing you can do to change how he feels about you. Nothing.

We spend so much time trying to make ourselves more lovable, from beauty regimens to gourmet baking, to being there for pretty much everyone. It's easy to forget we are already perfectly loved. Our Father loves us more than we can imagine, and he would do anything for us. Remember that throughout your day.

Lord, thank you that you care so much about me. At times, I have been that one lost sheep and you have come to find me. Thank you for your love for me.

"What do you think? If any man has a hundred sheep, and one of them has gone astray, does he not leave the ninety-nine on the mountains and go and search for the one that is straying? If it turns out that he finds it, truly I say to you, he rejoices over it more than over the ninety-nine which have not gone astray."

MATTHEW 18:12-13 NASB

You might have had a rough day or a really good day. Remember that your heavenly Father has been loving you throughout your day.

Who do you love most fiercely, most protectively, most desperately here on earth? What would you do for them? Know that it's a mere fraction, nearly immeasurable, of what God would do for you. Spend some time thanking him for his great love.

Father, I know that you will always search me out, no matter where I try to go. Help me to stay close to you so I can always bring you joy. Let me rest in your care for me as I go to sleep.

Are there areas of your life that you feel lost in? Let Jesus take care of those places.

All in Love

Let all that you do be done in love.

1 CORINTHIANS 16:14 ESV

Humans are emotional beings. We are motivated and impacted by our feelings and those of others. We speak harshly in anger, embark on adventures because of curiosity, lash out when embarrassed, and give to those in need through empathy. Emotion is a gift, but if we allow ourselves to be overly driven by our human passions, they will misguide us.

As followers of Jesus, we can check our hearts and continually remind ourselves to act in love. Everything God does is motivated and backed by overwhelming love for us, and that's the example we should follow.

Lord, love doesn't come naturally to me in every situation. Thank you for enabling me to do all things out of love through your love in me. Help me to always check my heart before I react to any situation, so I respond and act in love.

Do everything in love.

1 CORINTHIANS 16:14 NIV

We can't trust our emotions to drive us—they are too unpredictable. But we can choose to do everything in love. Acting in love is always the right course of action; it neutralizes any sinful attitude or motivation.

The positive effect of love on our lives is undeniable; love brings us closer to God and more into his likeness. As we become more like him, we are able to choose love over other emotions that spring up so quickly.

God, I know I can show love to those around me when I choose to love like you do. It isn't always easy, but I know it's what you want me to do. I choose love when I'm tired, stressed, annoyed, and angry. I choose love this evening because you chose to love me.

How do you take control over your emotions and choose to love?

Compassion

Share each other's burdens,
and in this way obey the law of Christ.

GALATIANS 6:2 NLT

Advertisers know your secret. They know the sight of a lost puppy, starving child, or grieving mother tugs at something deep inside your heart, giving you a powerful desire to do something—anything. They are counting on it.

When we accepted Christ, and he gave us his Holy Spirit, we became aware of his heart. Specifically, we became aware of what breaks his heart. The more in tune we are with him, the more those things break our own hearts.

God, I want to be in tune with you today. Guide me to have compassion on those in need.

Bear one another's burdens,
and so fulfill the law of Christ.

GALATIANS 6:2 ESV

Jesus was pretty clear: "Feed my sheep," he commanded. His actions said the same; he fed them by the thousands. He wept for Lazarus' sisters in their grief. He wept for those who did not recognize him. He wept for us. He took on our burden of sin, the full weight of it, so we might live and know his heart.

What breaks your heart? Do you find yourself aching at the sight of an orphaned child, a homeless mother, a neglected animal? As you rest in the stillness of another night, allow yourself to think and pray for those who need your compassion.

Lord, I pray for those who have come to mind tonight. Let me show them compassion in the days ahead. Holy Spirit, comfort, protect, and show these precious ones your love.

How can you act on compassion and obey Christ?

Powerful Kindness

I will tell about the LORD's kindness
and praise him for everything he has done.
I will praise the LORD for the many good things he has given us
and for his goodness to the people of Israel.
He has shown great mercy to us
and has been very kind to us.

ISAIAH 63:7 NCV

The Bible says that the kindness of the Lord leads people to repentance: not his anger, not his wrath—his kindness. There is power in kindness: a power that moves souls and changes lives. We can subconsciously equate kindness with weakness, but it's the exact opposite.

We can trust God and turn to him often, confident that his mercy is present, even in suffering.

God, I sometimes miss your point. I assume that you're angry with me or that I've distanced myself too far from you, but your arms are always open wide to me. Help me to walk in this truth today.

I will tell of the LORD's unfailing love.
I will praise the LORD for all he has done.
I will rejoice in his great goodness to Israel,
which he has granted according to his mercy and love.

ISAIAH 63:7 NLT

The Israelites turned their backs on God too many times to count. But what we see time and time again in their story is that God was still good. He showed them mercy; he gave them good things. He was kind to them.

Of course, Israel wasn't spared consequences and trials, but the people knew God's promises and trusted him. In the same way, we can trust God and turn to him often, confident that his mercy is present, even in suffering.

God, no matter how many times I turn my back on you, you're still constant in mercy. Thank you for your kindness and your unfailing love for me.

Can you see God's goodness in your life even through the consequences of your choices?

Growth

I do not mean that I am already as God wants me to be.
I have not yet reached that goal, but I continue
trying to reach it and to make it mine.

PHILIPPIANS 3:12 NCV

Do you remember when you realized you had stopped growing? Your height was going to be your height, your shoe size your shoe size. This second fact was pretty thrilling for many of us; no more hearing Mom say, "That's too much to spend on shoes you'll outgrow in a few months." And so the shoe collection began.

Our goal is to become mature in Christ. Maturity brings a sureness to your faith and steady trust that Christ is working through you. You might not reach this goal today, but you are on your way.

Lord, thank you that you allow me to grow in you each day. Help me to be a little more mature in you today than I was yesterday.

Not that I have already obtained this or have already
reached the goal; but I press on to make it my own,
because Christ Jesus has made me his own.

PHILIPPIANS 3:12 NRSV

Not too long after our bones finish growing, we realize the
real growth is just getting started. As we become young
adults, friendships either deepen or fade away as we begin to
figure out who we are. No matter what our ages today, most of
us are still working on that. When we are growing in Christ,
it's a process that never really ends.

Scripture says this is the way he made you, to grow in your
humanity, becoming physically and spiritually mature.
Reflect on your growth tonight and recognize where he is
stretching and challenging you.

God, I want to continue to grow in my knowledge and
understanding of you and your ways. Help me to listen to you and
to heed your advice so I can reach the goals you have set for me.

How does knowing that God wants to help you become your
best inspire you to attempt it this year?

Fear Factor

When I am afraid, I will put my trust in you.
I praise God for what he has promised.
I trust in God, so why should I be afraid?

PSALM 56:3-4, NLT

David did not hesitate to admit when he was afraid! King Saul
was pursuing him and so great was his terror that he ran to
the enemy's camp—an unlikely place to find refuge. It was
bold and risky, but perhaps King Achish would not recognize
him, or might consider him a deserter and an asset.

Unfortunately, David was found out, reported to the king,
and, motivated by more fear, acted like a mad man and was
sent away. Fear causes us to do things we normally would not.
Think about that as you go about your day.

*God, I am afraid today, but like David I am going to trust you! I
don't have to worry about anything because I know that whatever
you allow in my life is designed for my good. I rest in that
knowledge today.*

When I'm afraid, I put my trust in you.
I trust in God. I praise his word.
I trust in God. I am not afraid.

PSALM 56:3-4 NIRV

It wasn't long before David readjusted his thinking and put his trust once again in God. It is interesting that he says, "When I am afraid," not "If I am afraid." David knew he would experience fear again.

Fear is a human response, and unless counteracted by trust, is destructive at best. What are you afraid of this evening? Are you magnifying a concern into an impossible mountain of what ifs? Trust Jesus. Remember his promises to you. No matter the outcome, he is in charge!

God, your promises are good. I don't need to be afraid of anything because I trust in you. You are the powerful, all-knowing God so I have no reason to be afraid tonight. Help me to remember that when fear knocks at my door.

What are you afraid of today? Can you choose to trust God instead?

No Words

*Then they sat on the ground with him for seven days and nights.
No one said a word to Job, for they saw that his suffering was too
great for words.*

JOB 2:13 NLT

We recognize Job as a person who suffered greatly. It might
be easier to identify with Job because we have all experienced
suffering in our lives. But what about being a friend of a
person who is suffering?

We love to talk, don't we? Words of encouragement, words
of comfort, words of advice. Even if you are the quiet type,
you know someone who is rarely at a loss for words. It can
be all too easy to try and talk, but sometimes we just need to
be near to those who need it. As you go about your day today,
remember that sometimes your support is shown in actions
not words.

*Jesus, help me to know when you just want me to be silent and sit
with those who are suffering. Show me the needs around me today.*

Then they sat down on the ground with him for seven days and seven nights with no one speaking a word to him, for they saw that his pain was very great.

JOB 2:13 NASB

Occasionally, there really are no words. Someone you love is hurting, and you truly don't know what to say. Your presence says it all. Know that, in those moments you feel lost for words, if God occupies the central place in your heart, he'll make your heart known.

How easy or difficult would it be for you to simply be with someone in their sorrow and not try to "fix" them? Spend some time tonight reflecting on the friends who have done exactly that for you and be thankful for the support of good people.

God, I thank you that I can support my friends by just being near. Help me to be close to those that need me the most.

Do you know someone who would be blessed by the silent, loving presence of someone who loves them?

Twirling with Joy

You changed my sorrow into dancing.
You took away my clothes of sadness,
and clothed me in happiness.
I will sing to you and not be silent.
LORD, my God, I will praise you forever.

PSALM 30:11-12 NCV

Abandoned, abused single mother finds love, purpose, and healing. That's a movie most of us would watch. Who doesn't love a good restoration story? When God heals broken places and redeems lost situations, our hearts swell with possibility. If he can restore her life, he can surely come in and fix mine.

It's true. The mourners will dance, clothed in happiness. Voices silenced by sadness will sing loudest songs of praise. And you, regardless of what you face today, will be there: twirling with joy, singing your heart out. You will be there.

Lord, like a dancer spinning with grace, you turn things around. You restore what is broken and redeem what is lost. I praise you for your goodness. Hear my voice, delight in my dance—it is all for you.

You turned my loud crying into dancing.
You removed my clothes of sadness and dressed me with joy.
So my heart will sing your praises. I can't keep silent.
LORD, my God, I will praise you forever.

PSALM 30:11-12 NIRV

When we give God a chance to change our outlook for the day, he will gladly step in and do it. We don't need to focus on our sadness. In fact, we should be shouting his praises from the ends of the earth.

Even when we feel surrounded by grief, we can trust God to change us into our party clothes! There is an abundance of joy in his presence. We just need to spend time there to find it.

God, tonight I choose to change into the party clothes you have laid out for me. I take off my sadness and put on your joy instead. I lift my voice to you now and proclaim your goodness. I twirl around in joy and thanksgiving for all you have done in my life.

Thank God for the joy he has dressed you with today.

Truly Awesome

By the word of the LORD the heavens were made,
their starry host by the breath of his mouth.
He gathers the waters of the sea into jars;
he puts the deep into storehouses.

PSALM 33:6-7 NIV

"These cookies are awesome!"

"Wow, you look awesome today!"

The word awesome has slipped into American speech so thoroughly, we may have lost sight of its true meaning. The cookies, though delicious, probably don't inspire overwhelming reverence. Your friend looks gorgeous, but you're not truly taken aback, knocked to your knees. Only God does that.

Reread the Scripture above out loud, lingering over its meaning. Ponder all he has done and will do.

Lord God, I am in awe of you. When I consider the universe, formed by your breath, and the oceans as merely jars in your storehouse, I can barely contain my amazement. Truly, you alone are worthy of my praise.

34

The sky was made at the LORD's command.
By the breath from his mouth, he made all the stars.
He gathered the water of the sea into a heap.
He made the great ocean stay in its place.

PSALM 33:6-7 NCV

As you think about all the things you may have considered awesome today, compare each of those to the Creator of the Universe. They pale in comparison.

God, your Father, can hold an ocean in his hand, and yet he knows every hair on your head. He lovingly anticipates every move you make. He delights in you, and that is truly awesome.

God, you are awesome. There is no end to your goodness, your faithfulness, and your wisdom. The fact that you love me in all my imperfection is more than I can fathom. Let that thought rest over me as I wind down for the evening.

What have you seen today that you would consider truly awesome?

Follow the Arrow

Your ears shall hear a word behind you, saying,
"This is the way, walk in it,"
Whenever you turn to the right hand
Or whenever you turn to the left.

ISAIAH 30:21 NKJV

Decisions, decisions. It seems a week never goes by without our needing to make at least one important choice. Whether job related, relationship motivated, or something as seemingly innocent as how to spend a free Friday, wouldn't it be nice to have an arrow pointing us in the right direction—especially if we are in danger of making a wrong turn?

According to the Word, we have exactly that. When we truly desire to walk the path God sets us on, and when we earnestly seek his voice, he promises to lead us in the right direction. Stay on his path today!

Lord, I need your help with some important decisions today.
Let my ears hear your voice to guide me in the right direction.

Your own ears will hear him.
Right behind you a voice will say,
"This is the way you should go,"
whether to the right or to the left.

ISAIAH 30:21 NLT

Consider the decisions you have had to make today. What decisions will you need to make tomorrow? Whether you choose the right or the left, know that God is able to guide you into his best for the situation.

You might not get it right every time, but his ever-present Spirit is there, ready to put you back on the path each time you wander off.

Holy Spirit, thank you that you are the guiding voice behind me.
Help me to become more aware of what you are speaking to me.

What guidance do you need right now? To whom are you turning for guidance?

All Comfort

All praise to God, the Father of our Lord Jesus Christ. God is our merciful Father and the source of all comfort. He comforts us in all our troubles so that we can comfort others. When they are troubled, we will be able to give them the same comfort God has given us. For the more we suffer for Christ, the more God will shower us with his comfort through Christ.

2 CORINTHIANS 1:3-5 NLT

There are many things in this world we tend to look to for comfort. Sometimes it might be food, a hot shower, an air-conditioned room, family, friends, television, a good book... the list is endless.

The Word of God says our merciful Father is the source of all comfort. His promise is to comfort us in all of our troubles. How often do we look elsewhere for comfort when our true comforter is the one who created us and knows our every need?

Oh Father, I pray that today I would look to you to be my source of all comfort. I pray you would teach me to receive my comfort from you and in turn be a comfort to others.

Praise be to the God and Father of our Lord Jesus Christ. God is the Father who is full of mercy and all comfort. He comforts us every time we have trouble, so when others have trouble, we can comfort them with the same comfort God gives us. We share in the many sufferings of Christ. In the same way, much comfort comes to us through Christ.

2 Corinthians 1:3-5 NCV

Many things may appear to offer us comfort throughout the day. But when we really stop and think about it, our only real comfort comes from the one who loves us unconditionally.

While some things may satisfy our need for comfort and peace in the moment, they never last, and we are once again on the lookout for a new source. If we can learn to go to God first, we will be comforted in a way that is undeniable, and lasting!

God, thank you for being my true source of comfort. I don't want to look anywhere else for that. You are always with me, ready to wrap me in your arms and show me your unfailing love.

What are you seeking comfort in today?

Beyond Your Sight

From the end of the earth I call to you
when my heart is faint.
Lead me to the rock
that is higher than I.

PSALM 61:2 ESV

Have you ever wandered through a maze? Even though you may be good at solving mazes on paper, moving through shrubbery or stalks of corn at ground level you are bound to run into a dead end or two. If only there were a place to climb up high, and see the way through.

So what can you do? Call for help. Follow the voice of someone who can see more than you. Today as you run into situations that require a better view, ask God to guide you. He loves to answer those prayers!

Lord, how wonderful it is to know that when I am lost, I can call to you. Your voice will be my beacon and your hand will lift me up. Will you be that for me today?

From the ends of the earth,
I cry to you for help
when my heart is overwhelmed.
Lead me to the towering rock of safety.

PSALM 61:2 NLT

When life feels like a maze, and you're faint from the exhaustion of running into walls, call out to God. Follow the sound of his voice to the next turn. Allow his hand to lift you up—beyond your own sight—and show you the way through.

Do you know that God is your towering rock of safety? He is always listening, waiting to guide you through the overwhelming situations in your life. Call out to him whenever you need help. He will not let you down.

Father, thank you for showing me what otherwise can't be seen.
You know what turns I need to take and when I should take them.
Help me to continue to listen for your perfect guidance in my life.
I trust you, God.

Do you find it easy to ask God for guidance? Why do you think that may be?

You Are Perfect

By a single offering he has perfected for all time those who are being sanctified.

HEBREWS 10:14, ESV

Stop, go back, and read that again. You are perfect. Looking in the mirror, or thinking back over your week, it is easy to forget or disbelieve those words. Don't let that happen. A wrinkle here, a bulge there, an unkind word, or a jealous thought cannot change the way the Father sees you. And it's how he wants you to see yourself.

The dictionary uses about 250 words to explain what it means to be perfect, but we only need to know this: We are complete. When he chose to die on the cross for our sins, Jesus took away every flaw from those of us who love him. He finished what we never could; he made us perfect.

Jesus, please take my negative thoughts about myself today and help me walk into my day with a confidence of knowing that I am completely loved by you.

By that one offering he forever made perfect
those who are being made holy.

HEBREWS 10:14 NLT

If possible, go to the mirror you see yourself in most often. Stand before it and ask God to show you what he sees when he looks at you.

See past the flaws, past any hurt or anger in your eyes, past any perceived imperfection. See yourself as complete, just as you were meant to be. See yourself as perfect.

Jesus, I thank you that even though I do not feel perfect, I know that I am perfect because of you in me. I choose to think the best of myself because of what you have done for me. Help me to live in the confidence of knowing I am being the best I can be.

What imperfections do you need to hand over to God this evening?

Better than Life

Your unfailing love is better than life itself;
how I praise you!

PSALM 63:3 NLT

We've all heard about the dessert, or the necklace, or the dress that was "to die for." What is meant, of course, is delicious, beautiful, a perfect fit. As brownies, baubles, and body-flattering clothes go, they are the pinnacle.

Clearly, a girl's not about to throw herself in front of a moving train to get her hands on the perfect little black dress. Only one thing is truly better than life, and that's life with the Maker.

Lord, nothing compares to your love. On my worst day, I find comfort in your promise. On my best, I marvel at the knowledge that so much more awaits me in heaven. Help me to remember that as I go about my day.

Because your love is better than life,
my lips will glorify you.

PSALM 63:3 NIV

Do we believe that God's love is better than life? Can we believe it this side of heaven? It may be easier on the days when life's not so great, but when things are going our way, when life couldn't be better, can we see how great God's promise is? What awaits us is so much better than anything we can ask or imagine here on earth!

His love never fails, and nothing compares to it. Regardless of the season we are in or the day we have had, let's acknowledge this beautiful truth from his Word.

God, you are bigger than life, you are better than life, and you are the love of my life. How I praise you. Oh, how I love you.

Can you believe in your heart that God's love is better than life itself?

Choosing Well

"Revere the Lord, and serve him in sincerity and in faithfulness; put away the gods that your ancestors served beyond the River and in Egypt, and serve the Lord. Now if you are unwilling to serve the Lord, choose this day whom you will serve, whether the gods your ancestors served in the region beyond the River or the gods of the Amorites in whose land you are living; but as for me and my household, we will serve the Lord."

JOSHUA 24:14-15 NRSV

How different would life be if you decided, today, to be done with your job? Whether CEO, barista, or dance instructor, your choice would be noticed. Lives would change. What would happen if you simply chose not to get out of bed tomorrow? Even a change of hair color has the potential to affect our trajectory. Our decisions matter—and not just here on earth.

God is interested in the choices you make. He has plans for you and desires for your life, but you have the final say. You get to choose. As you make decisions today, remember to put Jesus first.

God, I want to serve you with my whole heart. I love you and choose to put aside my selfish ambitions so I can serve you alone.

"Fear the Lord and serve Him in sincerity and truth; and put away the gods which your fathers served beyond the River and in Egypt, and serve the Lord. If it is disagreeable in your sight to serve the Lord, choose for yourselves today whom you will serve: whether the gods which your fathers served which were beyond the River, or the gods of the Amorites in whose land you are living; but as for me and my house, we will serve the Lord."

JOSHUA 24:14-15 NASB

While the angels are probably not sitting around debating which shade of red you should try at your next salon visit, know that heaven is truly interested in how you choose to conduct your life. God waits for you to choose life—to choose him—every day.

At times, it can be hard to stand up for your faith. Maybe you experienced something today where you didn't know how to share your belief. Sometimes we need courage to share that we have chosen Jesus, and other times we just need to show it.

God, thank you for giving me a choice. I want to use the freedom that you gave me for good. There are many others in my life who have not chosen you, but I still say yes to your Word.

How will your choice to follow Jesus affect your decisions tomorrow?

Inherent Goodness

You, O LORD, are good and forgiving,
abounding in steadfast love to all who call upon you.

PSALM 86:5 ESV

We all approach God for different reasons, with different matters on our hearts. Sometimes, we come to him in joy and thankfulness. Other times, we come with our heads bowed low, nearly crushed by shame and sorrow.

No matter how we come to God, he meets us the same way— with goodness. As you move through your day today, make a point of seeing God's goodness in your life.

Thank you, God, for your inherent goodness. I never fear unfairness when I come to you. Thank you for your steadfast love and for always responding to me in goodness.

You, LORD, are good, and ready to forgive,
And abundant in lovingkindness to all who call upon You.

PSALM 86:5 NASB

God is full of love for us, his children. He doesn't receive us with quick anger or frustration, but with a love that is steadfast and unchanging.

God isn't just good some of the time; goodness is his nature. Whether he is passing righteous judgment or granting undeserved grace, he is good. Because of his perfect character, we can wholly trust him.

God, help me understand your inherent goodness, so I won't hesitate to come to you first in every situation. Thank you for showing me your goodness today.

How did you see God's goodness manifested in your life today?

Cherished

I am convinced that neither death nor life, neither angels nor demons, neither the present nor the future, nor any powers, neither height nor depth, nor anything else in all creation, will be able to separate us from the love of God that is in Christ Jesus our Lord.

ROMANS 8:38-39 NIV

It's good to be loved, isn't it? What feeling really compares to knowing someone has run through the rain, cancelled an international flight, driven all night—for you? Even if we've never experienced it, we've imagined it in our hearts. Or else we've had the realization that we, too, would move heaven and earth for the one we love the most. Whether spouse, child, parent, sibling, or dear friend, to love and be loved deeply may be the best feeling there is.

Remember that Jesus loves you even more than this. No matter what you face as you get going this morning, be assured that you are loved by the most perfect love there is.

God, sometimes I wake up and don't feel very good about myself or about the day. I thank you for reminding me this morning that I am loved by you, no matter how I feel. I choose to look forward to my day.

I am persuaded that neither death nor life, nor angels nor principalities nor powers, nor things present nor things to come, nor height nor depth, nor any other created thing, shall be able to separate us from the love of God which is in Christ Jesus our Lord.

ROMANS 8:38-39 NKJV

How much love you have given or received is a mere sampling of the way Jesus feels about you. You are cherished, loved beyond reason or measure. The one who really can move heaven and earth would do so in a heartbeat—for you.

Have you seen his love for you today? Have you been able to recognize his voice despite all the chaos and noise in your life? Let the incredible words of this Scripture wash over you as you realize there is nothing—absolutely nothing—Jesus wouldn't do for you.

Jesus, I know that nothing can separate me from your love. As I think on everything I have done, or haven't done, today, I choose to see how you have loved me in all it.

When do you feel most separated from God? How can you assure yourself of his love in these times?

Heavenly Rewards

Be patient, therefore, brothers, until the coming of the Lord. See how the farmer waits for the precious fruit of the earth, being patient about it, until it receives the early and the late rains.

JAMES 5:7 ESV

There is a prevalent message in today's culture that whispers sweet and appealing lies: rights to luxury and self-indulgence. You deserve it, Christian! God wants you to have it and to be happy. This whisper takes away the sweet truth of a God who rewards us, and injects the poisonous lie that that enjoyment must be immediate.

God wants to reward you. That is truth. He promises rewards to the faithful, and he keeps his promises. Those rewards are often not on this earth, and why would we want them to be? Earthly rewards are enjoyable, but they can be destroyed by moth and rust. Heaven's treasures are eternal.

Develop patience in me, God! Grant me endurance to wait for the gifts you have in heaven and not be satisfied with temporary things.

Be patient as you wait for the Lord's return. Consider the farmers who patiently wait for the rains in the fall and in the spring. They eagerly look for the valuable harvest to ripen.

JAMES 5:7 NLT

To lean into the pull of God's kingdom instead of the tug of instant gratification, requires enduring patience. When you are tempted to give in to temporary satisfaction, remember the rewards that wait for you in heaven.

Know that your loving Father is waiting to give you more than you could think to ask for. Let that spur you on in your works and actions, motivating you to live with a kingdom-driven mind-set.

I want to be fully satisfied by you, God, and by the promise of eternal life with you. I patiently wait for your return, knowing you have blessed me with everything I need.

What do you find it most difficult to be satisfied with in your life right now?

Troubled Heart

"Peace I leave with you; my peace I give you.
I do not give to you as the world gives.
Do not let your hearts be troubled and do not be afraid."

JOHN 14:27 NIV

I can't get a moment's peace. Sound familiar? We all go through seasons where it seems every corner hides a new challenge to our serenity, assuming we've actually achieved any semblance of serenity in the first place. Why is it so hard to find peace in this world? Because we're looking in this world.

True peace is found in Jesus. There will be a lot of things that try to take away your sense of peace today, but if you allow the Holy Spirit to speak to you, your day will be filled with moments of knowing that he is near.

Lord, let your words of life bring peace to my heart today.

"I leave you peace; my peace I give you.
I do not give it to you as the world does.
So don't let your hearts be troubled or afraid."

JOHN 14:27 NCV

After his resurrection, before Jesus ascended into heaven,
he left his disciples with something they'd never had before:
peace. More specifically, he gave them his peace, a gift not of
this world. Whatever the world can offer us can also be taken
from us. Any security, happiness, or temporary reprieve from
suffering is just that: temporary. Only the things of heaven
are permanent and cannot be taken away.

Do not let your heart be troubled, Jesus tells us. This means
we have a choice. Share the things with him that threaten
your peace, and then remember they have no hold on you.
You are his, and his peace is yours.

Thank you, Jesus, that I do not have to be afraid. Watch over me as
I sleep and let your peace rest on me tonight.

What have you been troubled about lately? Will you allow
God's peace to replace your fear?

Hearing God

Faith comes from hearing,
and hearing through the word of Christ.

ROMANS 10:17 ESV

The best way to know if something is true, or right, is to hear it for yourself—straight from the source. You believe you nailed the interview, but you don't believe you got the job until you get the phone call. You feel you might be pregnant, but you wait for the test results before telling anyone. The same is true for bad news, at least ideally. You get wind of a rumor about a friend's indiscretion, but you wait for her side of the story before believing a word.

What about God? How can we hear from him? How do we discern his will for our lives? Think about the voices that come into your life today and remember to keep his voice at the forefront.

Father God, thank you that you can speak to me through
your Word and through your Holy Spirit. Guide me in your
righteousness this day.

Faith comes from listening to this Good News—
the Good News about Christ.

ROMANS 10:17 TLB

We may not have a hotline, but we do have his book. God speaks to us through his Word, so if you are waiting for confirmation, direction, validation, or conviction, pick it up. Read, and listen.

How often do you feel God speaking to you through his Word? Were your conversations today as frequent and meaningful as you'd like? Share your heart with him right now, and listen for his reply.

Lord, tonight I make the space to hear from you. I know that your voice is kind and loving and that you know what is best for me. I choose to listen to you now.

What do you hear God saying to you?

Greater Wonder

When I look at your heavens, the work of your fingers,
the moon and the stars, which you have set in place,
what is man that you are mindful of him,
and the son of man that you care for him?

PSALM 8:3-4 ESV

The God of all—the universe and everything in it—is the same God who gave his life to know us. The God who spoke the world into being is the same God who speaks quietly to our hearts. His love for us is as unsearchable as the heavens.

It's hard to believe that the Creator of the Universe is not only interested in us, but he is invested in us. His love for us knows no limits or boundaries. Let your mind ponder this throughout the day today.

Father, I don't understand why you love me the way you do when you are as great as you are. But I am so thankful you do.

I look at your heavens,
which you made with your fingers.
I see the moon and stars,
which you created.
But why are people even important to you?
Why do you take care of human beings?

PSALM 8:3-4 NCV

The greatness of our God is displayed majestically throughout his creation. When we look into the night sky at all the twinkling stars and the far-off planets, we realize almost instantly how small we are in his universe.

A greater wonder than the grandeur of God's capacity is his value for mankind. He is an incredible Creator who wants to be fully engaged with his creation.

God, thank you that you see me as being important. Thank you for giving me life and the choice to follow you. You are the greatest wonder that exists in all the universe.

Spend time pondering the majesty of God's creation and the wonder of his desire to be directly involved in it.

He Is Faithful

Your faithfulness flows from one generation to the next;
all that you created sits firmly in place to testify of you.

PSALM 119:90 TPT

What is the oldest thing you own? How long have you had it, and what does it mean to you? Whether a decades-old diamond ring, twenty-year-old car, or a tattered baby blanket hanging together by threads, you probably know it won't last forever.

How about your longest relationship? How many years have you been connected to this person through the good and the bad? One way we decide where to place our faith is longevity. History matters. You can carry on the faithfulness of the generations even as you go about your day. Take Jesus with you in your heart and actions.

God, thank you that this life in you is the most real thing we can ever know. When I doubt you, let me remind myself that your love has been around since the beginning of time.

Your faithfulness endures to all generations;
You established the earth, and it abides.

PSALM 119:90 NKJV

Consider now what God made: the earth we live on. Scientists estimate it to be 4.5 billion years old, give or take fifty million. Whether we think it's been around that long or six to ten thousand years, it's some quality workmanship. If we're looking for someone to trust, we won't find better credentials than that.

Through every storm, every disaster, every war, and every attack of the enemy, our earth stands. Ponder all God has made and all he has done, and share your heart with him regarding his faithfulness. Have you embraced it today?

Father, thank you for showing yourself through your creation.
Thank you that the earth is still spinning and the world still
reflects your beauty even when things are difficult.

What good things in your life have come from past generations?

More than Gold

These troubles come to prove that your faith is pure. This purity of faith is worth more than gold, which can be proved to be pure by fire but will ruin. But the purity of your faith will bring you praise and glory and honor when Jesus Christ is shown to you.

1 PETER 1:7 NCV

We can waste much of our lives trying to answer the "whys" of our most difficult times. Most of the answers we seek will not be revealed to us until we meet the Lord in heaven, but Scriptures such as this one from Peter provide lovely encouragement while we wait.

We know gold is precious—so precious it's a universal standard for measuring the entire world's wealth. Here, we are told that faith that withstands troubled times is worth more than all the gold on earth. Be encouraged by that today!

Lord, I invite you to use my pain, present and future, as a proving ground for my faith. Allow my troubles to strengthen my trust in you; allow difficulty to increase my reliance on you.

*These have come so that the proven genuineness of your faith--
of greater worth than gold, which perishes even though refined
by fire--may result in praise, glory and honor when Jesus Christ
is revealed.*

1 Peter 1:7 NIV

Holding strong to God's promises regardless of what struggles
we face affords us an invaluable reward: the praise, honor,
and glory of Jesus himself.

This doesn't mean our difficulty is a test assigned by God, but
the outcome—a faith that withstands the fire—is used by him
to bless us beyond imagining.

*Father, when you prove yourself faithful, as you always do, I grow
to love you more and more. Thank you for being faithful to me as
I walk through difficult times and seasons. I want my faith to be
proven as genuine through all the tests.*

What testing do you sense in your life lately? Can you determine
to be proven genuine in your faith throughout the testing?

Remain Faithful

Hold on to loyal love and don't let go,
and be faithful to all that you've been taught.
Let your life be shaped by integrity,
with truth written upon your heart.

PROVERBS 3:3 TPT

A video of a small, white dog entering a hospital through the automatic doors and wandering its halls made national news a while ago. A short investigation revealed the dog's owner had been taken to the hospital for cancer treatment. The dog bolted from the yard earlier that day and ran all the way— nearly two miles—to the hospital to see her owner. No one is sure how she knew where to go. She was led by love.

God desires that kind of faithfulness from us. He wants his daughters to seek him, to love him, with all our hearts. May nothing stop you today from returning his faithfulness with your own!

God, thank you for your love and provision for me. Remind me of your words of truth today, so I can remain faithful to these words.

Never let loyalty and kindness leave you!
Tie them around your neck as a reminder.
Write them deep within your heart.

PROVERBS 3:3 NLT

Your day will have been filled with many challenges, some small, some big, but with God's truth in your heart you can have integrity in your decisions and actions. If you failed today, there is always tomorrow!

Do you see how much your Father loves you? He desires your faithfulness so much he wants you to write it on your heart. What would it take for you to seek him intently, to bolt from the safety of your surroundings in search of him? Even—or perhaps especially—if we don't know where we are going, let us be led by love to show our faithfulness to our Father.

Lord, sometimes I find it hard to do the right thing, especially when no one really notices. I pray for your truth to be written on my heart so deeply that I will allow myself to be shaped by you.

What areas of your life do you need to submit to his truth? Where can you show more integrity?

Found

"I will be found by you," says the LORD. "I will end your captivity and restore your fortunes. I will gather you out of the nations where I sent you and will bring you home again to your own land."

JEREMIAH 29:14 NIV

Lost. It's an uncomfortable word. Being lost is unnerving, and losing something is unsettling. Losing someone: unbearable. Losing God? Unthinkable.

Though they were sent far away from him for many years, Jeremiah 29 contains God's beautiful words of comfort to his beloved Israel. "I will be found by you…I will bring you home again." Thank God that he can always be found.

Father, there are days I fear I've lost you. I know it isn't true, but I can't feel your presence or find your peace. I never want to be away from you, Lord. Find me, Father. Draw me near. Bring me home.

"I will be found by you," declares the LORD, "and will bring you back from captivity. I will gather you from all the nations and places where I have banished you," declares the LORD, "and will bring you back to the place from which I carried you into exile."

JEREMIAH 29:14 NIV

Many believers encounter a season where God might feel far away, or even lost. The relief of finding what we've misplaced is nothing—nothing—compared to the incomprehensible joy of reuniting with the Lord. He will be found!

God intends good for you. He adores you, and if you continue to seek his face and claim his promises for your life, he will bring you home again.

Father, you deeply care about me. Thank you that you always know where I am, and that you are never far from me. Wrap me in your arms tonight.

How do you draw near to the Lord when he seems far away?

Surrendered Heart

O my son, give me your heart.
May your eyes take delight in following my ways.

PROVERBS 23:26 NLT

Watching the news we learn the losing army in a war has surrendered to their enemy. The fugitive has finally surrendered to police after a long standoff. Perhaps, closer to home, someone you know has surrendered to addiction. So how, given all these examples, are we supposed to feel good about surrendering to God? It can be scary to allow ourselves to be vulnerable. Doesn't surrender mean defeat, giving up?

It would…if God were our enemy. But because he is for us and not against us, surrender means something else altogether. It means freedom. Delight in his freedom today.

God, I choose to trust you with my heart today. Help me to make decisions that are pleasing to you.

My child, give me your heart,
and let your eyes observe my ways.

PROVERBS 23:26 NRSV

Surrender also means abandoning ourselves to God and no longer resisting him—accepting his plans and his perfect will for our lives. We don't have to strive any more once we give him our hearts. Consider that his plans are perfect, that his will for you is peace.

In a world full of chaos, it's nice to know that someone else is willing to guide you through. God wants you to delight in following his ways because they are the best.

God, I don't want to resist you or your plan for my life. Thank you that I don't have to strive for anything when I give you my whole heart.

Is there an area of your heart you don't want to let go of? Think about why that might be tonight.

Truly Special

You are a chosen people, a royal priesthood,
a holy nation, God's special possession.

1 PETER 2:9 NIV

We all want to believe that we are special. Most of us grow up being told that we are, and it feels good to believe it. But over time, we look around us and realize that, really, we are just like everyone else.

Sometimes doubt creeps in, making us second guess ourselves and damaging our self-confidence. Choose to believe today that God has called and chosen you for something truly special.

Thank you, God, that you see me as special. I revel in that knowledge today.

You are a chosen people, royal priests,
a holy nation, a people for God's own possession.

1 PETER 2:9 NCV

Long before you were even a wisp in your mother's womb, you were set aside and marked as special. You were chosen to be God's special possession, and that's a pretty amazing thing.

Of all the people in the world, God has chosen you to do something only you can do. Ask him to show you what he has for you as you continue to walk in his wonderful light.

Father, you have called me out of the darkness of the ordinary and have brought me into the light of the extraordinary. You have hand-picked me and you love me. I am so thankful.

Ask God to show you just how special you are to him.

Hope

May the God of hope fill you with all joy and peace as you trust in him, so that you may overflow with hope by the power of the Holy Spirit.

ROMANS 15:13 NIV

What differentiates hope from a wish? Think about the lottery. Does one hope to win or wish to win? How about a promotion, a pregnancy, or a proposal? Both hoping and wishing contain desire, but for wishing, that is where it ends. Hope goes deeper. The strong desire for something good to happen is coupled with a reason to believe that it will.

What do you hope for your day today? Do you hope for a peaceful moment, to complete a job, to have a meaningful conversation? Trust that the Holy Spirit can lead you to these things.

Holy Spirit, as you walk alongside me today, let my heart be full of your joy and peace. Let me realize your power to turn these desires into reality.

I pray that the God who gives hope will fill you with much joy and peace while you trust in him. Then your hope will overflow by the power of the Holy Spirit.

ROMANS 15:13 NCV

We see then how vital hope is, and why it's such a beautiful gift. Desire without hope is empty, but together they bring joy, expectancy, and peace. When we put our hope in Christ, he becomes our reason to believe good things will happen. Has he been your hope today?

Allow the blessing from this Scripture to wash over you tonight as the Holy Spirit reminds you of the hope, joy, and peace he brought to you today. Believe good things will happen tomorrow too —you have a wonderful reason to.

Jesus, I put my hope in your saving grace. I thank you for a day of experiencing your presence. Help me to carry this into my day tomorrow.

Where or when have you seen God bless you with his joy and peace today? Thank him for it!

Celebrate God's Blessings

For seven days celebrate the festival to the Lord your God at the place the Lord will choose. For the Lord your God will bless you in all your harvest and in all the work of your hands, and your joy will be complete.

DEUTERONOMY 16:15 NIV

When you hear the words spiritual discipline, what comes to mind? Usual responses include prayer, fasting, and meditating on Scripture. If someone mentioned celebrating, would you rebuke them? Is that answer unspiritual, irreverent?

Surprise! God actually commanded us to celebrate, rejoice, and have parties. Joy is overflowing exaltation. When you see a beautiful sunset, you want to grab someone and share it with them. It is right to celebrate the goodness of the Lord!

Thank you, God, for the abundance of blessing and joy in our lives! I celebrate you and the wonder of who you are. Let my rejoicing be a beacon for your glory.

Seven days you shall keep the festival to the LORD your God at the place that the LORD will choose; for the LORD your God will bless you in all your produce and in all your undertakings, and you shall surely celebrate.

DEUTERONOMY 16:15 NRSV

Celebration causes joy to overflow into the world around us. What if you heard a joyous celebration and found out people were praising the Lord? It would be difficult to not join in. It's okay to laugh, dance, and celebrate what God has done in our lives. He is a good father!

Gather around a campfire and sing your lungs out. Take your partner's hands and spin around the kitchen floor. Delight in a warm meal with true friends. These things are pleasing to God. They bring him glory.

God, thank you for creating special occasions for me to celebrate. I am so grateful for the many blessings you have showered on me. Help my celebration to be a light to those around me—leading them to you.

What can you celebrate today?

He Feels

Jesus wept.

JOHN 11:35 NASB

In the shortest verse in the Bible, but also among the most beautiful, Jesus saw how his dear friends were hurting and was moved to tears. He knew he was about to take their pain away by raising Lazarus to life again, but in that moment, their pain was his pain—and it broke his heart.

When someone we love is in pain, their ache becomes our ache. We cry openly with our newly jobless neighbors, recently bereaved friends, freshly disappointed daughters. Tears come easy when your heart is surrendered to the Holy Spirit, because they are his tears. He hurts when we hurt.

Lord, thank you for sharing in my pain. Help me to have that same compassion for the people around me today.

Tears came to Jesus' eyes.

JOHN 11:35 TLB

In telling the story of Lazarus' death and resurrection (see John 11:1-46), take some time this evening to reflect on why these words are set apart and given their own verse.

Reflect on the humanity of Jesus and how he deeply cared for others. Are you able to imagine Jesus openly weeping with Mary and Martha? As you reflect on your day, have you shared in the emotions of those around you?

God, I thank you for all the different people that you have placed in my life. Thank you for the range of emotions that we can feel. Remind me of your presence in everything that I feel, and help me to share in the joys and pains of others.

How have you felt Jesus' affection for you today?

Rejoice Today

This is the day the LORD has made;
We will rejoice and be glad in it.

PSALM 118:24, NKJV

When winter is fully upon us, it is not as warm outside, and there's not as much life in nature. If you live where winter is cold, you may be growing tired of boots, hats, scarves (well, maybe not scarves), and puffy, shapeless coats. Looking outside, there may not be much to feel particularly joyful about.

The simple truth is that God made today, and he made it with you in it. As you go into your day, either with excitement or dread, encourage yourself that this is a day purposed by the Lord, for you. Make the most out of it!

Lord, I wasn't that happy to get out of bed this morning, but now that I am up, I commit this day to you and thank you for making it!

This is the day that the LORD has made.
Let us rejoice and be glad today!

PSALM 118:24, NCV

We were called to rejoice today – were you able to see the joy in your day? There are days we see his handiwork everywhere we look, and there are days that just happen. Be certain; the Creator has created this day. Today was an offering from our Father to us. That in itself is cause for celebration, don't you think?

Let's look harder, closer, at today. Was there a patch of blue sky, did you share a hearty laugh with someone, did you find something great to eat for lunch? Turn your heart toward God, and rejoice and be glad for the day he made for you.

God, there are a few things that I didn't like about today and yet I can see some great things in my day too. Help me rejoice in all it, knowing that you purposed this day for me.

What can you look forward to about tomorrow?

Our Rock

There is no one holy like the LORD,
Indeed, there is no one besides You,
Nor is there any rock like our God.

1 SAMUEL 2:2 NASB

Most of us have been blessed by special relationships in our lives. We are surrounded by friends and family that love us. These are people we can turn to in times of trouble and pain. And it can be tempting to allow these people to feel like a rock: a stabilizer. As soon as something happens, we run to them and ask for their strength to get us through.

The Bible tells us that there is no rock like our God. He's the best; there's no one else that can take his place. Run to God today when you need strength.

Father, I give you my burdens. I'm so thankful that you are my rock and my daily source of strength. Help me to turn to you first in all that I do.

No one is holy like the LORD!
There is no one besides you;
there is no Rock like our God.

1 SAMUEL 2:2 NLT

When we start to worry, become afraid, or experience difficulty, our first source of comfort should be the Lord. He is so good to us! No matter what we are going through, he will be there for us. There is simply no one like him.

As the day comes to a close, let God the Rock be the place you rest. Let him take all of your worries and fears away.

God, my Rock, there is none like you. Thank you for being the only place I can turn to for real, lasting peace. I trust you for that this evening.

Can you trust God to be your first source of comfort?

Nothing to Fear

In the day that I'm afraid, I lay all my fears before you
and trust in you with all my heart.
What harm could a man bring to me?
With God on my side I will not be afraid of what comes.
The roaring praises of God fill my heart,
and I will always triumph as I trust his promises.

PSALM 56:3-4 TPT

A loud crash in the night. Unexpected footsteps falling uncomfortably close in a dark parking lot. A ringing phone at 3:00 a.m. No matter how brave we think we are, certain situations quicken the pulse. We've heard, over and over, that we have nothing to fear if we walk with God, but let's be honest: certain situations are scary!

You might be anxious about today, perhaps there is a big event that you are a part of, or maybe you have to engage in a difficult conversation. Maybe you are just nervous because you don't know what the day will bring. The Psalms say that you can trust him with all your heart, so do that today.

God, I don't know what is going to happen today but I make the decisions right now to trust in you with all my heart. Give me peace for the day ahead.

When I am afraid,
I will put my trust in you.
I praise God for what he has promised.
I trust in God, so why should I be afraid?
What can mere mortals do to me?

PSALM 56:3-4 NLT

At times, it is people that we fear the most. We are afraid of rejection, broken trust, embarrassment, or shame. We want to feel safe, loved, and accepted, but this feels like it comes at a risk.

Let's consider David's words from Psalm 56. When we are afraid, and we will be, we can give our situation to God and let him take the fear away. Notice it doesn't say he changes the situation, but that he changes our response to it. We have nothing to fear not because scary things don't exist, but because God erases our worry and replaces it with trust. Have you been able to trust him today?

Thank you, Lord, that I can pray with the same confidence that King David had. I believe that you are on my side, and I believe that you can help me to find peace instead of fear.

What are you afraid of? Have you truly tried letting go of that fear? If not, why? Talk to God about this.

Mind Games

Let the peace that Christ gives control your thinking,
because you were called together in one body to have peace.
Always be thankful.

COLOSSIANS 3:15 NCV

Our minds can be a baseball field with baseball-like thoughts hurtling every which way. Maybe you have your mitt out, ready to catch, or maybe you get hit with a thought out of left field.

Instead of allowing your thoughts to be set statements of truth, take thoughts as information, and then determine your response. Your response should be considered through this lens; earlier in Colossians, Paul says you are a new creation. As a new creation, learn to quiet your thoughts; don't let them knock you over.

Lord, help me to guard my thoughts and surround me in truth.
Lead me through sometimes muddy fields, that I may know what
is truth and what is not.

Let the peace that comes from Christ rule in your hearts.
For as members of one body you are called to live in peace.
And always be thankful.

COLOSSIANS 3:15 NCV

Are your "baseball thoughts" God-honoring? In God's eyes, you are dressed in the righteousness of Christ. Accept that thought as truth and act on it.

Dismiss wrong thoughts as a part of your old, sinful nature. Desire peace with other Christians, viewing them as new creations too. Allow your thoughts about them to promote peace among you. Trust God's promise that his peace can control your thoughts.

Your Word is truth, and I desire it more than anything else. Help me tonight to quiet my thoughts. I submit them to you and ask for your peace to rule my mind. I am so thankful for your peace, God.

What's the best way for you to let the peace of Christ rule your mind?

Grace upon Grace

Of His fullness we have all received, and grace upon grace.

JOHN 1:16 NASB

You know those days, the perfect ones? Your hair looks great, you nail a work assignment (whether client presentation, spreadsheet, or getting twins to nap at the same time), you say just the right thing and make someone's day, and then come home to find dinner waiting for you. It's good upon good, blessing upon blessing.

Today might not be a perfect day, but you can still take a perfect attitude with you. You can choose to be thankful for God's fullness in your heart and in your life. Be gracious to yourself and to others today.

Lord, thank you that I take your grace with me each and every day. Thank you that even if today isn't perfect, your love for me is.

Out of his fullness we have all received grace
in place of grace already given.

JOHN 1:16 NIV

Being a daughter of the Almighty gains us access to that blessed feeling of grace and beauty every day, even when our circumstances are ordinary or even difficult.

God's love is so full, and his grace so boundless, that when his Spirit lives in us, even a flat tire can feel like a blessing. Our status as beloved daughters of the King guarantees his endless grace; we need only claim it.

God, as I go to bed tonight, I pray for your grace to fill my heart. As I think about the different events that happened during the day, I pray that I would know you have lovingly guided me through them.

Do you see God's grace poured out upon you today? Thank him for it.

In Sunshine and Storm

When times are good, be happy;
but when times are bad, consider this:
God has made the one as well as the other.
Therefore, no one can discover
anything about their future.

ECCLESIASTES 7:14, NIV

It's easy to feel happy on a sunny day, when all is well, the birds are singing, and life is going along swimmingly. But what happens when waters are rougher, bad news comes, or the days feel just plain hard?

God wants us to feel gladness when times are good. He has made each and every day. We are called to rejoice in all of them whether good or bad. Make today a good day just because you know God loves you.

God, I don't want my happiness to be determined by my
circumstance. Help me discover true joy in you today.

In the day of prosperity be joyful,
and in the day of adversity consider;
God has made the one as well as the other,
so that mortals may not find out
anything that will come after them.

ECCLESIASTES 7:14 NRSV

Happiness is determined by our circumstances, but true joy comes when we can find the silver linings, hidden in our darkest hours—when we can sing God's praises no matter what.

We don't know what the future holds for us here on earth, but we can find our delight in the knowledge that our eternity is set in the beauty of full relationship with our heavenly Father.

Father, give me a deep and abiding satisfaction in each day that goes beyond human understanding. Help me to rest in your joy this evening.

Do you trust God with your future?

Delightful

The LORD takes delight in his people;
he crowns the humble with victory.

PSALM 149:4 NIV

If ever there was something to lift your spirits and get you through the toughest of days, it's the knowledge that the Lord our God takes delight in you. He tells you so in his Word!

God takes pleasure in your very existence. Your heavenly Father created you to be in relationship with him, and he gets great joy out of it. Take that delightful thought with you throughout your day.

Father, it makes me smile to know that you delight in me. I lift up others who haven't experienced your delight, and pray that they'd come to know you in a deep and real way. You are truly glorious, and I'm amazed by you!

The LORD delights in his people;
he crowns the humble with victory.

Revel in the knowledge of God's delight for the rest of the evening and into tomorrow. Embrace the fact that there is one who loves you and is truly captivated by you.

God loves spending time with you; he wants to get closer to you each day. Allow him to take you deeper! Dive in and experience his delight for yourself.

God, thank you for loving me and wanting me to draw closer to you! Help me to embrace your delight and walk in your victory each day.

Did you feel God's delight in you today?

Honor in Purity

The LORD has rewarded me according to my righteousness,
according to the cleanness of my hands in his sight.

PSALM 18:24 ESV

What do you think of when you hear the word purity? Perhaps a nun in her convent—someone who keeps herself completely untouched by the temptations of the world—an innocent child, or a great religious figure?

Often when we think about purity we think of a lack of obvious, outward sin. But both purity and impurity are birthed in the heart and developed in the mind long before they become expressed in action. Our purity is measured, not in what we do or what we have done, but in the hidden places of our heart's attitudes and our mind's wanderings.

God, help me to have a pure attitude today and to set my mind on the good and true things that are in my life. Let me walk in your righteousness.

The Lord rewarded me for doing right.
He has seen my innocence.

PSALM 18:24, NLT

If you ever wonder if your purity counts for anything—if refraining from the pleasures of sin is even worth it—be encouraged today. God will reward you according to your righteousness.

The Father sees the intentions of your heart and the thoughts in your mind. He knows how badly you want to please him with your life, and he will bless you for it. He is honored in your purity, and that honor is the most important reward of all.

Lord, I'm not sure how pure my attitude was today, and I'm sorry if I messed up. I thank you that it is worth trying to do the right thing, and that you love me no matter what. Thank you for your forgiveness.

What negative attitude or unhelpful thought pattern might God be trying to shine his light into at this moment? Ask him for help!

Abundant Rain

Be glad, O children of Zion,
and rejoice in the LORD your God,
for he has given the early rain for your vindication;
he has poured down for you abundant rain,
the early and the latter rain, as before.

JOEL 2:23 ESV

Our Lord is so good and faithful. He provides us with everything we need if we only look to him for it.

When our lives are in drought, parched from our daily grind, he sends us rain in abundance, to nourish our souls and keep us from drying out spiritually. The fields that are our lives begin to green up again after a season of becoming brown. We feel refreshed as his showers of love pour down over us.

Lord, thank you for protecting me from drying out. You give me everything I need to flourish, and for that I give you all the praise.

Rejoice, you people of Jerusalem!
Rejoice in the LORD your God!
For the rain he sends demonstrates his faithfulness.
Once more the autumn rains will come,
as well as the rains of spring.

JOEL 2:23 NLT

Let's celebrate and be glad! Our God in heaven cares for us so much. He wants to see us bearing good fruit, and he will continue to give us what we need to nourish and grow.

Turn to him when you are feeling parched, and he will give you rain for the exact season you are in. He always knows just what you need.

God you know which rain I need in which season. I rejoice in you because you are faithful to care for me just the way I need to be cared for.

What kind of refreshing rain do you need today?

Imago Dei

> God said, "Let us make man in our image, after our likeness. And let them have dominion over the fish of the sea and over the birds of the heavens and over the livestock and over all the earth and over every creeping thing that creeps on the earth."
>
> GENESIS 1:26 ESV

God created you in his image. Have you ever pondered what this really means? God intended for you and the rest of humanity to demonstrate what he is like to the rest of the world; to display the goodness of the Creator and to represent his name. That's a big task.

Remember that it isn't what you strive to do, it's who you are, so be encouraged today that you are representing your Creator just by being you.

God, it seems like a really big thing to be bearing your image, but I thank you that you created me and you love me as I am. I pray despite my imperfections I would still be able to reflect you in my life toward others today.

God created man in his own image,
in the image of God he created him;
male and female he created them. And God blessed them.

GENESIS 1:27-28 ESV

Was your day full of peace and love or have you had moments of quarrelling and tension? No matter what way it went, you are loved by God and his grace allows you to continue to be like him.

An image in ancient days were idols made from human hands with no life in them. We are a different image from any manmade thing because the God of this universe breathed life into us. We are alive, just as he is alive.

God, I need you to breathe new life into areas of my life where I am not fully representing the person you have created me to be. I choose to look ahead to the renewal that is going to take place in my heart and in my life.

What area of your life do you feel you need to reflect God more?

Swept into Him

Let that abide in you which you heard from the beginning.
If what you heard from the beginning abides in you,
you also will abide in the Son and in the Father.

1 JOHN 2:24 NKJV

Most homes, even those of the most organized among us,
end up with junk drawer. Maybe a junk closet, junk room,
or a garage you can no longer park in is more your situation.
No matter how large your clutter-catcher is, the problem is
the same: space. Everything that enters your home needs a
spot, and the more that comes in, the fewer the open spaces.
Eventually, be it a yard sale, donation, or a storage unit,
something's got to go.

Our hearts and minds are basically the same. Everything
allowed inside takes up room. One of the most wonderful
gifts of a relationship with Jesus is the space his Spirit claims
in our lives. The more we invite him in, the more junk gets
cleared away. His peace pushes out anxiety. His patience
banishes our short temperedness. His joy leaves no room for
contention.

God, abide in me! Take all the space you need; nothing I've
collected compares to the beauty of your Spirit. Let my heart make
way for all you want to bring.

Let that abide in you which you heard from the beginning.
If what you heard from the beginning abides in you,
you also will abide in the Son and in the Father.

1 JOHN 2:24, NASB

The reality of God in us, and we in him is a beautiful one. Because he is everywhere, when he comes to us we are swept into him.

Like a sponge in the ocean, at once saturated and contained by his vastness, our lives are forever connected. We are influenced and changed by God in us. We are protected through residing in him.

God, tonight I thank you for mysteries too big for me to fully comprehend. Beyond even the depth of the oceans, my life in you is limitless. Your life in me is a gift.

What does considering your oneness with God do in your heart?

He Is with Me

> *"Fear not, for I am with you;*
> *be not dismayed, for I am your God;*
> *I will strengthen you, I will help you,*
> *I will uphold you with my righteous right hand."*

ISAIAH 41:10 ESV

"I am with you." Sometimes, that's all we need to hear, isn't it? It's why we have those special few on speed dial: the friend, the sister, the mentor who says, "I'm here" and instantly the crisis grows smaller. The presence of another—minus even words or touch—is enough to quiet an anxious spirit. And when that "other" is God? What can this, or any day throw at us that we, with his strengthening help, can't handle?

Even weak, we are strong. Even trembling, we remain upright. Our God is just that strong, just that for us, just that good. Even on a day that's hard, his arms are waiting. He is with you.

God, how strengthening it is to know you are always with me! What a beautiful hope it gives me to sense your presence. I have nothing to fear, ever, because I have you.

"Fear not, for I am with you;
be not dismayed, for I am your God.
I will strengthen you, yes, I will help you,
I will uphold you with My righteous right hand."

ISAIAH 41:10 NKJV

Think back to your childhood, and a time you were frightened, then calmed. Perhaps Dad shone a flashlight under a bed you were certain housed a monster, revealing instead an old suitcase and a stuffed bear. That mysterious noise turned out to be a tree branch against the eaves, or a squirrel in the rain gutter. Once you understood how safe you were, your fears were even funny.

Take that joyous laughter to any grown-up fears you may be facing. Upheld by God, who never leaves you, you are strong enough to shine the light at anything.

Lord God, I'm so grateful for your presence! As I drift into sleep
tonight, may I dream of walking beside you. May I sense your
nearness as I face my fears, and together, may we laugh at them.

Where do you need to ask God to reveal his presence and quiet a fear?

Very Good Work

The heavens and the earth were finished, and all the host of them.
And on the seventh day God finished his work that he had done, and
he rested on the seventh day from all his work that he had done.

GENESIS 2:1-2 ESV

It must have taken a lot of energy for God to create this universe, this world, and the complexity that is humanity. God also planned rest into his creative work. After he had finished his very good work he rested.

As you go through your day, your various working activities will require energy from you. Think about God's intention for rest after hard work; he knows what is best for us. Take a few moments to rest from your very good work.

God, I thank you for the day ahead. I ask for your energy to get some very good work done. I pray that you would give me moments of rest so I can be restored to do more work that will bring glory to you.

God blessed the seventh day and made it holy, because on it God rested from all his work that he had done in creation.

GENESIS 2:3 ESV

At the end of a long day it's easy to feel a little down because your energy has been depleted.

You may have had very little time for yourself today, but now you have a moment to sit and reflect on the goodness of God with the idea that he wants you to be here right now and rest in him. God took a whole day out of his work to rest.

God, I thank you for this moment of rest, this time to be restored by reflecting on being like you and resting like you did. I pray for your strength; I pray for great sleep so I am ready to face another day.

What day can you take this week that will allow you to have time to rest?

Every Good Thing

Whatever is good and perfect is a gift coming down to us from God our Father, who created all the lights in the heavens. He never changes or casts a shifting shadow.

JAMES 1:17 NLT

Who in your life always seems to come up with the perfect gift? From a scarf that perfectly matches your eyes, to a care-package of herbal teas, an empty journal and a beautiful pen, this person just gets you, and so what they give you is always just right. Good gift-givers are themselves a gift.

Consider our Lord, and the intimate way he attends to us. What if we could start seeing not just the obvious gifts, but every good thing as a gift from above? Pay special attention today to all the good you see, hear and experience, and consider the Father as the author of it all.

God, you are the ultimate giver. From the smell of brewing coffee to a perfectly timed green light, you love to make me smile. Thank you! May I spend this and every day in grateful awe of all you do.

Every gift God freely gives us is good and perfect, streaming down from the Father of lights, who shines from the heavens with no hidden shadow or darkness and is never subject to change.

JAMES 1:17 TPT

Along with all the good and perfect things about our Father lies this incredible treasure: he never changes! Even the most loving relationships, the most stable job, the most well-behaved child is bound to change.

Only one thing is certain, and it's the goodness of our Lord. He simply can't be any other way.

God, what a good Father you are! I never have to wonder with you; you are always for me, always in the light, always good. Thank you for all the ways you love me, and all the perfect gifts you bestow.

What is the best gift God gave you today?

Hiding

They heard the sound of the LORD God walking in the garden in the cool of the day, and the man and his wife hid themselves from the presence of the LORD God among the trees of the garden.

GENESIS 3:8 ESV

It would have been a hard day for Adam and Eve, the day they were deceived and made the choice to disobey God. They were so ashamed that they hid, although they must have known that they would be found.

We all know what shame feels like, when we have committed wrong toward someone else. We want to run from our problems and not face those we have hurt, and yet the truth cannot escape us. Can you face your day with boldness, knowing that truth and owning up to your mistakes is better than hiding?

Jesus, I am going to need your help today to make sure that I don't hide from my mistakes, and to know that your presence is always there, not to condemn, but to give me grace.

The LORD God called to the man and said to him, "Where are you?"
And he said, "I heard the sound of you in the garden, and I was
afraid, because I was naked, and I hid myself."

GENESIS 3:9-10 ESV

Were there any mistakes or arguments in your day that made
you feel like covering up or hiding? We aren't often very good
at taking ownership of our wrongdoings, and sometimes we
think that ignoring them is the easiest way out.

Perhaps you have been hurt by someone and are waiting for
them to apologize. Whatever the wrongdoing, notice that God is
all about restoration. In the garden, it was God who went to find
Adam and Eve. He didn't wait for them to come out from hiding;
he sought them out. Don't be afraid, and don't hide. God will
always seek to restore relationship with you and with others.

God, there is a lot of brokenness around me, and sometimes I just
want to carry on and try to hide from my own sin. Thank you for your
forgiveness, for your grace, and for restoring relationship with me.

What relationship do you need God to restore to you? If you
need forgiveness, approach God—he is for you, not against you.

Even Though

"Whenever you stand praying, if you have anything against anyone, forgive him that your Father in heaven may also forgive you your trespasses."

MARK 11:25 NKJV

Forgiveness is one of those topics it's tempting to attach a "Yeah, but…" or an "Even though…?" to. We know forgiveness is important, and we know we're commanded to give it, but it's often easier said than done. "Yeah, but he did this," we think. "I'm expected to forgive her even though she did that?" we ask.

In a word, yes. Jesus was crystal clear. After all, forgiveness is why he came, why he suffered and died, and why he rose. And just as his forgiveness frees us from our sins, our forgiveness frees us from anger, resentment, and broken relationships. Did you catch that? Forgiving frees us! Oh, how he loves us. Even the hardest commands are for our good.

Jesus, you're simply amazing. Not only do you forgive me—daily—for all my failings, you do it for everyone who loves you. And still you keep giving, by helping us banish unforgiveness from our own hearts. Thank you, God, for your redemptive, gracious love.

*"Whenever you stand praying, if you find that you carry
something in your heart against another person, release him and
forgive him so that your Father in heaven will also release you and
forgive you of your faults."*

MARK 11:25 TPT

Which sounds more like you? "I have struggled to forgive,
despite a heartfelt apology and deep remorse? "or "I have
forgiven someone who wasn't sorry, who didn't even ask me to."

What feelings come up as you consider these two scenarios?
Where is Jesus in each?

*God, thank you for showing me it is I who am set free when I
drop the chains I've wrapped around people who have wronged
me. Make me gracious, offering release where it isn't deserved
or even wanted. I invite you to take over my heart in the area of
forgiveness, and I ask you to forgive me for the times it's hard.*

As you close your day, meditate on the healing nature of
forgiveness given and received.

Colorful Promises

God said, "This is the sign of the covenant that I make between me and you and every living creature that is with you, for all future generations: I have set my bow in the cloud, and it shall be a sign of the covenant between me and the earth."

GENESIS 9:12-13 ESV

Rainbows are beautiful wonders of nature that bring joy to those fortunate enough to see them. They come from a combination of rain and sun, and it is easy to see why God put such a beautiful reminder in the sky of his goodness.

Your day may be filled with some pain and some joy. Remember that the combination of different aspects can be turned into a beautiful reminder of God's promise to remember his children and to show them his lovingkindness.

Father, I need your lovingkindness in my life today. Whether I experience rain or shine, or a little of both, I pray I would see your beauty working in and through me.

"When I bring clouds over the earth and the bow is seen in the clouds, I will remember my covenant that is between me and you and every living creature of all flesh. And the waters shall never again become a flood to destroy all flesh."

GENESIS 9:14-15 ESV

It grieves God's heart to see his children in pain. It is good to remind ourselves that while we do not understand the ways of God, we believe in his goodness and knowledge of his creation to know what is best for the world. When the waters of life seem to be rising higher and higher, don't panic.

God has made a promise to keep you from drowning. Trust in him.

God, after a long day I am feeling overwhelmed. Help me to remember your promise to always be with me and to help me get through each and every day. Give me rest as I go to bed and give me hope for a new day.

What pressure are you feeling today that is causing you anxiety? Think of the rainbow that God put in the sky and remember that his promises are for you.

That Dream

> "I know that you can do all things;
> no purpose of yours can be thwarted."
>
> JOB 42:2 NIV

We all know someone who seems unstoppable, don't we? That person who, when she's on the job, we know it will get done. When he gets in the game, the other team might as well go home. As amazing as those people are, their will, tenacity, and capacity pale in comparison our Lord's.

That dream you get when you are praying and asking for direction, that desire in your heart to make a difference, the one that just won't go away? If God has planted this purpose in you, it's going to happen. Fear, resistance, and procrastination might as well go home.

Father God, I have dreams only you know about, and only you could have given me. I know this because there is no way I can realize them on my own. I know this because there are days I am not even sure I want to try, and yet my heart won't let go of them. Thank you, God, for God-sized dreams and the ability you plant and replant in me to bring them to fruition.

> *"I know that you can do anything,*
> *and no one can stop you."*
>
> JOB 42:2 NLT

Imagine for a moment this prayer of Job's is actually God speaking to you. "I know that you can do anything, and that no one can stop you."

When your will is joined with his, he does speak this over you. He believes in you; he is proud of you! God knows exactly why he made you, and he knows exactly what you need to fulfill your purpose. Listen to him, and believe.

God, I want to believe I can do anything you ask of me. Let your Holy Spirit fill me with the passion, confidence, and will to make you proud.

What is your God-given dream? How are you pursuing it?

The Good Portion

Abram said to Lot, "Let there be no strife between you and me, and between your herdsmen and my herdsmen, for we are kinsmen."

GENESIS 13:8 ESV

Abram and his nephew Lot had been on a long journey together to reach the land that God had promised them. When they got there, Abram had a choice to make; there was good land and there was very good land. Abram chose peace over greed and gave the very good land to his nephew. As a result, God blessed Abram abundantly.

You may have some choices to make today that will require you to give up something that seems very good for the sake of someone else. Let God bless you as you practice generosity.

Thank you, God, for the many blessings of this life. I pray that if an opportunity comes today to be generous to someone else that you would remind me of your generosity toward me.

"Is not the whole land before you? Separate yourself from me. If you take the left hand, then I will go to the right, or if you take the right hand, then I will go to the left."

GENESIS 13:9 ESV

Have you had to put aside your need or desire in order to benefit someone else today? Or did you lose the opportunity because you didn't want to give it up?

Either way God is still on your side and will be with you whether you are an Abram or a Lot. Allow God to continue to work on gifting you with a generous spirit.

God, I don't always get it right and I am particularly challenged to have to give up opportunities for the benefit of those around me. I pray you would remind me of your love and immeasurable goodness so I will have the desire to give more to others.

In what ways do you find it hard to be generous toward others? Is it money, patience, or a better opportunity? Allow yourself to be challenged to give more.

All Wise

Who is wise and understanding among you? Show by your good life that your works are done with gentleness born of wisdom.

JAMES 3:13 NRSV

What does wisdom mean to you? Do you picture a white-haired grandma, spouting out pearls of advice? The dictionary combines experience, knowledge, and good judgment to define it. With these terms, it's fairly safe to say we are all wise in some regard.

Rather than wait for the rocking chair days, let's pay attention to where our experience, knowledge, and good judgment could be a blessing today. As wonderful as it feels to be over, past, or through something, might we benefit someone by revisiting those days? Gently, lovingly, with an eye ever on the Father, is there someone you can bless with your wisdom?

God, give me eyes to see where my experience can ease the road of another. Show me where my knowledge can edify, and where my good judgement, gained through trial and error, can spare someone an error or two. Give me gentleness and humility, born of love, as I move to be of help. Remind me always that everything I've gained is from and for you.

If you consider yourself to be wise and one who understands the ways of God, advertise it with a beautiful, fruitful life guided by wisdom's gentleness. Never brag or boast about what you've done and you'll prove that you're truly wise.

JAMES 3:13 TPT

Just as there are areas of life in which we are wise, there are those where we are in need of wisdom.

Spend some time in prayer over an area of your life in which you feel stuck. Is there a mistake you repeat or a cycle you can't seem to break? Ask God to bring someone wise into your situation.

God, sometimes I marvel at how I can be so together in some ways and such a mess in others! Thank you for making me so complex. Thank you for opportunities to share the wisdom you've given me, and for bringing wise people into my life for the areas in which I have much growing left to do. Let both my wisdom and my lack be a blessing.

How are you wise? Where do you need the wisdom of another?

Well Pleased

Jesus came from Galilee to the Jordan to John, to be baptized by him. John would have prevented him, saying, "I need to be baptized by you, and do you come to me?" But Jesus answered him, "Let it be so now, for thus it is fitting for us to fulfill all righteousness." Then he consented.

MATTHEW 3:13–15 ESV

Jesus didn't just come to the world to show us perfection, he also came to show us a new way of life. Of course he didn't need to be baptized, he was God. He chose, however, to model what our righteousness was all about.

John baptized Jesus to represent how our old life can die with Christ and rise again. You will probably be challenged in some way today, to put behind your old self and to live in the new life Jesus has given you. Are you up for this challenge?

Jesus, thank you for showing me that you made a way for me to live a better life. I know you don't require perfection, so I ask that you remind me, as I face challenges today, to be a person of the new life you demonstrated to us.

When Jesus was baptized, immediately he went up from the water, and behold, the heavens were opened to him, and he saw the Spirit of God descending like a dove and coming to rest on him; and behold, a voice from heaven said, "This is my beloved Son, with whom I am well pleased."

MATTHEW 3:16-17 ESV

When you get to the end of the day you can feel a sense of accomplishment knowing that you achieved a few things and simply got through the day without any major catastrophe.

Sometimes you may have even gone that one step above and remembered to show love in some way to someone around you—you lived in the new life that Christ has given you. Well done. Let yourself be encouraged that the Father says these same words to you, just as he did to his beloved Son: "Child, I am well pleased with you."

Father, sometimes I feel as though I don't deserve your praise. Thank you that you have a different view. Thank you that you see me with love and acceptance and that simply because I am your child, you are well pleased with me.

Can you imagine these words being just for you? Reflect on your day and let God show you the heart attitude that he was well pleased with.

Ripples to Waves

Remember to welcome strangers, because some who have done this have welcomed angels without knowing it.

HEBREWS 13:2 NCV

Who is the best hostess you know—that dear soul whose door is always open and whose table is always full? It's not hard to think of someone, is it? The gift of hospitality is easy to recognize and wonderful to benefit from. Perhaps that warm hostess is you. Opening your home, filling it with friends, and filling their bellies is food for your soul.

While hospitality is a gift of the Spirit, coming to some as naturally as breath, others among us are more inclined to attend than to host. Just the thought of entertaining makes us uncomfortable. The cleaning, the shopping, the cooking, the cleaning again? "I'll bring the bread," we say tentatively. But what might we be missing out on? Who knows who God has sent to help us open our hearts along with our homes?

God, you know me so well. Whether you made me a born entertainer or whether I'm more of a bread-bringer, I want to experience every blessing you have for me! I want to know every angel you set in my path, and give my heart every opportunity to bless another. Give me a heart of hospitality, Father.

Do not neglect to show hospitality to strangers,
for thereby some have entertained angels unawares.

HEBREWS 13:2 ESV

Won't it be fun to get to heaven and have it all make sense?
To see all the interconnected threads, all the ripple effects of
every tiny act of kindness?

As you end your day today, imagine a world where hospitality
comes as naturally as breath. See ripples turn to waves as
strangers are revealed as angels.

Precious God, remind me! Remind me every single person I meet
is a child of yours or an angel in disguise. Make me generous with
my words, my time, and my table. Send me an angel to bless, that
I may know a heart that's truly open.

Where in your life can you show greater hospitality? Does
God bring anyone specific to mind?

Hard to Resist

Again, the devil took him to a very high mountain and showed him all the kingdoms of the world and their glory. And he said to him, "All these I will give you, if you will fall down and worship me."

MATTHEW 4:8-9 ESV

The world can offer a lot of great things. Careers offer success, relationships offer security, and riches can provide comfort. Nothing is inherently wrong with having these things, unless they are used for our own glory.

In the world, people want to glorify themselves. This is what the devil was after, too. He wanted to be worshiped. Thankfully, Jesus knew that the kingdoms of this world were nothing like the kingdom of God. He chose something greater. Are you able to resist the temptation of the world today?

God, thank you that you understand the temptations in this world. Please strengthen me for the day ahead and remind me that your kingdom is better than all the false glory that may come my way.

Jesus said to him, "Be gone, Satan! For it is written, 'You shall worship the L ord your God and him only shall you serve.'" Then the devil left him, and behold, angels came and were ministering to him.

There are many pressures in the day to serve things other than God's kingdom. Have you found yourself tempted to buy something new but not needed? Have you booked another beauty appointment because you feel like you can't show anyone your flaws? Did you say yes to just one more thing that you don't have time for because you didn't want to look bad by saying no?

We need to reassess our decisions in light of who we are serving—is it God, or humans? The Bible says we should only worship the Lord our God. Tell the devil who is boss and let God minister to you as you resist temptation.

God, I am sorry for becoming distracted with desiring the things of this world. Help me to say no to temptation and worship only you. Minister to me now as I rest in your presence.

What is drawing you away from worshiping God and him alone?

Passionate and Powerful

I love You, O Lord, my strength.

PSALM 18:1 NASB

"Don't you just love these?" There are words of great weight we have come to toss around as lightly as snowflakes. Words like love, the most powerful of all actions or emotions, get attached to things like cookies, colors, or athletes and celebrities we'll never actually know. Awesome can as easily describe a brownie as the power of God to lift an affliction or transform a heart.

Today, let's meditate on what it means to love God, then purpose to notice our casual use of heavy terms. Let the "I love you," we offer our Father carry a singular weight. Let the brownies be yummy, and God alone be awesome.

God, I want to honor you with the reverence you deserve. I know you know I don't consider you equal with a delicious dessert, but Holy Spirit, I invite you to show me how liberally I speak as though I do. Let my love be true love and my awe be genuine awe. I love you, Lord.

Lord, I passionately love you and I'm bonded to you!
I want to embrace you, for now you've become my power!
PSALM 18:1 TPT

The expanded version of this verse gives us further insight into how David was feeling when he wrote this Psalm. Feelings have degrees; we obviously don't love God and brownies, our children and the color green, or our parents and our favorite football player in the same way.

The love David had for God—the love the Lord wants us all to have—is passionate, binding, and powerful. It's also the way he loves us. How much strength can we gather from a love like that? How much hope?

Father God, I want to love you with all the passion I have. I want to need you, as David did, every moment. Increase my desire for you, God, and strengthen me through the bond of our shared affection.

Imagine yourself in a deep, loving embrace with your Creator. How does it feel?

Jesus Heals

Jesus was going throughout all Galilee, teaching in their synagogues and proclaiming the gospel of the kingdom, and healing every kind of disease and every kind of sickness among the people.

MATTHEW 4:23 NASB

It is hard to understand how and when God heals his children. Have you prayed for healing recently and haven't got any better? Do you know someone around you that is unwell and not recovering? It can be disheartening when you are sick, or see others that you care about not improving.

Our faith does not need to be great, but through our belief in Jesus, we can also acknowledge our belief in the miracles that he performed. Jesus showed us that what we think is impossible is not impossible with God.

Jesus, I pray for healing in my life and in the life of those who are unwell around me. I know you cared for others and had compassion to heal, but I also recognize that sometimes you don't answer us exactly how we want. Help me to trust that you are always good, no matter what.

News about him spread as far as Syria, and people soon began
bringing to him all who were sick. And whatever their sickness or
disease, or if they were demon possessed or epileptic or paralyzed—
he healed them all.

MATTHEW 4:24 NASB

Sometimes healing doesn't come, and we need to trust that
God is still faithful and gracious. He will restore perfect
health to us in eternity.

We may have to wait for healing and we may never really know
why. But let us still be encouraged today to believe in a God
of miracles, and pray with all our might that he will bring
healing to the sick.

God, I do trust that you are faithful and gracious. I believe there
are times that you have healed me, or those around me, and I
believe that you have also kept me safe in times I wasn't even
aware of. Thank you for your enduring love.

Are you praying for healing for yourself or someone else?
Can you see God's goodness in that situation?

Truth Matters

I have no greater joy than this,
to hear that my children are walking in the truth.

3 JOHN 1:4 NRSV

How is your relationship with the truth? The deeper we dig into this question, the more likely it is we're realizing it's a relationship that could do some growing. While few followers of Christ are outright liars, once we consider embellishment, exaggeration, omission, and the like, it's easy to see we all have room for improvement.

And why does this matter? Notice how often Jesus refers to the truth in the Gospels. Whether starting a sentence with "I tell you the truth," declaring himself to be the truth, or indicating truth as the gateway to freedom, it's clear truth matters to our Lord.

Dear Jesus, I want to walk in the truth, because I know that's where you are. I consider myself an honest person, and I know how much I value honesty in my relationships, so I ask you to show me any areas of my life where truth is lacking. Whether I am prone to exaggerate, embellish, or even behave differently alone that I do around others, show me the truth and give me the courage to join you there!

Nothing gives me greater joy than to hear
that my children are following the way of truth.

3 JOHN 1:4 NCV

Whether or not you have ever raised a child, chances are you've been lied to by one. It's almost charming, isn't it, the way they so boldly insist on something so clearly false? Gently, we explain the importance of being honest. "You need to be honest so people will trust you," we say. In later years, these stories become family legends, often the source of great laughter.

The older people get, the more that innocent charm wears off. There's nothing funny about being lied to by a teenager, a roommate, a co-worker, a spouse. Lies hurt, but honesty brings joy, and no wonder: Jesus himself is truth. A relationship based on truth is one where Jesus can live.

God, because you are the truth, I want more truth! Bring honesty
and openness to my relationships, so you can dwell among us.
Infuse my life with the joy that comes from following your way,
and help me be a safe place for others to share their truth with me.

How might you infuse more honesty into your walk?

There Is Joy

Those who sow with tears will reap with songs of joy.

PSALM 126:5 NIV

How do you define joy? Is it just intense happiness, or is it more complex, more unexplainable than that? Reading Bible verses that contain the word, a theme emerges. Biblically speaking, joy is often connected to its opposites: sorrow, pain, and tears. Frequently, joy springs from places we wouldn't expect it.

When we're able to celebrate a life while mourning a death, there is joy. When we have hope for the future despite a present disappointment or disaster, there again is joy. With God as our shepherd, our supply and our strength, intense happiness—joy—is possible, even in the saddest of circumstances. Could it be that the contrast between where we are and how the Lord is holding our hearts is the reason for the intensity? Could it be that God is not only the source of joy, but joy itself? What a joy it is even to wonder such things!

God, you are my joy! Because I've been able to smile on even my darkest day, I know you will redeem every circumstance of my life. You bring joy from every tear, laughter from every sorrow, and pleasure from every pain. May I remember this every day, and may I be a guiding light for others in their own search for joy.

Those who sow in tears shall reap with joyful shouting.

PSALM 126:5 NASB

It's a common experiment, the first many of us ever conducted: place a dried bean inside a wet paper towel, then place the paper towel in a plastic bag. Within days, sprouts emerge. Factors like the amount of moisture and the amount of light have an effect on how quickly your bean will grow, but almost without fail, your bean will grow.

In a time of sorrow or transition, God's Word teaches us that as we plant tiny seeds of hope, eventually we'll reap in joy. It probably won't grow as quickly as those beans, but it will grow.

God, you are so faithful! I can't see what you're doing underground, but because of your promises, I know roots are forming, hope is sprouting, and one day joy will burst forth from this place. Thank you for hope, for your faithfulness, and for joy.

When has God shown himself faithful by bringing joy to your heart?

Empty but Blessed

"Blessed are the poor in spirit, for theirs is the kingdom of heaven. Blessed are those who mourn, for they will be comforted."

MATTHEW 5:3-4 NIV

There are days where you might wake up a little more sluggish, with a little less energy and positivity about the day. That can feel kind of empty, a gap you're hoping to fill.

The great thing about the God you serve is that in him, you can be complete. He can be that gap-filler. As you sit with him, his light begins to burn brighter.

God, lift me up this morning. It's hard to get out of bed and sometimes I feel anxious or worried about the day ahead. Give me energy and strength to face another day.

*"Blessed are the meek, for they will inherit the earth.
Blessed are those who hunger and thirst for righteousness,
for they will be filled."*

MATTHEW 5:5-6 NIV

On this particular day, meet God in dependence. Come to him even when you don't feel like it. Present your helplessness and emptiness to him and he will bless you and fill your gap with warmth, joy, peace, care, and love.

As you spend time with God tonight, allow him to speak to you and rest knowing you were transformed and filled on one of the hardest days. He is faithful and loving no matter our circumstance or feeling.

I'm glad to be here in your presence tonight, God. It is a struggle for me to just sit down and think about you when my mind is so full of other things. As I seek you, let the things of this earth grow dim in the light of your glory.

Have you seen the fruit of this promise on one of your rough days?

Selflessness

"Greater love has no one than this:
to lay down one's life for one's friends."

JOHN 15:13 NIV

In a society that seems to grow more self-oriented every day, the New Testament notion of selflessness is certainly counter-cultural. Particularly as young women are finding a voice in the very important conversation about equality, the idea that we would willingly place our own wants below those of our friends, neighbors, and even people half way around the world can be controversial.

What then do we make of this call to selflessness? Are we to skip over it, or, can we look past our first, bristly reaction and find the imbedded gift? The moment we stop thinking about ourselves—start giving ourselves away—is the moment we realize that letting go of "me" is what makes way for "us." Standing up for "my rights" becomes standing up for "our rights." Laying down "my life" means joining with yours and together being swept up into Christ's.

God, I can't lie to you. This one is hard! Lay down my life? What if no one picks it up, or someone tramples it? Inspire me to forget "me"—even for a day—and become absorbed in loving and serving someone else. Show me that less of me makes room for more of you and that as I become more like you, choosing others becomes automatic.

"The greatest love a person can show is to die for his friends."

JOHN 15:13 NCV

What would you die for? Fortunately for most people, this is a question we'll never need to prove our answer to. It's the stuff of journal writing, or perhaps Bible study conversation, but not a serious decision.

And yet, for Jesus, it was. John didn't share these words of Jesus in his Gospel so we'd all rush into burning buildings and otherwise throw ourselves into harm's way to save one another; he shared it so we could try and comprehend the incredible depth of Jesus' love for us. Willingly, premeditatedly, and through indescribable pain, Jesus proved his answer. He was willing to die for you.

Jesus, as I lay down to rest, help me lay down my life. Your selfless love is more than I can fathom. Facing fear and unbearable pain, you literally gave your life. For me. For us. The next time I don't feel like participating in a meal train, or taking a turn in the toddler room at church, please, God, flood me with awareness of what you gave up for me. I am so very grateful.

How selfless or selfish do you believe you are? Ask the Lord to reveal the truth to you.

Salt and Light

"You are the salt of the earth. But what good is salt if it has lost its flavor? Can you make it salty again? It will be thrown out and trampled underfoot as worthless."

MATTHEW 5:13 NLT

You are blessed simply because you believe in Jesus and have eternal life. When Jesus was speaking to the disciples, he wanted them to know that this very good thing that they had received needed to be shared.

There is no point to a life in Christ if we lose the one thing that makes us different from the world. God wants you to display a life that shows how wonderful salvation is. Can you be like salt in an otherwise bland world today?

Jesus, thank you that you blessed me with the gift of salvation. Let my words and heart attitude toward activities and people be an expression of this gift so I don't just blend in with everyone else. Let my life be that point of difference that makes people wonder why I have peace and joy.

"You are the light of the world—like a city on a hilltop that cannot be hidden. No one lights a lamp and then puts it under a basket. Instead, a lamp is placed on a stand, where it gives light to everyone in the house."

MATTHEW 5:14-15 NLT

As you prepare yourself for bed tonight, the last thing you will probably do is turn out the lights. You need the light to see everything you are doing until then. You need the light to show you the way. There would be no point of turning on the light only to cover it up.

This is our journey of salvation. Jesus didn't want you to receive his light and then hide it. He wants you to shine brightly so others will also see the path to faith.

Father, as I reflect on those places where I have hidden my light, I thank you for your grace. I know that you understand and that you want to give me the boldness to live out my faith as brightly as I can. I pray that as I greet the light tomorrow, I would be ready to shine alongside it.

Where have you hidden your light lately? What situations make you want to hide instead of shine?

Sleep in Peace

I will both lie down in peace, and sleep;
for You alone, O Lord, make me dwell in safety.

PSALM 4:8 NKJV

Ah, peace. Just to speak the word starts to bring the feeling on. Long before his birth, Isaiah called Jesus the Prince of Peace, and Jesus himself mentions peace over 100 times in the Bible, so it seems reasonable to believe it's important to him.

Most of us would say it's important to us too, but do our lives reflect this? Do we lie down in peace, or do we bring unfinished business, worries, and our smart phones to bed with us? As we sleep, does Jesus inhabit our dreams or does the chatter of our busyness continue to occupy us even then? Awake now and ready for a new day, let us pray for the peace of Christ to rule our thoughts and actions.

Lord God, I do want peace! I want to bring you, your calm and loving Spirit, into all my interactions. As stressors arise, let your peace remind me it's just a moment, just a decision. Help me to choose well, and again flood me with peace as I move forward. All day long, bring me to peace.

I go to bed and sleep in peace,
because, LORD, only you keep me safe.

PSALM 4:8 NCV

Regardless of the day, how done the to-do list is, how resolved the issues, we can go to bed and sleep in peace. We may need to lay our concerns out one by one, giving them over to the Lord and his infinitely more capable plans. We may need to shift our minds entirely off ourselves by praying for others or reading the Word. We may simply need to pray, "Lord, bring your peace."

The method is not nearly so important as the intention. Let the Prince of Peace rock you to sleep tonight. May you drift off easily and quietly, and may you wake restored.

God, prince of peace, help me shed the day. Turn my thoughts to the comfort and safety you alone provide and let the certainty of your love for me bring my mind and body to peace. May I rest and be refreshed and dream of you.

How might you tweak (or establish) your nighttime routine to invite peaceful sleep?

Love All

"You have heard the law that says,
'Love your neighbor and hate your enemy.'
But I say, love your enemies!
Pray for those who persecute you!"

MATTHEW 5:43-44 NLT

The ways of this world are different from the ways of the kingdom. Jesus made this clear by contrasting what the world says to do with your enemies and what Christ-followers should do.

You probably have people in your mind that you see as a threat, or those who are unkind toward you. Sometimes we even get mocked for our faith, whether overtly or subtly. These are the very people who Christ asks us to love.

It's not easy to pray for those who have hurt you. Jesus understands this; he had to forgive all who brought him to his painful death on the cross. Allow Christ to be your strength as you practice goodness to those who have wronged you.

God, I need your help with loving my enemies. Give me your heart for them. Help me to see that everyone is loved by you, no matter what they do or say. I don't accept their wrong behavior, but I choose today to pray for their healing, forgiveness, and restoration.

"In that way, you will be acting as true children of your Father in heaven. For he gives his sunlight to both the evil and the good, and he sends rain on the just and the unjust alike."

MATTHEW 5:45 NLT

It can seem unfair that good people suffer and those seemingly less deserving prosper. Jesus wanted us to recognize the Father heart of God for all his children, even those who reject him.

God loves unconditionally and when we show impartiality for all his creation, even those who seem bad, we know that we are being the true children of God, imitating his love for all humankind.

Lord Jesus, forgive me for a heart that cannot always see your love for all people. Help me to love these people who feel like enemies. Give me the grace to change my ways.

Who are your enemies? Is there anyone that needs an extra measure of grace and forgiveness from you?

When I Worship

Oh come, let us worship and bow down;
*let us kneel before the L*ORD*, our Maker!*

PSALM 95:6 ESV

How do you worship God? At first, the answer might seem obvious. We go to church, we sing the songs, we read our Bibles. But are we worshipping? Are we sure? Somewhere along the line, Sunday worship became, for many of us, for us. We go to church to learn, to be inspired, to see our friends. We sing along because we love the song. We read our Bibles because again, we want to learn—or be inspired—or even out of habit.

While being inspired by the teaching and moved by the music and enjoying the fellowship of our brothers and sisters are all wonderful things, let us take an inventory of those things we do for God. Not to beat ourselves up, but to rightfully raise him up, let us be mindful of our worship.

Father God, I have allowed my worship of you to become about me. Forgive me. The next time I sing a song to you without even thinking of you, invade my heart with love for you. As I read my Bible to keep up with my plan, overwhelm me with gratitude for the one who breathed every word to life. God, let my worship be worthy!

Come and kneel before this Creator-God;
come and bow before the mighty God, our majestic maker!
PSALM 95:6 TPT

No matter how and where you worship, you've probably encountered someone more demonstrative than yourself. Hands a little higher, voice a little louder, maybe even dancing up front or face down in the aisle, they seem a little freer, a little more surrendered, a little less self-conscious.

How do you feel around these free spirits? Are you comfortable asking God to show you how surrendered he wants you to be when you worship him? If you're an aisle dancer, are you comfortable asking God if your focus is truly all on him?

Dear God, you and I both know how self-conscious or free I am when I worship. This is a little scary for me, but I want to ask you, Father, to help me forget everything but you during my worship. Whether alone in my room or in a church of thousands, help me turn all my attention to you, and let me give you all the glory you deserve.

What addition can you make to the ways and times you worship God?

Your Treasure

"Do not lay up for yourselves treasures on earth, where moth and rust destroy and where thieves break in and steal, but lay up for yourselves treasures in heaven, where neither moth nor rust destroys and where thieves do not break in and steal."

MATTHEW 6:19-20 ESV

Have you ever been sitting on a beach and watched a little child work tirelessly on an elaborate sand castle? These little children are unaware of the patterns of ocean waves and don't realize that as the day passes, their masterpieces will eventually be swept away by the swelling tide. All that work, all that concentration, all that pride, gone as the water erases the shore.

What castles are we building in our lives that could, at any moment, be simply erased? We must know what can last and what won't. There are temporary kingdoms and a kingdom that will never pass away. We have to recognize which one we are contributing to.

God, I want to build meaningful things for your kingdom. Give me the discernment to know what is truly of worth to you.

"Don't keep hoarding for yourselves earthly treasures that can be stolen by thieves. Material wealth eventually rusts, decays, and loses its value. Instead, stockpile heavenly treasures for yourselves that cannot be stolen and will never rust, decay, or lose their value."

MATTHEW 6:21 ESV

If your work and your heart are invested in a heavenly vision, then what you have spent your life on will continue to matter for longer than you live.

Spend your time investing in the eternal souls of people, in the eternal vision of advancing God's kingdom, and in the never-ending truth of the Gospel. In these things you will find purpose and treasure that will never be lost.

Father God, I know that you have created my life with meaning and purpose. Help me to see how the gifts that you have given me matter in terms of eternity. Let me see the value of all my time, energy, and talent.

What are you putting your time, energy, and talents into? Are they being used for God's glory?

As They Are

Accept one another, then, just as Christ accepted you,
in order to bring praise to God.

ROMANS 15:7 NIV

It's easy to come up with ways other people could change for the better, isn't it? If she could keep a secret. If he would stop bragging about his possessions. We know Christ calls us to live in harmony with one another, but sometimes others can make this challenging. We start to notice sins and flaws, and the next thing we know, it's all we can see.

Romans 15:7 reminds us to accept one another… as Christ accepted us. Broken, imperfect, and sinful, Jesus loves us just as we are. If this is how our Savior feels about us, then truly, who are we to place conditions on our acceptance of one another? Yes, everyone in our lives could improve. But we bring glory to God by loving them as they are.

God, thank you for accepting me in all my brokenness. You see past my sins and shortcomings and you love me for me. Help me to see others as you see them, and to glorify you by accepting them for them.

Welcome one another, therefore, just as Christ has welcomed you,
for the glory of God.

ROMANS 15:7 NRSV

It's one thing to be more accepting of the people in our lives, and quite another to be more welcoming and accepting in general. As much as we might struggle to be more gracious toward a gossipy friend or a neighbor with a bit too much braggadocio, how much more challenging is it to extend that grace to the addict on the corner, or the shockingly rude customer on the phone? How about that politician that gets under your skin?

And yet, this is exactly what we are called to do. Jesus loves that dirty, shivering addict exactly as much as he loves us. His heart beats for yours and the politician's with the same abiding love. How much glory, then, do we bring him when we extend grace, acceptance, and love despite agreement or understanding?

Dear God, let it be so! When treated rudely, let me respond with your kindness. When my initial reaction is disgust, replace it with your compassion. Grant me empathy, god that defies reason and instinct. Open my heart so others will see you there.

Invite the Holy Spirit to bring you an opportunity to practice true acceptance.

The Real Prize

"Be strong, and let us be courageous for our people and for the cities of our God; and may the LORD do what seems good to him."

1 CHRONICLES 19:13 NRSV

Pause for a moment and read the verse aloud. For many of us, the first part of this verse is easy to rally around. Be strong! Have courage! Let's do this! But how about that second half? Can you easily say, "Whatever seems good to you, God" or do you typically struggle for control, ask for certain outcomes, want things to go your way? Is surrender to his plan easy for you, or a constant challenge?

In the words of Joab to his army, we find a perfect model of surrender: be strong for those we serve; be courageous for the Kingdom of God, and may the Lord's will be done. Nothing for us, all for God and those he has given us to serve. Oh, that we could achieve such devotion!

God, I want to use my strength for others, my courage to carry out your will. I want to want only what seems good to you. Grant me the faithfulness of Joab, God, that I may willingly surrender to your perfect will.

*"Be courageous! Let us fight bravely for our people
and the cities of our God. May the LORD's will be done."*

1 CHRONICLES 19:13 NLT

"Your Kingdom come, your will be done, unless it interferes with my happiness." If we were fully honest before God, our version of the Lord's Prayer might sound more like this. What if what he wills for my team to lose? What if he wills the other candidate to get the job? What if God's plan is to grow my character through a season of loss and struggle?

This is where courage comes in. As we trust him, we see that it's in the brave fighting we best glorify him. It's how we fight: bravely. It's why fight: for our people and the cities of our God. Winning is a bonus; the real prize is surrendering to his will.

Perfect Father, grant me this courage! As I sleep this night, loosen my grip on my plans. Draw me toward your will, and show me where I can fight bravely to see it done.

What cause, issue, or people come to mind again and again when you think of fighting bravely? How can you step in?

Under His Care

"Look at the birds. They don't plant or harvest or store food in barns, for your heavenly Father feeds them. And aren't you far more valuable to him than they are? Can all your worries add a single moment to your life?"

MATTHEW 6:26 NLT

When you wake up in the morning you can begin to feel anxious about the day ahead. What will you wear? What do you need to organize? Will you make it in time to your important appointment?

Life is so full that we can feel overwhelmed with worry about getting it all done, and getting it all done right. Jesus didn't want us to feel like that. God cares for us and takes care of a lot of the small things that we probably don't realize he has had a hand in. Recognize his work in your life today, and head into it with confidence.

God, I need you right by my side today. Thank you for all the small things that you take care of. Thank you that you are a Father who loves to take care of me.

"Why worry about your clothing? Look at the lilies of the field and how they grow. They don't work or make their clothing, yet Solomon in all his glory was not dressed as beautifully as they are."

Matthew 6:28-29

What is it about coming home after a long day that makes you want to change into something more comfortable? You may have already done that and are ready to relax.

Sometimes we need to be reminded that we even have this option. We are privileged that God not only looks after our basic needs but often blesses us with more than that.

Father, thank you for taking care of me. Thank you that not only do I have my basic needs met, but that you bless me with other beautiful things. Help me to express more gratitude for all my blessings.

What blessings are you thankful for? Where can you see God's provision in your life today?

He Whispers

"I, the LORD your God, hold your right hand;
it is I who say to you, 'Fear not, I am the one who helps you.'"

ISAIAH 41:13 NIV

Looking back on the most frightening and difficult things we've ever done, we often wonder where we found the courage. It seems impossible now that we actually passed that test; we felt so unprepared! How did we face that diagnosis, and the months of uncertainty that followed? Where did the words come from, and where did our tears go, when we stood up and gave that eulogy?

Scripture tells us again and again our help comes from God himself. He is the inner voice saying, "You can do this. You are strong enough. I've got you." That sudden burst of inspiration, endurance, or eloquence? That was the Lord squeezing your hand.

God, what a thrill it is to know you hold my hand! You stay close enough, always, to sense when I need a whisper of encouragement. The courage, the strength, the power that seems to come from nowhere—it all comes from you. You are my constant help, and the only help I need.

> *"I am the LORD your God, who holds your right hand,*
> *and I tell you, 'Don't be afraid. I will help you.'"*
>
> ISAIAH 41:13 NCV

Look down at your right hand. Open and close it. Turn it over. In a moment, close your eyes and try to sense the presence of God beside you, holding your hand. Don't give up too quickly; give your thoughts time to settle on him. What is he giving your courage for? What is he promising you will not face alone?

Rest with him awhile, allowing his presence to wash over you. Whatever he whispers, believe it.

Father God, I confess I don't come to this sweet space with you nearly enough. How incredible it is to know you are right here, always, no matter how long it takes me to return. Speak to me, Father. Tell me I can do it, face it, make you proud, and then—help me believe it.

How often do you sense God's presence?

Hope in the Storm

"All who listen to my instructions and follow them are wise, like a man who builds his house on solid rock. Though the rain comes in torrents, and the floods rise and the storm winds beat against his house, it won't collapse, for it is built on rock."

MATTHEW 7:24-25 TLB

Jesus didn't just give instructions on how to live so we could be nice people. There are nice people everywhere: believers and unbelievers alike. He gave us ways to live so we could walk through the storms with peace and joy in our hearts.

Our confidence is not in everything that is happening around us; it is in knowing that with Christ we have a new, eternal life. That knowledge is our solid foundation.

God, thank you for reminding me that a life lived your way is a life that is able to weather all kinds of storms that may come my way. Help me to live by your instructions and to be wise so I will always carry the hope of eternity in all circumstances.

"Those who hear my instructions and ignore them are foolish, like a man who builds his house on sand. For when the rains and floods come, and storm winds beat against his house, it will fall with a mighty crash."

MATTHEW 7:26-27 TLB

When we ignore God's ways, we also ignore the hope that he has placed in our hearts for his eternal kingdom. Forgetting to live with this eternal perspective means that even the smallest of storms can beat us down, making us feel discouraged and hopeless.

As you take this time to think about your day, reflect on whether you have been facing your challenges with hope or despair.

God, I have faced a few challenges this week and I know there are times when I have responded with despair and a lack of hope. Remind me that the knowledge of a new, restored life is the very thing that will keep my head above the water. Give me joy and peace in all circumstances.

How have you been responding to the storms of life this week?

Ready to See

Open my eyes that I may see wonderful things in your law.

PSALM 119:18 NIV

Have you ever been the last to get a joke? As everyone else wiped tears of laughter from their eyes, you smiled and thought, "Huh?" But then, suddenly, the extra layer of meaning was illuminated and your laughter became as genuine as everyone else's. Or maybe, seeing an old movie through adult eyes, you understand why your parents didn't want you watching it as a child.

We call these "Aha" moments, and Bible reading provides an endless series of them. As we go deeper into the Word, God opens our eyes to fresh revelations, allowing stories we thought we knew to become fresh and exciting. Passages we've taken for granted take on sudden weight and significance when the Lord opens our eyes.

Father, in the words of the psalmist, open my eyes. Illuminate layer upon layer of meaning. Show me the beauty hidden within your Word. Surprise me with wisdom; delight me with depth. I'm ready to see.

Open my eyes, that I may behold wondrous things out of your law.

As a little girl, it may not have made sense to you that you couldn't have cake for breakfast, lunch, and dinner. By the time you reached a certain age, though, you understood the wisdom of this rule. Speed limits can feel like a nuisance, especially to a young driver, but as we gain experience, we appreciate the safety of slower-moving cars in neighborhoods and around blind curves.

So it is with God's law. The more he illuminates our understanding, the more we understand every command is handed down in love. Every rule is designed with our best life in mind.

God, I confess I don't always enjoy obeying your laws. They sometimes conflict with my comfort, and cut down on my fun. And yet, each time I do, I gain something. Open my eyes further, God! Show me all the good that awaits when I follow your ways.

Is there a rule or law in Scripture you struggle to embrace? Let the Holy Spirit help you by opening your eyes to its loving intent.

One in a Hundred

"What do you think? If any man has a hundred sheep, and one of them has gone astray, does he not leave the ninety-nine on the mountains and go and search for the one that is straying?"

MATTHEW 18:12 NASB

Regardless of how beautifully or how imperfectly your earthly father showed his love, your heavenly Father's love is utterly boundless. Rest in that thought a moment. There is nothing you can do to change how he feels about you.

It's easy to forget we are already perfectly loved. Our Father loves you more than you can imagine. And he would do anything for you. Remember that throughout your day.

God, thank you that you care so much about me. At times, I have been that one lost sheep and you have come to find me. Thank you for your love for me.

"If it turns out that he finds it, truly I say to you, he rejoices over it more than over the ninety-nine which have not gone astray. So it is not the will of your Father who is in heaven that one of these little ones perish."

MATTHEW 12:13-14 NASB

You might have had a rough day, or maybe a really good day. Remember that your heavenly Father has been loving you throughout all of your day.

Who do you love most fiercely, most protectively, most desperately here on earth? What would you do for them? Know that it's a mere fraction, nearly immeasurable, of what God would do for you. Spend some time thanking him for his great love.

Father, I know that you will always search me out, no matter where I try to go. Help me to stay close to you so I can always bring you joy. Let me rest in your care for me as I go to sleep.

Are there areas of your life that you feel lost? Let Jesus take care of those things.

Find Peace Here

*Those of steadfast mind you keep in peace
because they trust in you.*

ISAIAH 26:3 NRSV

If you were to form a mental picture of chaos, what would you see? Impossible deadlines, commitments on top of commitments, long lists and short hours? How about peace? What picture comes to mind?

Most of us picture getting away. Whether our minds took us to a hot bath or a tropical island, we're definitely not here. The trouble with this image, though it's wonderful, is that it's fleeting. Whether bathtub or Bali, we can't stay. Rather than going to a peaceful place, let's start over, inviting peace right into our chaos. Let the Holy Spirit quiet your movements. Let Jesus slow your thoughts. Say his name. Find peace here.

Lord Jesus, I love how you come into my chaos with your peace. As I slow my breath and think of you, you envelop me in quiet joy. As I trust you with this load, you lighten it. As I commit my weakness to you, you help me see the ways I'm being strengthened. Thank you, God, for bringing peace here.

You will keep in perfect peace all who trust in you,
all whose thoughts are fixed on you!

Isaiah 26:3 NLT

Earlier today, in order to picture peace, we shifted our thoughts. Imagining a place where cares were few and all was quiet, chaos diminished. God promises this peace can be ours any time, any place, anywhere. How? By thinking of him.

Fixing our thoughts on the Lord and all his goodness, we see it is simply impossible to remain unsettled. The more we train our minds to stay with him, the more perfect peace is ours—no matter the circumstances. The more we place our trust in him, the less we have to steal our peace.

God, as I end this day, will you help me shift my thoughts? Each worry, as it comes to mind, I turn over to you. I marvel at the creative ways you've cared for me in the past, and I imagine the glories you have in store for the future. Because I know you are faithful, because I know you are good, I will sleep in peace.

As you close your eyes tonight, speak the name of Jesus. Imagine his presence. Let him bring you peace.

Gathered Together

"I also tell you this: If two of you agree here on earth concerning anything you ask, my Father in heaven will do it for you."

MATTHEW 18:19 NLT

When was the last time you felt spiritually recharged from conversation or prayer with other Christians? Sometimes going to church or a Bible study seems like just another thing to add to your list of things to do.

Are you giving yourself an opportunity to be uplifted by other believers or to be an encouragement to those around you? Remember that God promises to be with you when you are gathered together in his name. Is there a gathering that you can commit yourself to this week? Make an effort to go so you can experience the rich rewards of fellowship.

Father God, sometimes I feel too tired to go to something else. Give me energy to say yes to something this week that I know will be good for me and good for others.

> *"Where two or three gather together as my followers,*
> *I am there among them."*

MATTHEW 18:20 NLT

God is a relational God. He knows that we need each other, and that life is better together. As a Christian, it is especially important to share time with other believers.

When we make time to pray together, study the Bible together, and share our faith stories, we can be supported, encouraged, and strengthened.

God, thank you for creating others in my life. I have so many wonderful friends and I really do love my family. Help me to encourage those who have faith and to be a witness of your love to those who do not.

Take a moment this evening to make a mental list of all the things you are involved in. Are these things encouraging you in your faith? Are they resulting in rewarding relationships?

Wrapped in Love

Blessed be the God and Father of our Lord Jesus Christ, the Father of mercies and God of all comfort, who comforts us in all our affliction, so that we may be able to comfort those who are in any affliction, with the comfort with which we ourselves are comforted by God.

2 CORINTHIANS 1:3-4 ESV

To be held by the Father is a comfort like no other. As we climb like children into that space that feels like it was made just for us, he holds us sweetly, but also with sureness. He's here to soothe and also to protect. No matter what we are going through, our Abba knows how to make it better. And once we're better, he invites us to pass it on.

Part of his beautiful design is that we would give away what's been so generously given to us. Once we've known his comfort in the face of disappointment, we can be there for a friend facing bad news. Once he's loved us through loss, we're uniquely equipped to walk alongside someone else through theirs. And through it all, we—and they—are drawn ever closer to him.

God, on the days I need your comfort, wrap me up and hold me close. On the days I need to be a comforter, open my arms toward the one who needs me. Give me words, wisdom, and compassion. Let me be a warm, soft blanket—a conduit of your comfort.

Praise be to the God and Father of our Lord Jesus Christ. God is the Father who is full of mercy and all comfort. He comforts us every time we have trouble, so when others have trouble, we can comfort them with the same comfort God gives us.

2 Corinthians 1:3-4 NCV

After a long day, sometimes all we want to do is crawl under the comforter and rest. The warmth, the weight, the softness and even the smell wrap us up and invite us to relax.

This is how our Father God wants us to think of him. The God of all comfort wants us to crawl under his weight, feel his warmth, experience the softness of his compassion.

Notice how many times the word comfort is repeated in the verse. This isn't an accident; it's so we don't miss the message. We are comforted so that we will comfort. Our Father wants us to experience the incomparable warmth of being the comforted and the comforter. He wants to wrap us in love, and he wants us to become love.

God, as I settle into bed tonight and sink into sleep, make me aware of your presence! Allow me to feel the warmth and reassurance that only you can provide. And when I wake, equip me to give it away. I can always come back for more, and you will always give it.

Are you more a seeker or a giver of comfort? How might God be inviting you to move toward the other?

Burden of Riches

"If you wish to be complete, go and sell your possessions and give to the poor, and you will have treasure in heaven; and come, follow Me."

MATTHEW 19:21 NASB

If only I had more money! The thought runs through our minds frequently, and though we may actually have enough to be content with, we are often thinking about what we could do with more.

Wherever you stand financially, you probably have a goal of accumulating more wealth than you have now. But did you ever notice how the Bible seems to view earthly riches as actually getting in the way of our relationships with God and others?

God today I will probably have to deal with money. Help me to show integrity and generosity in paying bills, shopping, and even in earning money. Show me ways that I can be generous too.

*When the young man heard this statement, he went away
grieving; for he was one who owned much property.*

MATTHEW 19:22 NASB

Wealth is rarely what we hope it is; the more we have, the
more we have to lose. Jesus wanted the rich man to have a
compassionate heart—one that was willing to give up what he
had for the sake of the kingdom. To do this, he would have
needed to give up the life that he was accustomed to.

Before asking God to bless you with wealth, ask him to bless
you with a heart of giving.

*Heavenly Father, thank you that you have given me more than
enough. Help me to be content with what I have and to think more of
others than myself. Bring generosity and compassion into my heart.*

Are there areas where God is asking you to be more generous?

Defeating the Mighty

We have this treasure in jars of clay to show that this all-surpassing power is from God and not from us.

2 CORINTHIANS 4:7 NIV

In the age of social media, every day brings another inspiring story. Here's a theme we're probably all familiar with: someone displays miraculous strength, saving someone else. A mother saves her toddler by lifting a car. A man saves a buddy by moving a 500-pound boulder. A vacationing couple swims out into a riptide, saving a drowning stranger. It's such a lovely image, the tiny defeating the mighty.

This is God at his most transparent. When our frail, fragile bodies do things they can't, it's because he can. And it doesn't have to be lifting a car: for some of us, not lifting that glass to our lips is a feat of equally miraculous strength. Either way, it's a chance to bring him glory.

God, I may not save anyone's life today, but I can still bring glory to you with my life. Every time I am more kind, more patient, more restrained, it's because of you. Let me never forget this, and let me give you all the credit.

*We have this treasure in earthen vessels that the excellence
of the power may be of God and not of us.*

2 CORINTHIANS 4:7 NKJV

When God calls us out of our comfort zone, our first instinct is often to think of all the reasons we can't. Or shouldn't. Or just plain won't. We dwell on our capacity, forgetting the One who calls us is the same one who will equip us.

We are like Esther, wondering, "What if I fail?" We are like Moses, saying, "But I'm not even a good speaker!" But that's the point, isn't it? That's always been the point. The weaker we are, the stronger he is. The more unlikely the hero, the more the signs point upward.

God, forgive me for the times I've felt you urging me toward something bigger, something possibly great, and stayed put. I don't want to fail, and I know I'm not great, so I pretend I didn't hear you. I hear you. And the next time you ask me, I'll remember where my strength comes from—and say yes.

Do you have a crazy, impossible dream that just won't go away? Maybe you've been ignoring an invitation to move toward something that feels beyond you. Could God be inviting you to display his glory?

You Are Beautiful

You are altogether beautiful, my love;
there is no flaw in you.

SONG OF SOLOMON 4:7 NRSV

Have you ever had a friend refer to herself as ugly? You didn't agree with her, did you? "No!" we say, "You're beautiful! You're so beautiful. I wish you could see yourself the way I see you." And we mean it. We mean it because we love her and we mean it because it's true. There is beauty in every face because we all reflect the face of God.

Imagine how the Bridegroom feels when we call ourselves ugly, poking at the parts we don't like and complaining about everything that makes us unique. "No, my darling. You are beautiful. So beautiful. Let me show you what I see when I look at you. Those aren't flaws; those are jewels. And you, my beautiful one, are a crown." Believe him.

Oh, Jesus, can it be true that you see only beauty in me? Will you give me your eyes? Help me believe I'm flawless. Let me radiate your beauty, with eyes that see, a mouth that encourages, ears that listen. Shine from inside me, God, and I will see it.

Every part of you is so beautiful, my darling.
Perfect is your beauty, without flaw within.

SONG OF SOLOMON 4:7 TPT

Let's be honest. This is a hard one. Every woman has a list of things she'd like to change; some spend thousands of dollars and hours pursuing an idealized beauty. Consider this: do you think Solomon's bride was truly perfect, inside and out? Of course not! Because he adored her, she was perfect to him.

The invitation to see ourselves as beautiful is an invitation to see ourselves as adored. It's a beckoning to forget the freckles, look past the lines, and see the radiance of a woman chosen by the King himself.

God, only you are flawless. When you speak these words over me, you are reminding me where beauty comes from. Thank you, Jesus for choosing, for loving, for cherishing me. What a beautiful thing!

How hard would it be for you to make a conscious choice to focus on seeing your beauty? Ask Jesus to lend you his eyes, and begin.

Ask for Favor

"LORD," he said, "if I have found favor in your eyes, then let the LORD go with us. Although this is a stiff-necked people, forgive our wickedness and our sin, and take us as your inheritance."

EXODUS 34:9 NIV

Even though Moses admits the sin and wrongdoing of the people of Israel, he still requests God's favor, not only for himself but for the people who would represent the way forward for all humanity.

From day to day we may forget that we are part of this greater plan and that God wanted us to be a part of his saving work. Even though you can admit that you aren't perfect, ask God for his forgiveness and be ready to receive his favor.

God, I am most certainly not perfect. I know I will not have a perfect day today but I ask for your favor. I know that your grace covers a multitude of sins and I will need your grace to face the day.

> *"I am making a covenant with you. Before all your people I will do wonders never before done in any nation in all the world. The people you live among will see how awesome is the work that I, the LORD, will do for you."*
>
> EXODUS 34:10 NIV

God accepted Moses' request to bless his people; he set up a covenant that would allow amazing things for and through the Israelites.

We know that God did many miracles, but we also know that the people didn't always obey and fulfill their part in that covenant promise. God remained faithful and showed his loving kindness toward them over and over again.

God, thank you for being faithful even when I am not. I know you still want to do amazing things in and through my life. I ask for your forgiveness. Open my heart to your loving advice.

Where and how do you need God's favor in your life this week?

Destiny

This vision is for a future time.
It describes the end, and it will be fulfilled.
If it seems slow in coming, wait patiently,
for it will surely take place.
It will not be delayed.

HABAKKUK 2:3 NLT

Watching a gifted athlete, or listening to a brilliant singer, words like "destiny" come to mind. Some talents are so extraordinary; they simply have to be used and shared. She was born for this, we think. What am I born for? we might think next.

We may not all sing like angels or swing a golf club like we were born holding it, but we do all have a destiny. Some of us know what it is; we're just not ready. The timing isn't right. Others among us aren't even sure we have one. Take heart. God knows exactly why he made you. He knows what he gave you to do, and who he gave you to love, and exactly how long it's going to be before you fulfill his plans. It might not feel like it today, but you're right on schedule.

God, I love believing I have a purpose. It doesn't need to be grand, but if it is, I'm willing to step up when you call me. And if it isn't, remind me it's big to you. Help me prepare by paying attention to the people, places, and assignments you put in front of me. I trust your timing, God, and I ask you to help me wait—with patience and with faith.

The vision is yet for an appointed time;
but at the end it will speak, and it will not lie.
Though it tarries, wait for it; because it will surely come,
it will not tarry.

HABAKKUK 2:3 NKJV

Not only do you have a destiny, but all of humanity does. Daily, we are moving toward a promised end, where heaven and earth are renewed and we will live together with God forever. Whether you long for this day, or whether eternity seldom crosses your mind, allow this promise to assure you: what God promises, God delivers.

If something feels late, or even forgotten, know that it is not. His timing is perfect and his love is boundless.

Father God, thank you for your Word! Promises in Scripture, though made to people living thousands of years before me, speak to me and remind me you are faithful. You are truthful. You are good. Whatever you have for me, I eagerly await. Whatever you want from me, I will eagerly do.

Does God's timing feel slow in an area of your life? What reason might he have for waiting?

Call to Follow

As Jesus passed along the Sea of Galilee,
he saw Simon and his brother Andrew casting a net into the sea—
for they were fishermen. And Jesus said to them,
"Follow me and I will make you fish for people."

MARK 1:16-17 NKJV

Simon and Andrew were just doing their ordinary job when Jesus called out to them. It wasn't like they were doing anything particularly special. Jesus must have known that they longed for significance in their lives. He put his call to them in their language. They knew that catching fish was sometimes difficult and that it required determination and strength.

This is what the Christian life is like for us. It is sometimes difficult. Think of Jesus calling out to you as your do your ordinary things today. He wants you to follow him into a life full of significance.

God, thank you for the call to follow you. Thank you that you give me that chance again and again. I am reminded today that I want to follow you, and I ask you to give me the strength and determination to share the good news with others.

Immediately they left their nets and followed him.

MARK 1:18 NKJV

The disciples responded immediately to Jesus' call to follow him. They must have known about Jesus and his ministry, and they were eager to be a part of God's work on earth.

In our busy lives we can be quick to dismiss Jesus' voice, or it can be drowned out in the noise of everything else competing for our time and energy. As you take some time this evening to stop and still your heart, listen for what Jesus wants to say to you, and commit to responding quickly.

Jesus, thank you for calling out to me. I know that there are times in the day that I find it hard to hear your voice, but I thank you for this time and for the words that you are speaking to me right now. I ask for a diligent heart to respond to your words tonight.

What can you hear Jesus speaking to you in this moment?

Moment of Solitude

In the morning, having risen a long while before daylight,
He went out and departed to a solitary place; and there He prayed.

MARK 1:35 NKJV

When do you find time to pray? Even if we are intentional and passionate about prayer, the everyday activities in our life will almost always take priority over time with God. It is often said that prayer can happen at any time, and of course it does, but is there value in setting aside a specific time to communicate with God?

Did you ever realize that the notion of quiet times comes from the example set by Jesus? We see in the Bible that Jesus would get up before daylight and pray in a solitary place. We are not often told what Jesus prayed about. It's not the content that matters; it's the willingness to maintain our relationship with the Father and seek his will. What better time to do this than at the beginning of our day?

Jesus, I give you this time, now. Thank you for the opportunity to spend some quiet time with you.

Simon and those who were with Him searched for Him. When they found Him, they said to Him, "Everyone is looking for You."

MARK 1:36-37 NKJV

Does this sound like you tonight, as you try to step away from the busyness of the day? Are people looking for you, pressing in on your alone time? Instead of trying to fit prayer into your busy day, pray before it gets busy, so you can cope with the pressures of life.

Were you able to give God some time in the early morning? Did you find a solitary place to hear from him? If not, fight for your time now. Be like Jesus and find the time and space to wait upon the Father.

Father, I know you are gracious and that you are not concerned with religious practice. Help me, however, to get into a good routine of introducing you into my morning and evenings so I am equipped to love you and to love others throughout my day.

How will you fit prayer time into your busy life?

Beautiful Day

I will recount the steadfast love of the Lord,
the praises of the Lord,
according to all that the Lord has granted us,
and the great goodness to the house of Israel
that he has granted them according to his compassion,
according to the abundance of his steadfast love.

Isaiah 63:7 ESV

We can claim the truth of this verse each and every day, regardless of our circumstances or emotions. His goodness is plentiful; his steadfast love is abundant.

Show God how thankful you are by remembering his goodness and telling others about what he has done for you.

You are so good, God! Your goodness cannot be recounted in one day alone, but I will rejoice in attempting to remember as many blessings as I can. Thank you for your steadfast love and compassion.

*I will tell of the kindnesses of the L*ORD,
the deeds for which he is to be praised,
*according to all the L*ORD *has done for us—*
yes, the many good things he has done for Israel,
according to his compassion and many kindnesses.

ISAIAH 63:7 NIV

God's goodness never waivers and his love for you never decreases. Even if life seems like drudgery and today feels rotten, the list of blessings in your life is quite long.

Recall the steadfast love he has granted to you, his goodness and compassion, and know that according to those, this day has been beautiful.

Loving and kind Father, thank you for all you have blessed me with. You are full of compassion and you care for me deeply. I am amazed by your love and I want everyone around me to know about it.

How have you seen God's kindness in your life today?

Constant Love

Above all, maintain constant love for one another,
for love covers a multitude of sins.

1 PETER 4:8 NRSV

Have you ever been shown kindness that you didn't deserve?
What did it feel like to be given love when you deserved hate?
To be given a second chance when all you should have gotten
was a door slammed in your face?

We will wrong one another and we will be wronged by others.
It's the human condition. But that is why the love of God is
the only perfect solution for us. Love can cover even a million
wrongs. When we choose love and kindness over anger and
revenge, the sins that seemed so intense suddenly fade away.
Love is the presence of Jesus in us, and Jesus is the only true
anecdote for sin.

Jesus, thank you for your grace, I am going to need it today! I pray
that you will give me your love for the people that I interact with
today. If I am wronged, help me to choose kindness.

Above all, keep fervent in your love for one another,
because love covers a multitude of sins.

1 PETER 4:8 NASB

As you reflect on your day, did you find yourself challenged to choose love instead of anger? It might have been a hard day and you may have struggled to see Jesus working in your life.

Constant love won't come naturally to you. Your humanity will cry out from within you and anger and rage will bubble forth without conscious invitation. But when you rely on the Spirit of God to intervene in your life and in your relationships, he can make kindness your response and love your reaction. Ask him to fill you with his Spirit and release his love in your heart so you can walk fully in his presence.

Holy Spirit, fill me with your presence. Renew your love in my heart so I can be ready for tomorrow. I need your guidance in my actions and decisions. Thank you for your grace.

Who can you identify in your life that needs to see the heart of God? Can you commit to showing them love this week?

One Step at a Time

To him who is able to keep you from stumbling and to present you blameless before the presence of his glory with great joy, to the only God, our Savior, through Jesus Christ our Lord, be glory, majesty, dominion, and authority.

JUDE 24-25 ESV

This race called life is a tiring one; sometimes the road gets long and our legs threaten to buckle underneath heavy burdens. How, then, do we persevere?

Hear this glorious news: God, whose majesty is matchless, is waiting to hold you up under the weight you are carrying. He lifts the burden to his own strong shoulders. He keeps you from slipping and falling away. He brings you into his presence! Rest a while in his presence today and draw strength from your time with him.

Father, whether the path is rugged or smooth, thank you for staying by my side, keeping me upright, and encouraging me with every step. I pray that I would hear your joyous voice today!

God is strong and can help you not to fall. He can bring you before his glory without any wrong in you and can give you great joy. He is the only God, the One who saves us. To him be glory, greatness, power, and authority through Jesus Christ our Lord for all time past, now, and forever. Amen.

JUDE 24-25 NCV

When the cold rains of sorrow or the sharp winds of discouragement are at our backs, how do we press on and finish the race?

Run your race listening to the encouragement of your heavenly Father—his mighty shouts of everlasting joy! Take it one holy step at a time. Keep your eyes on him, and you will finish victorious.

Lift me up, mighty God, when I stumble. Let me hear your whispers and shouts of encouragement along the way. I need your strength and your joy to be victorious in this life.

Listen for God's encouraging voice as you take one step at a time.

Stress

*Those who love your instructions
have great peace and do not stumble.*

PSALM 119:165 NLT

We are all well acquainted with stress. There are so many things in our life that cause us to be worried, pressured, and anxious. The world constantly presents us with unknowns and predicaments that steal our joy and rob our peace. You might be facing some of those predicaments today.

Spend time in his presence today, letting his peace wash over your heart. Focus on his truth and his capability rather than your problems and incapacity. God is able to take everything that is troubling you today and exchange it for peace that is beyond what you can imagine.

God, you are the most loving father, and you care about my wellbeing. I choose to follow your instructions, knowing that it will bring me peace.

Those who love Your law have great peace,
And nothing causes them to stumble.

Psalm 119:165 NASB

When we get in the presence of God and spend time in his Word, we are able to escape the stress of our lives and place our problems in his hands. God gives a peace that is unlike anything the world offers. He is focused on preparing us for his permanent kingdom, and, as a result, his presence offers hope and everlasting joy that is opposite to the trivial stressors of this life.

If you are feeling weary and a little down-trodden tonight, ask God for his guidance. He loves you enough to show you a way through your troubles and stress. Let his love for you bring peace deep within your being.

Lord, as I rest tonight, I pray for a really deep peace that will settle in my heart and allow me to have a wonderful sleep. Thank you for the wisdom that you bring to my life.

In what ways is the Lord directing you through your worries and stresses? Will you submit to his instructions?

Sacrifice of Praise

Bring your petition.
Come to the Lord and say,
"O Lord, take away our sins;
be gracious to us and receive us
and we will offer you the sacrifice of praise."

HOSEA 14:2 TLB

Songs of praise and worship are sometimes the last thing we feel like singing. A lamentation or a dirge feels more appropriate if we feel lonely, disappointed, or angry. How can we continue to praise our worthy God when we cannot find anything worthy of praise in our lives?

First, recognize the little things that are truly blessings: air in your lungs, God's love pouring over you, the salvation you have in Jesus Christ. Begin with these truths today and see how it changes your outlook.

You alone, God, deserve my praise. Thank you for your mercy and every good thing in my life. I praise your holy name!

> *Take words with you,*
> *And return to the LORD.*
> *Say to Him,*
> *"Take away all iniquity;*
> *Receive us graciously,*
> *For we will offer the sacrifices of our lips."*
>
> HOSEA 14:2 NKJV

Just as Hosea was instructed, sometimes we have to offer God the sacrifice of praise. Sometimes praise comes at the cost of humbling ourselves and giving God what he deserves. God restores hearts a hundred-fold when they are submitted to him.

Choose the sacrifice of praising God tonight. Even if you don't feel like it, he is worthy of your praise, and he will restore your joy.

You are always worthy. I am undeserving, yet you bless me. I am always falling, yet you lift me up.

Can you choose the sacrifice of praise tonight?

Wisdom of Solomon

"You did not ask for a long life, or riches for yourself, or the death of your enemies. Since you asked for wisdom to make the right decisions, I will do what you asked."

1 KINGS 3:11-12 NCV

If you could ask for one thing from God, what do you think it would be? Money, happiness, love, success... any one of us would love to be given any of these in full measure.

Solomon, a man who we know had an appetite for pleasure, took hold of his opportunity and asked for the best thing he possibly could have—wisdom. And God gave it to him. In all of life, don't we need wisdom the most? Wisdom to know what to do, how to act, and how to understand? As you launch into a day full of decisions, make sure you ask God to help you make the right decisions. You'll be a whole lot richer with good choices.

God, you created wisdom and you know all the best ways to get through this life. I ask you now, to guide me in all my decisions today and give me grace to choose the right ones!

"Because you have asked for wisdom in governing my people with justice and have not asked for a long life or wealth or the death of your enemies—I will give you what you asked for! I will give you a wise and understanding heart such as no one else has had or ever will have!"

1 KINGS 3:11-12 NLT

We have the same privilege as Solomon: to ask God for wisdom, knowing that he will give it. Maybe you're on the edge of a huge decision, a choice that will affect your life forever. God says that what you need—wisdom—is yours for the taking.

Ask God to come into the midst of whatever confusion you are faced with. Ask him to give you the same wisdom that he gave Solomon.

Lord, sometimes I become frozen when it comes to making big decisions. I am not always certain of which way you are telling me to turn, or what is the best decision. In these times, I ask for wisdom that comes from your Word, wisdom that comes from others, and wisdom that you speak into my heart.

What area of your life do you need wisdom for?

All I Need

Happy are those
who do not follow the advice of the wicked,
or take the path that sinners tread,
or sit in the seat of scoffers;
but their delight is in the law of the LORD,
and on his law they meditate day and night.
They are like trees
planted by streams of water,
which yield their fruit in its season,
and their leaves do not wither.
In all that they do, they prosper.

PSALM 1:1-3 NRSV

Thanks to a modern diet of technology and social media, women today can feast on heaping portions of gossip, envy, boastful pride, and selfishness. It is not a nourishing diet, but it is deviously sweet.

What sicknesses are we susceptible to when we replace time with our Father with time in front of a screen? Can you choose today to spend time in God's Word and be refreshed by the rich promises found there?

God, I admit that at times I am underfed on your Word. I'm malnourished from overeating at the modern-day buffet of social media and entertainment. Help me get rid of these unhealthy habits and embrace you more fully each day.

Blessed is the man
Who walks not in the counsel of the ungodly,
Nor stands in the path of sinners,
Nor sits in the seat of the scornful;
But his delight is in the law of the Lord,
And in His law he meditates day and night.
He shall be like a tree
Planted by the rivers of water,
That brings forth its fruit in its season,
Whose leaf also shall not wither;
And whatever he does shall prosper.

PSALM 1:1-3 NKJV

Praise God for his nourishment! His Word is as relevant for us today as it was for David thousands of years ago. Meditate on these words, and hear his voice calling to you.

When we spend time with God and read his Word, we are on the path to joy and delight. Under his nourishment we yield delicious fruit without the threat of withering. We prosper! Did your day yield good fruit? It can when you spend time in God's Word.

Father, thank you for your wonderful Word. Thank you for the joy and life it brings to my spirit. Help me to yield good fruit and prosper as I meditate on your Word.

Delight in God's Word today!

Loss of Control

My flesh and my heart fail;
But God is the strength of my heart and my portion forever.

PSALM 73:26 NKJV

Have you ever had a moment where you've felt completely out of control? A car accident, a diagnosis, or some other frightening moment? There are instances in our lives when our own flesh fails us. We recognize in a flash that we are no longer in control of our own outcome—and it terrifies us.

In that moment, when control is lost and fear overcomes us, there is one thing we can know for certain. God is our strength, and he never loses control. When your life, and the outcome of it, is ripped from your hands, it's still resting firmly in his grasp. He is our portion. He is our ration. He is enough. Release yourself today into the control of the only one who will never lose control.

Heavenly Father, when my heart feels weak, I thank you that you are my strength. I thank you that you will never fail me and I choose to rely on your strength today.

My flesh and my heart may fail,
But God is the strength of my heart and my portion forever.

PSALM 73:26 NASB

There are times when we feel strong and independent and there are times when we realize that we are completely dependent on others. Did you have either of those moments today? God gave us gifts and strengths but we are still finite creatures. At times, we just have to admit that we can't do it all on our own.

The Psalmist recognized this and acknowledged that God is the source of strength. There is great relief in knowing that God is your rock, now and forever.

Lord, sometimes my heart and my flesh fail. There are times when I am sick, and there are times when I am heartbroken. Thank you that you are my rock during all these times. Your love gives me strength to carry on.

What have you been trying to do all on your own? How can you rely more on God and others that he places in your life?

Intimacy with God

God demonstrates His own love toward us,
in that while we were still sinners, Christ died for us.

ROMANS 5:8 NKJV

God desires intimacy with you. He fashioned you to be sustained by him, to be holy and pure, faultless and blameless, fully accepted and completely bound up in his love.

You have been chosen to enjoy increasing measures of God's favor and grace. At this moment, take time to step into greater intimacy with him. You have the opportunity now to accept greater measures of his unconditional, limitless love.

God, thank you for your perfect love. Please pour it into every area of my life that is thirsty and dry. I love you.

God demonstrates his own love for us in this:
While we were still sinners, Christ died for us.

ROMANS 5:8 NIV

Jesus' blood has washed you clean, and nothing stands between you and his benefits. When you drift, you only need to call upon him and step back into the interaction of love.

Bring everything to God, exchanging stumbling points for stepping-stones. He relentlessly works for your good and desires for you to remain close to him. Draw near tonight as you spend quiet time with him.

Father, it is my goal to please you, not because you need it, but because I need it. I want to overflow with love for you the way you do for me. Thank you for your demonstration of love.

Can you sit with the Father for a while tonight?

Conscious Choice

"Today I have given you the choice between life and death, between blessings and curses. Now I call on heaven and earth to witness the choice you make."

DEUTERONOMY 30:19 NLT

Would you want someone to love you if they didn't really want to? If someone were forced or even paid to love you but you knew their love wasn't genuine, would you enjoy that type of love?

You have a choice that no one can make for you. Life or death, it's up to you. God longs for you to choose life because he knows what wonderful things await those who respond to his love. He wants lovers who will worship him in spirit and in truth. He doesn't want false love, so he allows you to choose. What will you do with that choice today?

God, thank you for the gift of choice. Thank you that you don't force me to love you or to follow you, but that you will bless me as I choose life in you.

"I call heaven and earth to witness against you today, that I have set before you life and death, blessing and curse. Therefore choose life, that you and your offspring may live."

DEUTERONOMY 30:19 ESV

We have the conscious ability to choose whether or not we will love God. God will not make us love him or force us to follow him. The freedom that we have to choose is the most wonderful and the most fearful gift we have been given.

Your choices don't only affect you, they affect all the others in your life. When you choose life, you become a blessing to others around you. When you choose to be positive, to act in kindness, and to speak well of others, you are choosing a life of blessing.

Lord, sometimes I don't feel like life is a choice. I feel trapped in the day-to-day and I don't see a way out. I pray you would remind my heart of the hope and promises that you will bring blessing as I continue to choose your ways.

What choices do you need to make today that will positively affect you and others around you tomorrow?

Rich Rewards

Do not throw away your confidence; it will be richly rewarded. You need to persevere so that when you have done the will of God, you will receive what he has promised.

HEBREWS 10:35-36 NIV

Remember the early days of your relationship with God? Perhaps you were a child, full of wonder and excitement. Maybe you were an adult when you discovered his love, and it filled you to the brim with joy.

Continue to persevere. Breathe in God's peace today and rejoice in it. He will give you the strength you need to continue in him.

Lord, I pray I'd be restored to the excitement of the early days of our relationship. Thank you for the promises you've made to be with me. I know you are faithful.

Do not lose the courage you had in the past, which has a great reward. You must hold on, so you can do what God wants and receive what he has promised.

Hebrews 10:35-36 NCV

As you walk with Christ, life's ups and downs can get to you. The confidence that you placed in God to save you from yourself may waver.

Don't lose heart! God promises to reward your faith. Place your trust in him, and he will help you persevere through any situation. When you feel like you may falter, turn to him and seek the joy that only he can provide.

God, help me to remember your joy and peace when I feel like I'm going to stumble. I place my continued confidence in you.

Where is your confidence today?

Vulnerability

He gives us more grace. That is why Scripture says:
"God opposes the proud
but shows favor to the humble."

JAMES 4:6 NIV

Some of the most substantial and ultimately wonderful changes in our lives come from moments of vulnerability: laying our cards on the table, so to speak, and letting someone else know how much they really mean to us. But vulnerability takes one key ingredient: humility. And humility is not easy.

Isn't it sometimes easier for us to pretend that conflict never happened than to face the fact that we made a mistake and wronged another person? It's not always easy to humble ourselves and fight for the resolution in an argument—especially when it means admitting our failures.

Jesus, show me grace for people in my life who have wronged me. In the same way, help me to be humble when I have wronged others, and prompt me to be quick to apologize when I am wrong.

> *God gives us even more grace, as the Scripture says,*
> *"God is against the proud,*
> *but he gives grace to the humble."*

JAMES 4:6 NCV

The wrong kind of pride is not pretty. We are more likely to listen to those who are honest about their situation than those who are trying to make excuses for it. Do you know people who are too proud to admit their mistakes and who blame their failures on others?

Who are you in the face of conflict? Do you avoid apologizing in an attempt to save face? Does your pride get in the way of vulnerability, or are you willing and ready to humble yourself for restoration in your relationships? God says that he will give favor and wisdom to the humble.

Lord, I know that often I let pride win in my life. I don't like to be vulnerable and to show my weakness. I ask for confidence in the wonderful person that you have made me to be. With a true understanding of my value in you, I pray that you would help me to be honest and vulnerable in front of others.

What can you do this week to humble yourself for the sake of a restored relationship?

Eternal Kingdom

Since we are receiving a Kingdom that is unshakable,
let us be thankful and please God
by worshiping him with holy fear and awe.

HEBREWS 12:28 NLT

Kings and queens hold their throne for a time, but ultimately their reign ends, either through defeat or death. The kingdom of God is not like the kingdom of men. It is undefeatable and unshakeable.

Take heart today that the king you worship will be on the throne forever! Worship him as he deserves.

Lord, you are my king and I honor and adore you. Help me to remember that your kingdom has the authority over all, and that it will not be defeated.

Let us be thankful, because we have a kingdom that cannot be shaken. We should worship God in a way that pleases him with respect and fear.

HEBREWS 12:28 NCV

You belong to God's kingdom, and it will never be defeated. His power will not be surpassed by any other principality or power. Be thankful that you belong to this kingdom.

God is the king of this universe and the king of your heart. This evening as you reflect on his majesty, worship him in awe for all he has created and all he has done.

God, even though you are a great and awesome king, you love me as your child. Teach me to worship you reverently.

What does an unshakeable kingdom look like in your mind?

Come Close

Come close to God, and God will come close to you.
Wash your hands, you sinners; purify your hearts,
for your loyalty is divided between God and the world.

JAMES 4:8 NLT

Do you ever feel like you can't feel God? Like you've lost sight of him somehow? Sometimes we aren't sure how to get back to that place where we feel his presence strongly and hear his voice clearly.

God will not push himself on you. He will not share his glory with another, and he will not try to compete with the world for your heart. But, beloved, if you draw near to him, he will wrap you in the sweetness and power of his presence. Welcome him into your life today above all other loves.

Lord, be close to me today. There have been times I don't know where you are or what you are doing, but I recognize that those are probably the times when I am not drawing close to you. Let me feel your presence surround me in all that I do.

Draw near to God and He will draw near to you. Cleanse your hands, you sinners; and purify your hearts, you double-minded.

JAMES 4:8 NASB

We go through seasons where we feel distant from God, but the beautiful truth is that he has never gone anywhere. He's in the same place he was the first time we met him. God is unchanging and unwavering. His heart is always to be with us, and he never turns his back on his children.

As you think about your day, where do you see your loyalty? Sometimes it feels like our lives are so full of the world that we hardly have time to think about God let alone allow him to be active and speaking. Allow God to renew your heart tonight.

God, I accept your forgiveness in those times that I have chosen things of this world over you. I thank you that you give me the grace to start afresh tomorrow, and I ask for a sense of your presence in every part of my day.

Where has your loyalty been recently? Have you been so consumed with this world that you have forgotten to allow God into your day-to-day life? Let him back in tonight.

Governor

Those who are dominated by the sinful nature think about sinful things, but those who are controlled by the Holy Spirit think about things that please the Spirit.

Romans 8:5 NLT

We think constantly about what we feed our bodies. Whether we eat healthy food or junk food, we are at least aware of what we are consuming. It's a simple principle: what you put in, you will get out.

We know that if we continually feed ourselves junk food and candy, we will have low energy and poor health. We also know that if we eat balanced meals, we will feel better, look better, and function better.

Holy Spirit, when I think about eating today, remind me that I am also making choices about what I feed my heart and mind. Help me to surround myself with healthy thoughts and ideas and to feed on things that are good for me.

Those who live according to the flesh set their minds on the things of the flesh, but those who live according to the Spirit set their minds on the things of the Spirit.

ROMANS 8:5 NRSV

How well did you eat today? Did you give in to unhealthy foods, or did you allow yourself to stick to healthier habits?

Our thought patterns can easily be compared to our eating habits. When we fill our minds and hearts with things that aren't of God, our thoughts will follow those directions. Our thoughts determine our actions and our words. When we meditate on Scripture and fill our minds with Godly things, our thoughts, words, and actions will naturally be those of life, peace, and truth.

Jesus, there are so many things that have been going on in my mind and heart. Thank you for reminding me that I need to be allowing good and healthy things in. Help me to develop strategies to keep the unhealthy things out.

What is governing your mind? Your flesh, or the Holy Spirit? Think carefully about what you put in, recognizing that it has a direct effect on what will come out.

Promoted

"His master said to him, 'Well done, good and faithful slave.
You were faithful with a few things, I will put you in charge
of many things; enter into the joy of your master.'"

MATTHEW 25:23 NASB

Faithfulness brings exponential rewards in the kingdom
of God. Not only do we receive the joy of obedience, but we
receive more rewards from the trust God places on us. All of
us can look forward to the day we stand before God, by his
grace, having used our gifts well.

As we look ahead to the final day, let us use our gifts to further
glorify our Lord.

God, thank you for your faithfulness. You have longed to give me
certain gifts. Guide me through the opportunities you present.

"The master said, 'Well done, my good and faithful servant. You have been faithful in handling this small amount, so now I will give you many more responsibilities. Let's celebrate together!'"

MATTHEW 25:23 NLT

Here on earth, the application of that increased trust can come into our lives in the forms of greater responsibility and influence. It could look like promotions and prestige, earthly responses to the glory God has placed upon us and we have ably carried.

When earthly blessings come your way, accept them with humbleness and gratitude.

Father, show me where you want your faithfulness to make a difference in me. I choose to accept your challenges; help me see them through to completion.

What gifts do you feel like you use frequently?

Grief

Your promise revives me;
it comforts me in all my troubles.

PSALM 119:50 NLT

Grief is a strange thing. It shows up in the oddest of places. As time passes, it becomes threaded into your life in a subtle way you don't quite notice at first. When you smile and feel real joy but at the same moment tears spring to your eyes, that's when you know that grief is not absent even in happiness.

As time passes and life goes on, we must learn to bear all our varying emotions in sync. We can smile, we can laugh, and we can be perfectly happy, but the ache of grief is still there deep down. We don't forget it, but we don't betray that which we grieve by smiling either.

Father, I know that you care deeply for me and that you care deeply about my pain. I ask for comfort in the times that seem the hardest to bear, and I ask for your joy, even in the middle of difficult times.

This is my comfort in my affliction,
For Your word has given me life.

PSALM 119:50 NKJV

As a child of God, you have been promised a hope that
has the power to revive you even in the most sorrowful of
moments. And though your pain is real, deep, and sometimes
overwhelming, your God is strong and able to lift you out of the
deepest pit, and—even when it's hard to imagine—give you joy.

Ask God for joy tonight in the middle of your grief. Ask for
moments of laughter and peace in places you would least
expect to find them.

*Lord, let me search your Word for your promises. I know that you
will never leave me and that you are my constant companion. Be
my great comforter as you promise to be, and deliver me from all
my troubles.*

What grief or trouble are you experiencing right now? Can
you let the Holy Spirit be your comfort and share God's
promises with you as you take some time to lean on him?

Thirsty for Mercy

"Come, all you who are thirsty,
come to the waters;
and you who have no money,
come, buy and eat!
Come, buy wine and milk
without money and without cost."

ISAIAH 55:1 NIV

Money is used for what we want, but mostly for the things that we need—like food and even water. Imagine walking into a grocery store and being offered anything you want without having to pay a cent! This is a picture of the mercy that Jesus has shown all of us through his sacrifice.

Think about God's amazing free gifts as you go through your day. If that doesn't put a smile on your face, what else could?

God, I am so thankful for the free gifts you have so richly blessed me with. Help me not to take them for granted, and to remember to give you glory for everything I have.

"Is anyone thirsty?
Come and drink—
even if you have no money!
Come, take your choice of wine or milk—
it's all free!"

ISAIAH 55:1 NLT

We need God's mercy in the same way that we thirst for water. Wine and milk were expensive items in the time this was written, and to offer these free of charge would have been a great sacrifice.

What Christ did for you on the cross came at a great price, but it was all because of his great love for you. Embrace the free gift of forgiveness and rest in freedom tonight.

Lord Jesus, I come to you as a thirsty child in need of your mercy.
You have paid the price for me to receive your forgiveness. I am
thankful for the grace that you have freely given me.

Are you thirsty for God's mercy tonight?

Each New Morning

Tell me in the morning about your love,
because I trust you.
Show me what I should do,
because my prayers go up to you.

PSALM 143:8 NCV

There are many verses in the Bible that talk about morning prayer. Jesus himself set an example by getting up early and going to a quiet place to pray and talk with God. There is something about the morning that God values. Mornings symbolize new life, strong hope, and fresh beginnings—all things that we know God is passionate about.

When we seek God in the morning, we consecrate the first moments of the day. By coming and placing ourselves at his feet before we do anything else, we literally put him first in our hearts, souls, and minds.

Lord Jesus, I put you first in my heart and mind this morning.
I set my eyes on you and ask you to calm the storm of the day as
I follow you into it.

Let the morning bring me word of your unfailing love,
for I have put my trust in you.
Show me the way I should go,
for to you I entrust my life.

PSALM 143:8 NIV

To start the day basking in the love of God is an amazing privilege. To spend some time with him after the day will also give you encouragement. As you sit at his feet and read his Word, you gain strength, wisdom, direction, and perspective for the day that has just been.

Give him your day today and ready yourself for tomorrow. Find a quiet place to be in his presence and read his words of love to you. Listen to him tell you about his great affection toward you, and walk in that love as you face every obstacle and moment ahead.

God, I love spending time with you! So often I get busy and forget to stop and read your Word, or send you a quick prayer. I do that now, knowing that it is a blessing to let you into my life in a tangible way.

Are you struggling to make God part of your morning or evening routine? Take one moment to stop, read, listen, and pray. It doesn't have to be long, but it will be like food for your soul.

Give Thanks

Enter his gates with thanksgiving
and his courts with praise;
give thanks to him and praise his name.

PSALM 100:4 NIV

The morning alarms came too soon today. Whether they were in the form of children, an alarm clock, or a heavy heart that is restless even when sleeping, your slumber is over. Your mind immediately starts going over your to-do list for the day as you stumble through your morning routine. You glance at your watch. How can you already be running late?

It is at this moment that you must stop to thank God. That's right, actually stop what you are doing, get down on your knees (to ensure you are stopping), and thank him. Pausing to thank God gives him the honor he's due, but it also kisses your heart with peace and joy in the midst of busy morning routines.

Loving Father, I enter into your presence now on another one of your creations—this day. Thank you for giving me another day on earth. Thank you for life in my body and your love.

Come into his city with songs of thanksgiving
and into his courtyards with songs of praise.
Thank him and praise his name.

PSALM 100:4 NCV

A thankful heart prepares the way for you to connect rightly with God's heart. He isn't someone we use to get what we want. He is a sincere, loving provider for everything we will ever need.

As you close out your day, spend some time singing praise to God. Thank him for your day, no matter how hectic, sad, or boring it was. And if it was a great day, tell him that too! He loves to hear your praise.

God, help me walk in an attitude of thanksgiving every day. You are worthy of my grateful heart.

Sing a song of thanksgiving to God today.

Winter to Spring

*"Let us acknowledge the L*ORD*;*
let us press on to acknowledge him.
As surely as the sun rises,
he will appear;
he will come to us like the winter rains,
like the spring rains that water the earth."

HOSEA 6:3 NIV

Spring teases us, playing its own game of "catch and release."
A few balmy, sunny days awaken our senses to the freshness
of spring air and promise the end of winter. We fall into bed
after hours of sunshine and laughter, only to reawaken to a
white blanket covering any evidence of warmth. Spring sun
hides behind winter clouds, teasing us as though they know of
our longing for the great light they hide. When the sun finally
re-emerges, we are bathed in instant warmth.

Jesus is with us in every season. At times we feel the cold of
winter, at times we feel a warm breeze, and still other times
we welcome the freshness of the rain. Jesus is our constant
presence in it all. Whatever the weather is like out there
today, know that he is with you.

I thank you, Jesus, that you are forever near to me no matter what
season of life I am in.

Oh, that we might know the LORD! Let us press on to know him. He will respond to us as surely as the arrival of dawn or the coming of rains in early spring.

HOSEA 6:3 NLT

Our lives have winters, don't they? We live through seasons where we feel cold, hidden, and trapped. We feel buried under the snow of circumstance with an absence of clarity, warmth, and light. But, if we looked closer, perhaps we could see the rushing of the clouds, the gilded outlines that promise there is hope just past them. And though winter can be long, the moment when the sun returns will be worth it all.

Perhaps you are in the middle of one of life's winters. Remember that for every winter there is a spring. As you press in to God, he will come to you like the sun rushing from behind the clouds. You have only to wait, to hope, and to look for him.

Heavenly Father, your presence has been with me today and will be with me tomorrow. I know that I can trust in you, come what may.

What season of life do you feel you are in right now? Can you see Jesus in this season?

In His Timing

Rest in the LORD and wait patiently for Him;
Do not fret because of him who prospers in his way,
Because of the man who carries out wicked schemes.
Cease from anger and forsake wrath;
Do not fret; it leads only to evildoing.
For evildoers will be cut off,
But those who wait for the LORD, they will inherit the land.

PSALM 37:7-9 NASB

Man can spend a lifetime studying God and never really understand the ways in which he moves: unexpected and unpredicted despite the prophecy of man, subtle yet monumental despite the theology of his character.

Abraham was told to look to the skies; his descendants would be as many as the stars. He was promised the future of mankind and a legacy that would shake history. Abraham was handed his dreams in one stunning moment by an almighty God. And then God was silent. All Abraham was left with was a barren, scoffing wife, a shocked expression, and an inky black sky filled with millions of stars representing impossible promise. But in his own timing, in his own way, God moved.

Lord, at times I can be very impatient. I am impatient with my family and friends, and sometimes I am impatient with you! Thank you for reminding me this morning that waiting patiently for your promises is rewarding. Give me grace to be patient today.

Be still in the presence of the LORD,
and wait patiently for him to act.
Don't worry about evil people who prosper
or fret about their wicked schemes.
Stop being angry!
Turn from your rage!
Do not lose your temper—
it only leads to harm.
For the wicked will be destroyed,
but those who trust in the LORD will possess the land.

PSALM 37:7-9 NLT

You may feel like God has forgotten about you or that he's grown silent over the years. But God will honor the promises he's made to you. He will not forget to complete the work that he has begun.

God is the master of every plan, and he will accomplish his work in you. Be faithful even in the waiting and the quiet. At the right time, in the right way, he will move.

Jesus, I have learned a little more about patience today. I don't want to worry about the future, and so I wait for you. Help me to be faithful in the waiting.

What have you been waiting for? It's okay to continue to ask God for these things, just remember that he asks for your patience!

Relationships

Spend time with the wise and you will become wise,
but the friends of fools will suffer.

PROVERBS 13:20 NCV

Humans were created for relationship; we are hardwired to want and need others. Because of our design, friendships are vitally important to our lives and also to our walk with God.

It is a widely known fact that friends either bring us up or drag us down. Likewise, friends can either encourage or discourage us in our pursuit of godliness. As we seek counsel from our friends for the decisions we make in life, it is important that those friends are pushing us to follow Christ and not our own desires.

Jesus, I know that you desire that I have good friends. Give me discernment, even today, to spend time with those people that are good and uplifting and to keep away from the company of the unwise.

He who walks with wise men will be wise,
But the companion of fools will be destroyed.

PROVERBS 13:20 NKJV

Your friends have the power to lead you closer to God or push you away from him. Surround yourself with people who will echo God's words to you rather than lead you off course with their advice.

Evaluate yourself to make sure you are being the kind of friend who will lead others closer to Christ by your influence and your advice.

As I reflect on my day, Lord, I can see those people that have been very encouraging to me. I want to be with people who are wise and able to lift me up in my faith. I also ask for the love and grace to be a good and wise friend to others.

Who have you spent time with today? Are they people that are wise and encouraging? Who might you need to keep a healthy distance from?

Scandalous Forgiveness

"Be on your guard! If your brother sins, rebuke him; and if he repents, forgive him. And if he sins against you seven times a day, and returns to you seven times, saying, 'I repent,' forgive him."

LUKE 17:3-4 NASB

There are few things worse than being unjustly wronged. It's not easy when you are hurt—especially by someone close to you. A deep part of each of us cries out for justice. It's a God-given trait, meant to call us to stand in the gap for the hurting, the widow, the orphan—it's our longing for true religion. When we identify injustice, that longing rises up strongly. We feel pain, hurt, confusion, and pressure. And more than all those emotions, we feel the deep need to see justice served.

We have been forgiven much; therefore, we must love much. No matter how hard it is today to forgive someone who has hurt you, remember how much you have been forgiven. How can we extend any less grace than that which we have received?

God, give me the grace today to forgive those who have wronged me. Lord, I don't feel like these people deserve to be forgiven, and so I rely on your heart of love for them.

> *"Pay attention to yourselves! If your brother sins, rebuke him, and if he repents, forgive him, and if he sins against you seven times in the day, and turns to you seven times, saying, 'I repent,' you must forgive him."*
>
> LUKE 17:3-4 ESV

Forgive—over and over again. This is the scandal of the Gospel. This is the very essence of the Jesus we follow. Someone wrongs you? Forgive him. He wrongs you again? Forgive again. But, Lord, he was wrong. He was sinful. He hurt me deeply. His answer will still be the same: "If he repents, forgive, as I have forgiven you."

Forgiveness does not mean that you have to keep accepting the same behavior over and over. God gives us wisdom to know when to move on from something that is unhealthy. Forgiveness is handing the hurt to God and leaving the judgement to him.

Lord, I need your wisdom in situations where I have been hurt over and over again. I know that you do not want me to be in harm's way, and so I ask for a way through or a way out. I still choose to forgive those who have wronged me, and I ask that you give me peace in my heart.

Who do you need to forgive today? Is God asking you to remove yourself from harm?

Fully Alive

When you follow the revelation of the Word,
heaven's bliss fills your soul.

PROVERBS 29:18 TPT

Everyday living can suck the life right out of us. Somewhere in the middle of being stuck in traffic, sweeping floors, and brushing our teeth, we can forget to be alive.

What does it mean to be alive, rather than just to live? Not to only exist in life, but to know it, to understand it, to experience it—to live it. What would it be like? Freefalling from an airplane. Running through the grass barefoot with sun on your face. Bringing babies into the world, screaming and strong with power and life. What would it be like if we lived each moment in the spirit of those fully alive moments?

Jesus, thank you for filling my soul with your hope and your wonder. Help me to face today as a person who is aware of being fully alive in you.

Where there is no revelation, people cast off restraint;
but blessed is the one who heeds wisdom's instruction.

PROVERBS 29:18

Without a reason for life, without purpose, we perish. We falter. We lose our way. We lose hope. We begin to casually exist instead of breathing in the reverence of a fully alive life. We need to re-cast vision for ourselves daily.

Open your mind and your heart to the vision that God has for you. If there are dreams he gave you that you've lost along the way, trust that they will be returned to you. God breathed life into you so that you could live it to the fullest.

Lord, sometimes I get to the end of the day and I really don't feel like I have any life left in me. Thank you that you can breathe new life into me even now. Thank you for giving me hope, joy, and peace in the middle of all the other things.

What do you need God to breathe life back into tonight?

Never Too Late

> *Behold, the LORD's hand is not so short*
> *That it cannot save;*
> *Nor is His ear so dull*
> *That it cannot hear.*

ISAIAH 59:1 NASB

Do you have regrets in your life that you wish you could take back? Things that you aren't proud of? You lay awake at night thinking about mistakes you've made and you wonder if you've gone too far to ever get back.

When Jesus hung on the cross, there were two thieves hanging beside him. One of those thieves, as he hung in his final moments of life, asked Jesus for grace and a second chance. That thief—minutes before death—was given forgiveness and eternal life. The very same day he entered paradise as a forgiven and clean man. In light of his story, how can we ever say that it's too late to turn it all around?

Give me a fresh start, today, Lord. I need to remember that your mercy and forgiveness awaits me every single morning. I trust in that forgiveness today and ask for a renewed sense of purpose.

> *Listen! The LORD's arm is not too weak to save you,*
> *nor is his ear too deaf to hear you call.*

ISAIAH 59:1 NLT

If you feel like it's too late to change something in your life for the better, remember the story of the thief on the cross. There is always hope in Jesus.

The God we serve is the God of second chances. That might sound cliché, but it couldn't be more true. His love has no end and his grace knows no boundary. It is never too late for you to follow him with your life.

Lord, thank you for reminding me that your love is always ready to save me from worry, fear or self-doubt. Help me to rest tonight in the knowledge that you are always willing and ready to rescue me.

What do you need saving from this evening? Ask God to help you and trust that he will listen.

Rebuilt

And from far away the LORD appeared to his people and said,
"I love you people
with a love that will last forever.
That is why I have continued
showing you kindness.
People of Israel, I will build you up again,
and you will be rebuilt.
You will pick up your tambourines again
and dance with those who are joyful."

JEREMIAH 31:3-4 NCV

We were originally created to bear the mark of our Creator. We were masterfully designed to reflect his image and to reveal his glory. The corruption of sin has masked us, disguising our initial intended purpose. When we respond to salvation and give ourselves back to God, he begins reworking us to once again appear as he intended.

Sanctification is a process that can be painful. But its end result is beautiful. God empties our hearts of the things that could never satisfy us to make room for himself—the only thing that will always satisfy.

Lord, you continue to show me kindness and I need that as I am figuring out how to live out my faith well. I accept your grace, today, for the times when I don't reflect you, and I ask you to empower me to be more like you.

*The L*ORD *appeared to us in the past, saying:*
"I have loved you with an everlasting love;
I have drawn you with unfailing kindness.
I will build you up again,
and you, Virgin Israel, will be rebuilt.
Again you will take up your timbrels
and go out to dance with the joyful."

JEREMIAH 31:3-4, NIV

There are times in life, perhaps even today, where you feel like God has taken a wrecking ball to your life. He has flattened everything you had—your desires, your interests, your pursuits—but fear not. He will rebuild you. He is creating a masterpiece with your life that will bring him glory and honor.

Everything God removes he will restore to mirror the image of his likeness—your intended created purpose.

Tonight, Lord, I feel a bit like a broken wall. I don't feel like I have a lot left to give. I feel like there is not a lot to look forward to. Thank you for this Scripture that reminds me that you are a God that rebuilds his people and turns their sorrow into joy. Turn my heart to joy so I can dance and sing once again.

What do you feel has been broken in your life? Can you trust God to build you up in this area again?

New Life

We died and were buried with Christ by baptism. And just as Christ was raised from the dead by the glorious power of the Father, now we also may live new lives.

ROMANS 6:4, NLT

The entire human race is living on borrowed time. We spend our lives with the innate knowledge that we never know when it will all end for us. Death comes, as it always does, to every man.

When it came to Jesus, death didn't have the final say. And in that death—the one death that represented all humanity— the greatest form of life was born. The Gospel truth is that Jesus' death wasn't just a man's life ending on a cross. It was the death to literally end all deaths. Jesus died and took the full wrath of a righteous God upon himself so that our death sentences would no longer be ours to serve. And the story doesn't end there. The most glorious part of all is his resurrection: his conquering of death, and the ultimate display of power, glory, victory, and grace.

Jesus, you are literally my life saver! I am overjoyed when I think of the wonderful thing that you did for humanity, the wonderful thing you did for me. Let me serve you today in the joy of the eternal life that you gave me.

We have been buried with him by baptism into death, so that, just as Christ was raised from the dead by the glory of the Father, so we too might walk in newness of life.

ROMANS 6:4 NRSV

The whole point of the entire Gospel, summed up in one life giving phrase is this: you can have new life. Life that doesn't run out, expire, or end. This beautiful truth isn't just a charming thought. It's your reality as a Christian.

By accepting the finished story of the Gospel, you are written into the best ending in existence. Life is yours—glorious, powerful life. Ponder that for a while tonight.

Jesus, I reflect this evening on what you had to endure in order to restore eternal life back to humanity. I am humbled by your suffering, but I am overjoyed that the cross was once and for all. As I go to sleep, let me rest in the assurance of salvation.

What impacts you the most tonight about the saving work of Christ? Reflect on what this means for you.

Heaven's Promise

"God will wipe away every tear from their eyes;
there shall be no more death, nor sorrow, nor crying.
There shall be no more pain,
for the former things have passed away."

REVELATION 21:4 NKJV

When terrible things happen in this world, people cry out to God in desperation. They ask how he could have let it happen. How could the one who is in control of everything possibly be good when there is so much hardship?

But when we look at the system of heaven, we realize that God never intended for us to have sorrow, pain, or death. All these things only exist as a result of man's sin. When the kingdom of heaven is established on earth, we will live as God intended. All wrong will be righted and all pain will disappear.

God, some days I am faced with these questions of why? On these days, remind me of your promise of the hope that we hold of a good and perfect future. Thank you that your eternal plan for my life is beautiful.

"He will wipe away all tears from their eyes,
and there shall be no more death, nor sorrow,
nor crying, nor pain. All that has gone forever."

REVELATION 21:4 NLT

It is good to live and love with eternity's values in view. On some days, it can be the difference between despair or hope. What kind of day did you have today? Was it filled with hope or filled with hardship?

As a child of God, you know that any pain you have in this life is temporary because your eternal home will be devoid of it all. When the pain and sadness of the world threatens to overwhelm you, cling to the promise of heaven and the hope that one day every tear will be wiped from your eyes.

God, I look forward to the day that there will no longer be all these struggles and pain around me. Help me to face each night with courage and each day with hope as I live with the expectation of a wonderful future.

What sorrows are you feeling right now? Are there people in your life that are experiencing difficult times? Ask for the hope of eternity to settle in your heart and then pray for those around you.

What It's Worth

If people say they have faith, but do nothing, their faith is worth nothing. Can faith like that save them? A brother or sister in Christ might need clothes or food. If you say to that person, "God be with you! I hope you stay warm and get plenty to eat," but you do not give what that person needs, your words are worth nothing.

JAMES 2:14-16 NCV

As Christians, we are called to be the representation of Christ to the world; we are the visible expression of an invisible God. In order to express the heart of the Father, we have to know what is on his heart. God tells us in Scripture that he cares deeply about the "least of these": the orphan, the widow, the poor, the needy.

We cannot preach Christ to someone who is needy while leaving them in their need. Our words will not communicate the love of our Father unless accompanied by the actions that make him tangible to them.

Lord, let me show my faith in action toward those in need. Holy Spirit, guide me to the needs of others, whether it is someone close to me or needs of people in another country. Help me to respond quickly to help others today.

What use is it, my brethren, if someone says he has faith but he has no works? Can that faith save him? If a brother or sister is without clothing and in need of daily food, and one of you says to them, "Go in peace, be warmed and be filled," and yet you do not give them what is necessary for their body, what use is that?

JAMES 2:14-16 NASB

What is your faith worth? How far are you willing to go to express the love of God to a dying world? Will you give of yourself when it isn't convenient? Will you love on someone who is unlovable and give to someone who can never repay you?

The cost may seem great, and the work insignificant, but God sees your heart and what you have done, and he counts it as work done directly for him.

God, I see needs all around me. I saw a lot of needs in the people I encountered today. As I go to sleep tonight, I ask that you show me what I can do to help. I pray that you would give me ideas and courage to give to those that most need it. I want to be a part of advancing your kingdom on earth.

What needs did you see around you today? What are the needs that are tugging at your heart the most, and how can you respond to those?

Already In

When you live a life of abandoned love,
surrendered before the awe of God,
here's what you'll experience: Abundant life.
Continual protection.
And complete satisfaction!

PROVERBS 19:23 TPT

As advertisements go, Proverbs 19:23 puts forth a rather persuasive pitch for joining your life to God's. Abundant life? Yes, please! Continual protection? Let us in! Complete satisfaction? Where do we sign?

Here's the best part of all: we already signed. We're already in. The day we fell in love with Jesus and asked him into our hearts, all this and more was ours. To claim it, we need only remain in his love. To experience it, we need only give the Father our awe.

God, thank you for letting me in on the best deal ever. An overflowing life, completely safe and satisfying, is more than I could hope for before I met you. now it's mine to live and to share. What an awesome, generous God you are!

The fear of the LORD is life indeed;
filled with it one rests secure and suffers no harm.

PROVERBS 19:23 NRSV

When we are reclined on the beach, hearing gentle
waves rhythmically hit the shore, the ocean doesn't seem
particularly fearsome. Jumping from a ship into twelve-
foot swells and with no land in sight? It's hard to imagine
anything more terrifying. It's a matter of perspective. From
land, it's easy to forget the ocean's vastness and power. From
the center, it's impossible to think of anything else.

This is what it means to fear God. To fear him is to respect
him—to remember his vastness, to stand in awe of his power.
Let us remain at the center of our faith, constantly aware of
all he can, has, and will do, and find our secure rest there.

*Father God, I am awed by you. What little I know is more than
enough for me to realize your greatness is beyond measure, and
your power without limit. This knowledge gives me life. how easy
it is to rest secure knowing I am protected by a limitless God.*

Does your fear of the Lord bring you a feeling of safety? Work
through this with the Spirit and allow your awe of him to fill
you with peace.

Open Doors

"Keep on asking, and you will receive what you ask for. Keep on seeking, and you will find. Keep on knocking, and the door will be opened to you. For everyone who asks, receives. Everyone who seeks, finds. And to everyone who knocks, the door will be opened."

LUKE 11:9-10 NLT

It is hard to reconcile some of the promises in God's Word with our disappointment with things that we have asked for but haven't yet received. Jesus wouldn't have said these words if they were not the truth.

Perhaps you are waiting for an answer or are hoping for a miracle. Be encouraged that Jesus says we need to be persistent and resilient and that he is always willing to open the door to you so you can find him. When you allow Jesus into your life, you will receive all that you need.

Jesus, I ask for a resilient mind so I can keep asking, knocking, and seeking in faith that I will find what I need. I put my trust in you, knowing that you care for me and that you open the door to answer me. Encourage my faith in you as I head into my day.

"You fathers—if your children ask for a fish, do you give them a snake instead? Or if they ask for an egg, do you give them a scorpion? Of course not! So if you sinful people know how to give good gifts to your children, how much more will your heavenly Father give the Holy Spirit to those who ask him."

LUKE 11:11-13 NLT

It's a humorous picture that Jesus paints, of asking for one thing and getting something not only entirely different, but entirely unwanted. This is not the kind of father that God is. He not only wants the best for us, but he wants to give us the true desire of our heart.

We know that God is not a genie to give us anything that we want, so search your heart and ask him for those things that you truly desire. It may surprise you that when you spend time with him, your heart isn't after the superficial things of this world.

Holy Spirit, I give my heart's desires to you this evening. I know that you can discern what is right and what is selfish. I ask, in faith, that you bless me with the good gifts that I ask for.

What is on your heart to ask for God for tonight? Ask him now in faith.

Heart Directions

May the Lord direct your hearts to the love of God and to the steadfastness of Christ.

2 THESSALONIANS 3:5 ESV

Popular culture says the key to happiness is to follow your heart. The idea is that by pursuing our passions we're most likely to end up in a good place. It seems like lovely advice, but only as long as we're sure our hearts know the way. Could your heart use directions from time to time?

A young woman choosing partying with friends over hard work or study, or a middle-aged, married woman acting on a flirtation that makes her heart flutter—both women could be following their hearts. Yet the heart can be deceptive. The heart's wants can be based on selfish, unhealthy, or irresponsible desires. God's heart, though, is steady and true. He knows exactly where we need to go. His unwavering love for us will make certain we get there.

God, direct my heart. Speak into my heart and fill it with your love for me. Lead me toward purpose and stability. Direct me to Jesus, my ultimate home.

*May the Lord lead your hearts into God's love
and Christ's patience.*

2 THESSALONIANS 3:5 NCV

Visit any public venue and you're likely to see a child sprinting away from their parents. Their excitement can't be contained in their little bodies. They bolt because they are so certain they know where to go. We hear their harried parents call out to their child. "Slow down!" Whether by allowing her to temporarily believe she is lost, or by explaining the potential dangers of running off, the parents will try and teach her to stay close.

As a little girl, how often did you charge ahead, running headlong without looking back? How often do you do it still today? We know the Lord has plans for us, so each time we think we see a glimpse of what's next, we bolt. No looking left and right, no checking the rearview mirror, we just go. "Slow down," our Savior calls. May we listen and learn to stay close.

I confess it, Father. I try to rush you sometimes. Like a little girl in pursuit of the ice cream truck, I run ahead. I'm eager to arrive where you're leading me, so sometimes I forget to wait and follow. Thank you for your loving patience. Thank you for making sure I'm never lost.

Still your mind and ask the Father where he's leading your heart.

Pain Has Purpose

*Jesus answered, "It was neither that this man sinned,
nor his parents; but it was so that the works of God
might be displayed in him."*

JOHN 9:3 NASB

In Jesus' time, it was common to believe people with afflictions were being punished for either their own sins or those of a family member. Among the many incredible lessons about the heart of God that Jesus taught, he also set the record straight on this account. The man referred to in the verse, blind since birth, was sightless so that everyone witnessing—and everyone who would ever read this story— would see the awesome power of God.

Pain has purpose, dear friend. It draws us to the Father and gives us a chance to experience his compassion and healing. It may feel like punishment but believe Jesus' words, it's not.

Father, I know you don't punish me. Things beyond my control and messes I get into all on my own are opportunities for me to witness all you are able to do. Don't let me be blinded by pain. Heal me, Lord. Show me your glory and restore my sight.

Jesus answered, "Neither this man nor his parents sinned,
but that the works of God should be revealed in him."

JOHN 9:3 NKJV

Stories like the one in the verse above may seem unfair.
Especially if we have been in our own season of affliction,
we may even think God is being cruel. This poor man had
to spend his entire life blind just so Jesus could perform a
miracle? Ask yourself, though, what the man would say.

Always in darkness, he met Jesus who brought him into the
light. The first face he ever saw was that of the Son of God.
The hands who healed him were the hands of the Christ. Do
you suppose he'd tell you it was worth it?

Oh, Jesus, I hope to one day proclaim your glory has triumphed
over every affliction in my life! Already I see where I was and
where I am, and I can say with certainty it was worth it. I didn't
love the pain, but oh, how I love the healer.

What opportunities has the Lord taken in your life to display
his glory? Where would you like him to reveal it next?

Considered Surrender

> "Suppose a king is about to go to war against another king.
> Won't he first sit down and consider whether he is able with ten
> thousand men to oppose the one coming against him with twenty
> thousand? If he is not able, he will send a delegation while the
> other is still a long way off and will ask for terms of peace."

LUKE 14:31-32 NIV

Surrender is offering what you have to someone else because
you have considered your options and know that doing it your
way would do more harm than good. Once you surrender
something, you give up your ownership and your rights along
with it.

What does a life fully-surrendered to Christ look like? It's
holding nothing back from God, and surrendering every part
to him. Full surrender to a holy God cannot be fabricated.
God, the omniscient one, cannot be fooled by eloquent words
or false commitment. Complete surrender to him can be
nothing less than sincere, legitimate, full abandonment.

*God, I don't know how to fully surrender myself to you, so instead
hear my heart behind the words. I really want to have a life that is
dedicated to you and even though I fail, I still want to give it all up
for you. Give me a chance to show you that today.*

"In the same way, those of you who do not give up everything you have cannot be my disciples."

LUKE 14:33 NIV

Being a disciple of Christ requires complete and total surrender of everything you have and everything you are. He is not asking you to give up anything that he wasn't willing to give for you. When he gave up the glory and rights of his heavenly throne, he surrendered more for you than you ever could for him.

Jesus never sold this life as being casual, simple, or inexpensive. But he did promise that the reward would be great.

Jesus, let me remember the rewards that I have for a life surrendered to you far outweighs any earthly treasure. I choose to serve you today and every day. Give me the strength and grace to pursue you with all my heart.

What is God asking you to surrender to him? Trust that he knows what is best for you.

Light in Darkness

In him was life, and that life was the light of all mankind. The light shines in the darkness, and the darkness has not overcome it.

JOHN 1:4-5 NIV

Unless you are trying to sleep, what is the first thing you look for in the dark? Light. We require illumination to find our way. When light and dark are used figuratively, the same truth applies. There is a reason a tough season is referred to as a dark time. It's hard to see the way through. Obstacles are everywhere.

In our own darkness, Jesus is a constant source of life-giving, soul-nurturing light. He is likewise constant for all those who love him. For those who have yet to know him, let us be light. Let us bring his words, his presence, and his grace and peace everywhere we go.

Because you never leave me, God, I am never lost in darkness. I need only turn to face you. As you are ever with me, I can also light someone's way. Thank you, precious Jesus, for your constant glow.

The Word gave life to everything that was created,
and his life brought light to everyone.
The light shines in the darkness,
and the darkness can never extinguish it.

JOHN 1:4-5 NLT

In God's creation total darkness is rare. Halfway around the world, the sun still finds a way—on all but the cloudiest of nights—to reflect off the moon. The lights of a billion stars, unfathomably far away, still make their way to earth. There is always a little light because light is stronger than the dark.

In the darkest room, a single candle will change everything. It doesn't matter how dark that room is meant to be, that tiny flame will always succeed. As long as it's there, the room cannot be shrouded in darkness.

God, on the days my hope is as big as the sun, you are that light. You are life. On the days darkness tries to overtake me, you send a star. You light a flame. You bring hope on the light, God, and light always wins.

Go to the darkest place you can. Is there yet a beam of light beneath the door? The glow of an appliance? Total darkness is rare. If you do find it, you can always light a candle or flashlight. Thank Jesus for being light in the darkness.

When Others Fail

"Be on your guard! If your brother sins, rebuke him;
and if he repents, forgive him."

LUKE 17:3 NASB

There are few things worse than being unjustly wronged. It's not easy when you are hurt—especially by someone close to you. A deep part of each of us cries out for justice. It's a God-given trait, meant to call us to stand in the gap for the hurting, the widow, the orphan—it's our longing for true religion.

When we identify injustice, that longing rises up strongly. We feel pain, hurt, confusion, and pressure. And more than all of those emotions, we feel the deep need to see justice served. No matter how hard it is today to forgive someone who has hurt you, remember how much you have been forgiven. How can we extend any less grace than that which we have received?

God, give me the grace today to forgive those who have wronged me. I don't feel like these people deserve to be forgiven, and so I rely on your heart of love for them.

> *"If he sins against you seven times a day,*
> *and returns to you seven times, saying,*
> *'I repent,' forgive him."*

Luke 17:4 NASB

Forgiveness does not mean that you have to keep accepting the same behavior over and over. It does not mean that you have to continue to get hurt. God gives us wisdom to know when to move on from something that is unhealthy and not for our wellbeing.

Forgiveness is handing the hurt to God and leaving the judgment to him.

God, I need your wisdom in situations where I have been hurt, over and over again. I know that you do not want me to be in harm's way, and so I ask for a way through or a way out. I still choose to forgive those who have wronged me and ask that you give me peace in my heart.

Who do you need to forgive today? Is God asking you to remove yourself from harm?

Loving Intercession

We constantly pray for you, that our God may make you worthy of his calling, and that by his power he may bring to fruition your every desire for goodness and your every deed prompted by faith.

2 THESSALONIANS 1:11 NIV

Do you have someone in life who often tells you they are praying for you? Maybe a parent, a sibling or a close friend? What a gift they are! Since they have a heart to see you thrive, why not help them by sharing your God-given dreams with them?

We know the Lord answers the prayers of the faithful, so, as we invite others to pray for us, we can be confident he will hear them. Our desire to find and fulfill our purpose, our longing to be worthy of the great love of Christ, and the acts we perform in obedience to his calling: all will be blessed by their loving intercession.

God, thank you for the pray-ers in my life. I don't want to take them for granted. Knowing they want to see me reach my every dream is a gift. Having their sincere prayers for my growth and success is a blessing. Hear their prayers.

We always pray for you, that our God may make you worthy of his calling and may fulfill every resolve for good and every work of faith by his power.

2 Thessalonians 1:11 esv

It is with good reason that most churches encourage small groups. We are wired for connection. We are called to intercede for one another. We are made for love. Do you believe this?

To study God's Word with others and encourage each other to grow in faith is a beautiful, life-giving experience. Having people who constantly pray for you—and having people to constantly pray for—is a wonderful gift. As we take our eyes of our own concerns to lift up those of our friends, the Lord sees and rewards our compassion. As we share the load together, our own burden grows lighter.

Father, thank you for the gift of Spiritual friendship. A friend in Christ is a priceless blessing. May I treasure mine, and may I be a treasure to them.

Friend, do you have a group of women to pray with? If you do, thank the Father for them. If you do not, ask the Lord to lead you to the ladies he's chosen for you. Pay attention: this is a prayer he longs to answer.

Stones to Remember

Those twelve stones, which they had taken out of the Jordan, Joshua set up in Gilgal, saying to the Israelites, "When your children ask their parents in time to come, 'What do these stones mean?' then you shall let your children know, 'Israel crossed over the Jordan here on dry ground.'"

JOSHUA 4:20-22 NRSV

We have markers in our lives to remind us of special times and events. We have photos and landmarks and even special dates or smells that trigger our memory. It is important to have ways to remember significant things in your life so you can share the story with others.

For Joshua, setting up a pillar of stone was his way to mark out a very important event that would be told over and over again. Take some time today to think of the times when God has done something special in your life. See if you can share that story with someone.

God, you have been good to me. I'm glad that I can say that despite the things that haven't always gone right in my life, because when I reflect on the past, I can see your hand in all of it. Remind me to share these good stories with others.

"The Lord your God dried up the waters of the Jordan for you until you crossed over, as the Lord your God did to the Red Sea, which he dried up for us until we crossed over, so that all the peoples of the earth may know that the hand of the Lord is mighty, and so that you may fear the Lord your God forever."

JOSHUA 4:23-24 NRSV

It is not always easy to share the wonders of God with people today. Our day-to-day life is filled with the ordinary, but important, things like work, kids, meals, study. At the end of your day today, you may wonder where the time went and where your opportunity to share God's story was lost.

Rest assured there will be more opportunities, and prepare for it by reading up on all the amazing things God has done for his people in the past—like drying up the water so the Israelites could walk through and be saved. He is mighty.

God, you are mighty and powerful. It doesn't always seem like you are going to part the waters for me, but I trust that you are always working in my life. Help me to be more responsive and attentive to your guiding hand.

How has God shown his power in your life? How can you mark these special times so you will remember them?

Flung Wide Open

Though you have not seen Him, you love Him,
and though you do not see Him now, but believe in Him,
you greatly rejoice with joy inexpressible and full of glory,

1 Peter 1:8 nasb

What are your thoughts on love at first sight? Does a soul recognize its other half instantly, or are we stitched together with our mates slowly over time? How about love in the absence of sight? Could you fall for someone based solely on the words he wrote to you and the things he did for you, even if you never saw his face?

Of course, you can, and you have. The day you fell in love with Jesus, the eyes of your heart were flung wide open. Though you won't lay eyes on him until you meet in heaven, your soul has already seen his beauty and found its missing half.

Oh, Jesus, how I love you! The most beautiful thing I'll ever see is something I've never seen at all, and yet I know it will be amazing. My heart knows. Oh, what joy, what inexpressible joy, I will feel the day I see you face to face.

Whom having not seen you love. Though now you do not see Him, yet believing, you rejoice with joy inexpressible and full of glory.

1 PETER 1:8 NKJV

This beautiful picture of love is also a picture of faith. It is through faith we can rejoice in a promise. Trust allows us to revel in that we have yet to witness. We believe he is who he says he is and, believing, we love. Oh, how we love.

And how he loves us for it! We didn't ask for proof, we just opened our hearts and let truth in. We didn't demand evidence, our souls simply accepted what he offered, and we loved. How can this be? How can we, doubting and fickle, have such great capacity for love and faith? Only through him. In this truth, we find yet another reason to love.

God, thank you for this joyful love! It's as if you are rewarding me for my faith, or thanking me for believing you, by granting me glory. It's almost more than I can handle, and It's definitely more than I can describe. Thank you, Jesus. I love you.

How did you first fall in love with Jesus? Was it slow, like a friendship that grew into more, or all at once, like a bolt of lightning?

Many Parts

If the whole body were an eye, it would not be able to hear. If the whole body were an ear, it would not be able to smell. If each part of the body were the same part, there would be no body. But truly God put all the parts, each one of them, in the body as he wanted them.

1 CORINTHIANS 12:17-18 NCV

It's nearly impossible to experience a spectacular display of talent—whether painting, song, novel or even a touchdown run—and not feel a longing to be able to perform at that same level. A captivating speaker is bound to make us yearn for the podium. A beautiful dance may stir us to dig out the old pink slippers. These feelings are both natural and a lovely tribute to the way God gifted the artists.

The important thing is not to become fixated on someone else's gifts, lest we miss out on discovering our own. If I, a mediocre singer at best, am obsessed with becoming a vocalist, I may never realize my potential as a chef, nurse, or accountant. The world needs us to use the gifts we do have far more than to work on acquiring the ones we wish we had.

Father God, thank you for the way you made me. Thank you for the way you made everyone else and the amazing gifts you've given them. By making us all unique, you ensure a world of endless delights, provision, and beauty.

If the whole body were an eye, where would be the hearing? If the whole were hearing, where would be the smelling? But now God has set the members, each one of them, in the body just as He pleased.

1 Corinthians 12:17-18 nkjv

Imagine a country with nothing but athletes, a state with only doctors, or a city with only singers. It's unthinkable, almost laughable. No great athlete can become so without coaches, teachers, groundskeepers, equipment designers, assembly line workers, farmers, and so on.

We need each other. Even right now, someone else's greatness depends on yours.

God, I love your creativity! Your endless capacity for weaving things together amazes me. Let this inspire me to do my part with excellence, gratitude, and pride. Remind how significant my purpose is, and how vital my role is.

How important do you consider your "work?" Ask God to help you grasp the big picture and realize just how many people are affected by what you do.

Sincere Serving

"Fear the LORD and serve Him in sincerity and truth; and put away the gods which your fathers served beyond the River and in Egypt, and serve the LORD."

JOSHUA 24:14, NASB

You might be able to remember the time when you were not a Christian or not following the ways of Christ. In Bible times, people served other gods because they wanted health, wealth, and all forms of prosperity.

Instead of serving stone idols, we can be lured into finding other ways to achieve prosperity—from beauty products to the pursuit of high paying jobs. God's ways direct us in different forms of prosperity like healthy relationships, healing, and strength of character. Serve the Lord in sincerity and truth; his ways will give you all you need.

God, I am so often drawn to the things that used to make me feel better and yet I recognize that some of these things are shallow and not truly fulfilling. I come to you now, in sincerity and truth, and choose to serve you to the best of my ability today.

"If it is disagreeable in your sight to serve the LORD, choose for yourselves today whom you will serve: whether the gods which your fathers served which were beyond the River, or the gods of the Amorites in whose land you are living; but as for me and my house, we will serve the LORD."

JOSHUA 24:15 NASB

It's important to understand that not everyone will choose to serve the Lord. We live in a world that has temptations that some will not be able to resist. We live in a world where we may be mocked for our decision to follow Christ.

It is important, just as Joshua did, to make a decision one way or another. Scripture says elsewhere, we cannot serve two masters. When you make the choice, be brave and bold about your choice to follow God.

God, I am sorry when I chase other things in this life that will not bring true joy into my heart. The truth is that I will only ever be satisfied with a choice to follow you. Give me peace as I go to sleep tonight, knowing that my decision remains to serve the one true God.

Are you tempted to serve other things in this world? Choose today who you will serve.

Get Wisdom

Wisdom is the most important thing; so get wisdom.
If it costs everything you have, get understanding.

PROVERBS 4:7 NASB

Can you imagine needing to understand or explain traffic
if all the lights were shades of green? If it's grass-green, go
ahead. If it's tulip-green, you'd better hurry because once it
gets to pine-green, you have to stop. We'd all be hopelessly
confused.

Green means go. Red means stop. This basic pattern is one
that is easily taught and learned, even for young children. Our
safety depends on understanding and following this system,
so it was designed to be simple. While a lot of the Bible is
poetic and symbolic, certain instructions, like this one, are
as straightforward as a stoplight. Why? Because they're that
important. Wisdom? It's a really big deal.

God, thank you for making sure I can't miss the really big lessons.
Because you want me safe and wise, you make your most
important instructions the easiest to follow. Help me get wisdom,
God, and thank you for reminding me how much it matters.

The beginning of wisdom is: acquire wisdom;
and with all your acquiring, get understanding.

PROVERBS 4:7 NCV

Solomon, the author of Proverbs widely attributed to be the wisest man who ever lived, goes out of his way to emphasize the value of wisdom. Nothing matters more. Start here. His urging reflects the importance of constantly seeking greater understanding.

If we want to have something, we need to go get it. Want to be strong? Get strong by exercising or working hard. Want to be fast? Get fast by running a little harder and faster every time. Want to be wise? Get wise by learning from every experience.

God, I want wisdom! Help me to ask and understand why so I can grow wiser with every success, and every mistake. I see how much it matters to you, which makes it important to me. As I would run fast in order to get faster, let me think wisely in order to get wiser.

How much effort have you placed on acquiring wisdom?

Not Again

"I brought you out of Egypt into this land that I promised to your ancestors, and I said that I would never break my covenant with you, if you, on your part, would make no peace treaties with the people living in this land; I told you to destroy their heathen altars. Why have you not obeyed?"

JUDGES 2:1-2 TLB

It can be heartbreaking to read the failure of Israel to remain faithful to God. It is like watching a movie where everything is going wrong and you want the characters to see that they are headed for disaster. Just when God sets them back on track, they choose to go back to their past mistakes.

We recognize this pattern in ourselves. There are times when we realize that we are making the same mistake again. God is calling you forward into his promises, don't go back.

God, you are so loving. I know that you saved your people because of this great love. I believe I am forgiven for my past mistakes, and I ask that you help me to move forward into the good things you have called me to do.

"Since you have broken the contract, it is no longer in effect, and I no longer promise to destroy the nations living in your land; rather, they shall be thorns in your sides, and their gods will be a constant temptation to you."

JUDGES 2:3 TLB

God doesn't punish, but he can't promise that we will be blessed if we continue to live our own way. Until God's final return, we know that the world will always offer us temptation that lures us away from him.

While it may seem an impossible mission, God's grace allows us to live a life that is not only in obedience to his will, but that will also allow us to prosper.

God, I know that I can be lured back to my old ways and things in the past. Be with me tonight as I rest and help me to look forward to a future that begins as I wake.

What are you being tempted to go back to? Remember God's promise and ask for his help to resist.

Source of Peace

Great peace have those who love Your law,
and nothing causes them to stumble.

PSALM 119:165 NKJV

If you could be guaranteed a lifetime of peace with only one small requirement, would you be interested? According to this Scripture, you can. If we love the Lord's law, we will have great peace. Nothing can trip us up. Can this be possible? Rule-following sounds anything but peaceful; it sounds tedious and exhausting.

Rule-following is exhausting but, mercifully, that is not what it means to love the law. Loving God's law means trusting his will for our lives. It means we desire to please him above everything else. When our hearts are focused on making his happy, we needn't follow a list of rules. He will keep our hearts in line with his, and this will be the source of our peace.

God, as I desire more and more to walk in step with you, I am
learning to trust your will. Help me to see your law as a path to
peace, God. keep me from stumbling as I go.

*Those who love your instructions have great peace
and do not stumble.*

PSALM 119:165 NLT

Which sounds more peaceful: attending an elaborate
wedding or planning every detail of it? Even those of us who
dearly love to be in charge would have to admit it is more
relaxing to be a guest at a carefully planned event than it is to
be responsible for it.

How lovely of the Lord to have taken care of our lives, down
to the smallest detail! It's up to us to accept all his careful
planning. We can be "that guest" who smuggles her own food
in and tries to persuade the DJ to play her party mix, or we
can eat the beautiful meal prepared for us and then dance for
joy no matter the song.

*Oh Father, how I love the life you've planned for me. Your
instructions are clear and true. Every choice you have made is for
my good. What steadiness and peace I find on your sure-footed
path.*

Does the idea of following God's plans and instructions create
a peaceful or unsettled feeling in you? Discuss this with him.

Reassurance

*The angel of the LORD came and sat down under the oak in Ophrah
that belonged to Joash the Abiezrite, where his son Gideon was
threshing wheat in a winepress to keep it from the Midianites.
When the angel of the LORD appeared to Gideon, he said, "The LORD
is with you mighty warrior." "Pardon me, my lord," Gideon replied,
"but if the LORD is with us, why has all this happened to us? Where
are all his wonders that our ancestors told us about when they
said, 'Did not the LORD bring us up out of Egypt?' But now the LORD
has abandoned us and given us into the hand of Midian."*

JUDGES 6:11-13 NIV

How often have you had an encouraging word from the
Lord, only to respond with your doubts and insecurities?
Gideon had plenty of good reasons to be skeptical and yet
God reassured him that he had provided him with enough
strength to make it through.

It's in our nature to question why things happen the way that
they do, but when God speaks, he wants you to be confident
and trust that his Word is truth.

*Jesus, I need to hear your reassuring voice today. At times, I doubt
my ability to overcome obstacles or to share my faith, or to forgive
wholeheartedly. Thank you that the strength of you dwelling
within me is enough to do these things.*

The Lord turned to him and said, "Go in the strength you have and save Israel out of Midian's hand. Am I not sending you?" "Pardon me, my lord," Gideon replied, "but how can I save Israel? My clan is the weakest in Manasseh, and I am the least in my family." The Lord answered, "I will be with you, and you will strike down all the Midianites, leaving none alive."

JUDGES 6:14-16 NIV

We compare ourselves to others when assessing our ability to do something. Gideon felt like he was the least according to family hierarchy and his birth order.

God has created each of us as a unique person and he doesn't look at outward factors. Instead God looks at the heart and will use anyone who is willing to trust that God can work through them. It is not about you, but about your willingness to let God work through you.

God, I have been surrounded today by people and comparison is everywhere. Protect my heart and mind from thinking less of myself because of others. I am willing for you to work through me; be my strength as I live in your Word and the life you have chosen for me.

In what ways do you compare yourself to others? Can you trust God to work through you?

Only Pray

Then he will pray to God, and He will accept him,
that he may see His face with joy,
And He may restore His righteousness to man.

JOB 33:26 NASB

We all long to be accepted. Some people are willing to go much farther than others to gain acceptance, but we are all united in our desire to have it. Which material possessions or physical attributes will ensure we fit in? By worldly standards, the answer changes daily.

By God's standards, though, the system is always the same: we pray to him and he accepts us. No makeover or freshly-renovated house is required. Just as we are, we are accepted. To the King of kings, we fit in.

God, when I think of the effort I've expended trying to be accepted here, I can only shake my head in bemusement. How beautiful it is to realize I need only speak your name to be welcomed by you. I pray, and you usher me in. Thank you, God, for accepting me just as I am.

He shall pray to God, and He will delight in him,
He shall see His face with joy,
For He restores to man His righteousness.

JOB 33:26 NKJV

Can you imagine if everyone you encountered found you utterly delightful? For most of us, such a favored time in our lives ended around the age of two. Yet, no baby is preoccupied with how to make people like them. These days, we tend to wonder if we're doing it right from the way we look, the actions we take, and the very words we speak. Who is it we're trying to impress? What makes their acceptance so important?

The only one worthy of such effort is the Lord, and, amazingly, he is the only one who doesn't place conditions on us becoming part of his "in crowd." He restores, he welcomes, and he loves, while we need only pray.

Oh, Lord. Heal me of my desire to attain approval by obtaining the things of this world. With joy, I accept your acceptance of me. You alone are worthy of my striving, yet you don't ask me to do so. You delight in me. You restore my joy.

In your relationships, where do you feel the most authentic? Call to mind the precious people who love you as you are. Recognize them as little glimpses of Jesus' perfect love.

The Word

In the beginning was the Word, and the Word was with God,
and the Word was God. He was with God in the beginning.
Through him all things were made;
without him nothing was made that has been made.

JOHN 1:1-3 NIV

Jesus was the Word from the beginning, with God in the creation of this world, and the creation of humanity. Jesus had a hand in creating you. It's great to know of Jesus as he was on earth, but it's also important to remember where and who he was from the beginning.

Jesus not only can empathize with you from a human perspective, but he knows you inside out. Talk to him today as the person who knows you the best.

Jesus, thank you that you are a divine and human person and that you know me so well. As I go into my day today, help me to recognize your Spirit speaking to me and working in me. I love you, my Savior and my friend.

In him was life, and that life was the light of all mankind. The light shines in the darkness, and the darkness has not overcome it.

JOHN 1:4-5 NIV

Jesus created life and then he came to rescue the very thing he had created. We don't have to fear the darkness because Jesus is the light that came to overcome it.

As the darkness sets in this evening and you turn on lights so you can clearly see, remember Jesus, the light that came into this world so we could see the truth.

Jesus, thank you for coming to earth and saving humankind. Thank you that you are not only the light of this world but the light of my life. Help me to sleep with the peace of knowing that darkness has been overcome by your love.

What are the fears that threaten to surround you? Allow Jesus' light to expel all darkness.

Show Me

The LORD said to Moses, "I will do the very thing you have asked, because I am pleased with you and I know you by name." Then Moses said, "Now show me your glory."

EXODUS 33:17-18 NIV

If a person you'd never exchanged more than a few words with asked to borrow your car, you'd most likely hesitate. If your best friend asked, though, you'd hand the keys over in an instant. Intimacy welcomes openness. We love to do things for those we are closest to.

How intimate are you with the Lord? Has it "been awhile?" Would he be a little surprised to get a request from you, or do you talk so regularly that he already knows exactly what you need? How delighted will he be to show you his glory, to answer your prayer?

God, I want to delight you! Not simply to have my requests answered, but because I want you to know me by name. I want to be your friend, God. Will you show me your glory?

The Lord said to Moses, "This very thing that you have spoken I will do, for you have found favor in my sight, and I know you by name." Moses said, "Please show me your glory."

EXODUS 33:17-18 ESV

"Anything you want, anything at all, it's yours." Who hasn't fantasized about hearing something like that? What would we ask for? Depending on the day, our minds might jump to something simple, like a good night's sleep, something practical, like a fully paid mortgage, or something altruistic, like an end to hunger.

Having pleased God, Moses chose to see God. Specifically, to see his glory. What an awesome request. Would you have thought of it? Yet, what could be better? What could possibly compare?

God, am I thinking too small? I'm so fixed on things in and of this world, I forget you hold us all in your palm with room to spare. Show me your glory, Lord! Give me a glimpse of what is possible with you.

What would you ask for? Invite the Holy Spirit to show you just how big you can dream.

Uncountable Blessings

The LORD will command the blessing upon you in your barns and in all that you put your hand to, and He will bless you in the land which the LORD your God gives you.

DEUTERONOMY 28:8 NASB

"Count your blessings" has become cliché. It's one of those things we say without really even thinking about, but have you ever tried to actually do it? It only takes a few minutes to consider the people, experiences, opportunities, beauty, and second chances we've been given to realize it can't be easily done. We have been given too many blessings to count.

What kind of day might you have if you make a conscious effort to notice every good thing, thank God for giving it, and collect the blessings like tiny lights? How brightly would you glow by day's end?

God, every good thing is from you. I usually thank you for the obvious ones, but I know I often miss the little ones. No more. Holy Spirit, help me recognize every element of goodness in this day. Overwhelm me with how blessed I am to be showered with good and perfect gifts.

The LORD your God will bless you with full barns, and he will bless
everything you do. He will bless the land he is giving you.

DEUTERONOMY 28:8 NCV

How was your day? Were you overwhelmed by the
immeasurable lightness of God's goodness, or were you
overwhelmed by routine and responsibility, forgetting your
"blessing watch" before lunch. Either way, what ordinary
blessing did you see for the first time? Did anything
extraordinary happen?

End today as you began it by trying to count what cannot be
counted: the innumerable ways he has blessed you.

Father, you're overwhelming. The way you rain heaven down,
whether I am paying attention or not, in order to bathe me in your
love is so very beautiful. Thank you, God, for your constant goodness.
Thank you for the gifts, good and perfect, you so freely give.

What blessings did you notice today that you had been taking
for granted? Ask the Spirit to open your eyes even wider as you
dream tonight that you may see all the blessings in your life.

Prepare the Way

> *"You yourselves know how plainly I told you, 'I am not the Messiah. I am only here to prepare the way for him.'"*
>
> JOHN 3:28 NLT

John the Baptist was a radical man with a fire in his belly to prepare the earth for the coming of Jesus. He didn't live for himself but was completely sold out on the message of the Messiah. He had a thirst for eternity and an agenda to bring glory to God.

Just as John was the voice in the wilderness preparing the way for Jesus to come the first time, we now are the voice crying out to ready the world for the second coming.

God, give me boldness to proclaim your name today, and in the days to come.

"It is the bridegroom who marries the bride, and the best man is simply glad to stand with him and hear his vows. Therefore, I am filled with joy at his success."

JOHN 3:29 NLT

In order for Jesus to have his rightful place in the hearts of the people, John knew he had to fade away. You cannot save the people you're preaching to. You can't rescue them from sin or keep them from hell. Only Jesus can do that. But you can prepare the way in their hearts for his presence.

Don't keep the glory of God shut up. Let it out and make him known, so when he comes, those who have known you will know who he is because you proclaimed him clearly.

God, sometimes it is hard for me to know how to proclaim who you are and what you are doing in this world. I know, however, that I am your image bearer and that I can be a reflection of you. Let me represent you well.

How can you deliver the message of Jesus that is relevant to the people in your life?

Papa's Here

"As a mother comforts her child, so will I comfort you;
and you will be comforted over Jerusalem.
When you see this, your heart will rejoice
and you will flourish like grass."

ISAIAH 66:13-14, NIV

Few images are more precious than a mother soothing her child. She holds them close, gently swaying and whispering comforting words. "It's okay. Mama's here. I've got you." Through the prophet Isaiah, the Father promises his children that same loving comfort.

You will be comforted. You will rejoice and flourish. Papa's here. He's got you. All will be well. Believe it, friend. No matter how things look today, settle into the sway. Listen to his words and be comforted.

Abba Father, I love that I will never outgrow your arms. Your lap will always have a spot that fits me perfectly. Thank you for your loving comfort, God, and for promises of a joyful.

"I will comfort you there in Jerusalem as a mother comforts her child.
When you see these things, your heart will rejoice.
You will flourish like the grass!"

ISAIAH 66:13-14 NLT

Even if not today, a day will come when you are fighting tears.
Guess what? There is no need to fight! Store this truth up
for the day you need it, and the next time you find yourself
holding back, holding it in, and barely hanging on…don't.

On that day, go ahead and cry. Cry like a baby and let your
Abba's comfort wrap around you and hear his whispered
words of comfort.

I may just do it, Lord. I may just open the floodgates and let all
my tears come rushing out the next time they try. Who knows what
comforts I've been missing by not inviting you to see and dry my
tears!

What does it take for you to let your pain out? Why do you
think it's easy or difficult for you?

Believe in the Son

*"God so loved the world that he gave his one and only Son,
that whoever believes in him shall not perish but have eternal life.
For God did not send his Son into the world to condemn the world,
but to save the world through him."*

JOHN 3:16-17 NIV

It is good to be reminded of the simple truth of the gospel.
This verse is so well known because it sums up our faith so
well. This was God's plan for the world, and his plan for you.

God loved you so much that he gave his Son, Jesus. When
you believe in him, you have eternal life. It's a great thought
to take into your day. Let the hope of eternal life give you the
perspective you need to face today's challenges.

*God, thank you for reminding me that there is hope of eternal life
with you. Thank you that as a believer, I am no longer condemned
to death, but I am saved. Remind me of this amazing grace today.*

"Whoever believes in him is not condemned, but whoever does not believe stands condemned already because they have not believed in the name of God's one and only Son."

JOHN 3:18 NIV

It really is as simple as believing. We can often approach this faith with the idea that we need to be better people. Sometimes we expect others to be better, to do better, to live more of a righteous life. It's important that we live in God's ways, but more importantly is our faith in Jesus. This belief is what saves us, and what saves every other person.

When you love God, you will be better—not through your effort, but through the revelation of love that God shares with you because you believe.

Lord Jesus, I am sorry when I have expected the wrong things from other people or become self-righteous about my faith. Thank you that all you require from my heart and that of others, is a belief that you are the Son of God and that you came to save us. Thank you that I am made righteous through this belief.

What expectations do you have of yourself and others? How do they relate to belief in Jesus Christ?

What Is Right

Pursue peace with everyone,
and the holiness without which no one will see the Lord.

HEBREWS 12:14 NRSV

Is there a peacemaker in your life? Perhaps you have a friend or relative who can't rest while others are at odds? It's likely that they are always butting heads with those who can't let go of a grudge or agree to reconciliation. What is it that makes both the peacemakers and grudge-holders so passionate?

Both have a strong conviction of what is right. Sometimes when we feel we have been wronged, all we can focus on is assigning blame and standing our ground— that's what feels like the right thing to do. For peacemaker, what's right is peace, regardless of fault or blame. According to Hebrews, we are likewise called to pursue peace this way. We are to love each other unconditionally, continually forgiving any wrongs. It is by becoming the peacemaker ourselves that we grow in holiness and see the Lord.

God, knowing I can only have you if I have peace, all my squabbles now seem silly. Holy Spirit, bring to my heart any relationships in need of healing. Inspire me to pursue the peace that leads to where you are. I don't need to be right; I need to be with you.

Make every effort to live in peace with everyone and to be holy;
without holiness no one will see the Lord.

HEBREWS 12:14, NIV

"Make every effort to live in peace…and to be holy." Lest we be tempted think these are two separate instructions, let's notice they are contained in the same sentence. They are not mutually exclusive concepts, rather one fosters the other – it's a process. Lie down and rest. Stand up and walk. One leads naturally to the other and so we conclude: the path to holiness is peace.

Why does this matter? Because the path to Jesus is holiness. The author of Hebrews spells it out for us simply, so we can understand this important truth. If you want to run, you need to stand. If you want to see the Lord, you need to live in peace.

Jesus, I see. I understand. You are holy, and holiness does not allow for strife. You want us—all of us—with you. For this harmony to become reality, you urge us to reconcile. When we find this peace, we will find you waiting.

Pray about your relationships. Are you making every effort to live at peace with everyone and be holy? Do you feel the Lord nudging you to take a step towards reconciliation with anyone?

From the Heart

"The time is coming—indeed it's here now—when true worshipers will worship the Father in spirit and in truth. The Father is looking for those who will worship him that way."

JOHN 4:23 NLT

When was the last time you gave yourself over fully to a time of worship? Not just singing along to the words in church, not just bowing your head in prayer, but letting yourself be completely consumed by the presence of the Lord?

Take some quiet time today to allow his mighty presence to wash over you. Revel in the time that you have with him, worshiping him in whatever way feels natural to you. You'll discover that he is indeed worthy of your adoring reverence.

God, I worship you with my whole heart this morning. Give me time in my day to reflect on how truly wonderful you are.

"God is Spirit, so those who worship him must worship in spirit and in truth."

JOHN 4:24 NLT

True worship is quite different than just singing along. We serve a God who is awesome and powerful. He is deserving of our utmost devotion. When we discover just how amazing he is, we know that he is worth our full praise.

People can talk about worshiping God, and show all kinds of outward devotion, like lengthy prayers, hands in the air, or intense biblical debate. But God is after the heart, that's why he made it known that there are true worshippers and false worshippers.

God, I know that sometimes I compare myself to other people who seem to be more spiritual than me, or who like to "worship" more than I do. Thank you for confronting me with the truth, that it isn't about the songs that I sing, or the way I show my worship, but that you care about a heart that is directed to you. I give you my heart's attention tonight.

How will you worship in truth this week?

Our Sustenance

You are the fountain of life,
the light by which we see.

PSALM 36:9 NLT

When lost in the desert, do we long for water or sand? Fumbling in the dark, do we search for light or squeeze our eyes shut? When thirsty, we crave water. In darkness, we seek light. Our bodies know what we need.

Spiritually, God is both our sustenance and the light that leads us to it. His truth is what nourishes us while his Spirit is what draws us into it. His grace is our salvation while his Son leads the way. He is author and perfecter, beginning and end, and supplier and supply. He is Lord.

God, you set me up so I cannot fail to find you! You designed me to thirst and because you love me, you became living water. You created me to seek light, and then made yourself the brightest star in the sky. Thank you, God, for being both light and life.

With You is the fountain of life;
in Your light we see light.

PSALM 36:9 NKJV

God is our standard bearer. His beauty helps us recognize beauty. His truth reveals truth. His light is how we know light. This is opposite from the world. Here, light is easier to pinpoint in darkness. Beauty more obvious against a backdrop of dreariness. A fountain more prized in a parched land.

So how can this be, that in his light—incomparably, incomprehensibly bright—we see light? Because he is light. He is beauty. Without him, refreshment, beauty and light simply wouldn't be.

Beautiful God, you don't just set the standard, you make it possible. You don't just illuminate the path, you make the path and open my eyes to see it. You don't just make things good, you are goodness itself. You are awesome, God. You are everything beautiful, bright, and sustaining. You are life.

What has God's light helped you to see?

Ripe

"My food," said Jesus, "is to do the will of him who sent me and to finish his work. Don't you have a saying, 'It's still four months until harvest'? I tell you, open your eyes and look at the fields! They are ripe for harvest."

JOHN 4:34-35 NIV

Food is a necessary part of our existence. Sometimes it feels like we eat to live and live to eat. Jesus explains that doing the will of the Father is necessary and fulfilling. He says that unlike the crops that we wait for, we do not need to wait for souls that need saving, they are already ready.

Jesus wants us to know that there are many still waiting to hear and receive the gospel.

Jesus, help me to see salvation as a necessary part of my calling as well. Thank you that you have involved me in your plan for humanity and that you want me to share my faith. Give me boldness to help reap what has been sown.

"Even now the one who reaps draws a wage and harvests a crop for eternal life, so that the sower and the reaper may be glad together. Thus the saying 'One sows and another reaps' is true."

JOHN 4:36-37 NIV

Jesus needs both those who are willing to sow seeds and those who are bold enough to reap when the harvest is ready. God needs to use all gifts to achieve his purpose.

Whether you are quietly showing kindness to a neighbor or boldly declaring the gospel to unbelievers, God can and will use you. We need to appreciate one another and the different ways that God uses us to build his kingdom.

God, thank you that you place all kinds of believers in the field and that we all have different ways of contributing to your kingdom. Help me to rise up to the calling to share my faith in big or small ways.

Is God asking you to sow or reap this season?

Lifted Higher

From the end of the earth I call to you, when my heart is faint.
Lead me to the rock that is higher than I.

PSALM 61:2 NRSV

Have you ever walked through a maze? Even if you can easily navigate one on paper, it's quite a different experience without the bird's eye perspective. In the thick of it all you can see is the hedge or row of corn directly in front of you. Having no other choice, you take it one turn at a time. Inevitably, without that overhead view, you'll make a wrong decision. You may even get lost, repeatedly coming up to the same dead end.

When life feels like that maze, call out to God. Follow his voice to the next turn, and the one after that. Allow his hand to lift you up—higher than your own sight—and show you the way through.

Father God, you are always listening and waiting to guide me. You see whether I am headed the right or wrong way. What a comfort it is to know I can call to you and follow the sound of your voice. I can extend my arms and you will lift me up, showing me more than I can see on my own.

I call to you from the ends of the earth when I am afraid.
Carry me away to a high mountain.

PSALM 61:2 NCV

We can call to the Father for direction and perspective. We can also call to him for rescue. Rather than sink into fear, huddled into a corner of the maze in defeat, we can cry out to God. No matter how far we've travelled, he will hear us. His loving hand can pluck us straight out of our fear and onto the mountaintop of his promises. Our circumstances may not change right away, but our hearts will lighten immediately.

In that high, safe place with him, what could possibly trouble us?

God, you are both guide and rescuer, and you know which I need. When I am just a little lost, your voice gives me direction; your wisdom provides perspective. When I am truly off course, trapped by fear and faced with too many decisions, you lift me up, carrying me to a place where nothing can touch me.

Which could you use more of in your life right now: perspective, direction, or rescue? Call out to him and let him take you higher.

Divine

> *"Whoever believes in me, believes not in me but in him who sent me. And whoever sees me sees him who sent me."*
>
> JOHN 12:44-45 ESV

It was one thing to believe and follow Jesus as a man doing amazing miracles with great teaching, but Jesus made it clear that he was sent by God and that he was the Son of God.

Believing in Jesus for us means that we can know the Father by understanding who Jesus was and is. The Holy Spirit is our helper to reveal all of this to us, so be encouraged that when you believe in the acts and character of Christ, you are beginning to understand the heart of the Father.

Father God, thank you for sending your Son, Jesus, into the world so we could see who you are. Help me, Holy Spirit, to understand more about you.

"I have come into the world as light, so whoever believes in me may not remain in darkness. If anyone hears my words and does not keep them, I do not judge him; for I did not come to judge the world but to save the world."

JOHN 12:46-47 ESV

Jesus came to earth because it was the will of the Father. He did not come in the way the Jews had expected—with a sword to destroy all their enemies. He came to save and bring people from darkness to light.

This is our responsibility too, as imitators of Christ. We are not here to judge others, but to give them the message of love and salvation. When we come home from a hard day at work, with the kids, or at school, we may forget about the light that we carry inside of us. Don't hide it. Keep it burning brightly for all to see.

God, help me to remember your words and to keep them in my heart so I am always ready to share the light of your life with others.

Who are the people in your life, or in the outside world that need to see the light, rather than hear about judgment?

Seek Him First

Fill us with your love every morning.
Then we will sing and rejoice all our lives.

PSALM 90:14 NCV

Seek him first. Why are we encouraged both in the Word and by our fellow believers to begin our days with the Lord? If you already begin your mornings with him, you know what a perfect start to the day that is. Settling into his Word and his will first thing creates an awareness of his nearness, a desire to remain close to him, and an overflowing of his love.

We see through his eyes, rendering everything beautiful. We feel with his heart, making everyone lovable. We act with his purpose, giving meaning to our every action. With God's Spirit so near, what else can we do but sing for joy?

Precious God, make my day! Show, move, and lead me in your way. Fill me with compassion, purpose and awe. Allow your overflow to touch everyone I encounter so that together, we'll make their day better too.

Oh, satisfy us early with Your mercy,
that we may rejoice and be glad all our days!

Psalm 90:14 NKJV

Good news and bad news. Which do you prefer to hear first? Most of us choose the bad news, so we can get it over with. We want to deal with the negative, then move on to happier matters. The New King James translation of Psalm 90:14 offers a similar perspective.

By pleading early for mercy, we can turn our attention to the praise, rejoicing and gladness of life with our Lord. By handing him our burdens first thing, we are unencumbered when it's time to dance. Seek him first each day, and joy will follow.

Here they are, God, all the burdens I carry. Take the weight of worry, guilt, and shame from me so I am free to sing of your great love. Remove my doubt so I can dance in your glory. Have mercy on my sins so joy may rule my days.

What mercy do you need from your Savior, so you can dance and be glad in his goodness?

Acts of Humility

When he had washed their feet and put on his outer garments and resumed his place, he said to them, "Do you understand what I have done to you? You call me Teacher and Lord, and you are right, for so I am. If I then, your Lord and Teacher, have washed your feet, you also ought to wash one another's feet. For I have given you an example, that you also should do just as I have done to you."

JOHN 13:12-15 ESV

Jesus showed just how great his love was by doing the job that was reserved for a lowly servant. He was revered by his disciples as a great teacher and yet he gladly showed the disciples his affection through an act of humility.

Jesus wants us to show this same humility for one another. It doesn't matter if we have a higher position, career, or place in society, we need Jesus' heart of compassion to serve one another in love.

Jesus, thank you for showing me humility. You have such great love for all people and I want to honor your words that tell me to do what you have done. As I go into the busyness of life today, I ask that your Holy Spirit gives me the grace to love as you do.

"Truly, truly, I say to you, a servant is not greater than his master, nor is a messenger greater than the one who sent him. If you know these things, blessed are you if you do them."

JOHN 13:16-17 ESV

The workplace is one of great hierarchy. You probably have had a boss in the past that has acted with a superior attitude toward you, and perhaps you have been guilty of it yourself. Jesus wasn't suggesting that a servant is any less of a person than his master; rather, he was showing that he was gladly doing the will of his Father, even if it meant he had lower his status to do so.

Jesus says we are blessed if we also can humble ourselves for the sake of the higher calling.

God, I am sorry when I have not acted in humility toward others. Help me to acknowledge that you have sent us to do your will and that this requires serving others rather than serving myself.

What superior attitude do you need to let go of or forgive someone for?

Clinging to Dust

My soul clings to the dust;
revive me according to your word.

PSALM 119:25 NRSV

How did this verse sit with you? Your response can tell you about the current condition of your soul. Was your heart pierced with feeling for the writer, and for those you know who are clinging to the dust as well? If your heart responded with compassion is a sign your soul is feeling strong. If this surprises you, take heart, you are doing better than you realized.

If, when you read this, you felt as though you could have written it, sweet friend, then you are laid low. Take care not to let the ground claim you. It will try. Reach up your hand. Grab onto God's and let him revive you. Cling to the promise in his Word: promises of better days, rejoicing, healing, mercy, and grace. Hold on, dear one, and feel your spirit rise.

Savior, what a comfort it is to know that no matter how low I fall, how low I feel, you are there to meet me. I need only cry out and your hand of mercy will begin to lift me. I need only hang on, and your promise of healing will continue my rise. I need only remain in your grasp, and your restoration will be mine.

I lie in the dust;
revive me by your word.

Psalm 119:25 NLT

Perhaps it's been one of those days. Wearily, you wave your white flag and lie down. "I'm done," you declare. "I give up." It may seem like the best place to be, but we're vulnerable lying low. The enemy doesn't respect the white flag. As we curl up in defeat, he layers on sadness. Above the guilt, he piles on shame. But God offers a solution.

"Revive me by your Word." Contained in the pages of Scripture is more hope, encouragement, healing, and promise than you imagine. The next time you find yourself curled up in defeat, rise up from the dust to be revived by the power of the Word.

Oh God, how I love your Word! Whatever I need to hear, you've written it down. Thank you, God, for the living, breathing power of Scripture to revive me. Holy Spirit, remind me when I taste defeat that you offer a better way.

How big a part does the Bible play in your story? Talk it over with God and see if there is more he wants to say to you through his Word.

Choices that Build

The wise woman builds her house,
but the foolish pulls it down with her hands.

PROVERBS 14:1 NKJV

If you were to see a mother bird ripping her nest apart, how would you feel? Confused? Concerned? A mother dog refusing her hungry puppies tugs similarly at our hearts. It's unnatural. Now imagine a woman too busy to make it to volleyball too harried to pack lunches, or too overwhelmed to accept an invitation to coffee. It's not as hard to picture, is it?

Twig by twig, we have the option to build our homes— our relationships, our lives—or to destroy them. Every "harmless" complaint about a husband, every forgotten birthday of a friend, every time sleep is more important than a morning hug goodbye, the nest is weakened. Keeping close to our Lord, he leads us to the choices that build, sustain and strengthen our homes. He fortifies us with the love and the will to keep building.

Dear God, remind me today of what is important. Help me to be a builder, to reinforce the structures of connectedness, affection, and respect that make my house strong. Make me wise, Father, and make me strong.

The wisest of women builds her house,
but folly with her own hands tears it down.

PROVERBS 14:1 ESV

"If I knew then what I know now…" Who hasn't thought
or said these words before? If only wisdom were innate!
Instead, it seems we often get wise by making—or
witnessing—foolish mistakes. If only gentle warnings were
enough to make us steer clear of choices that weaken our
foundation.

Perhaps they can be? Perhaps, if we lean into God's Word,
and trust his wise, perfect plan for our lives, our most recent
bad decision can be our final bad decision. Of course, we
know we will still make occasional mistakes, but how lovely
that we grow wiser with each one.

Father, make me wise! Let me bypass learning the hard way by
leaning on you and building my house upon your wisdom. Each
time I forget and tear down another brick from my house, Let me
replace it with one that is stronger.

Does your nest need some attention? Ask God to show you
the areas you should focus on rebuilding.

Hear My Prayer

"If my people, who are called by my name, will humble themselves and pray and seek my face and turn from their wicked ways, then I will hear from heaven, and I will forgive their sin and will heal their land."

2 CHRONICLES 7:14 NIV

Cause and effect may be the earliest concept we grasp. A baby cries, and someone comes to soothe her. A toddler sees different results when she asks sweetly or throws a tantrum. We sometimes approach prayer from this simple mindset. If I cry out to God, he'll come running. If I ask nicely, he'll give me what I want. However, that's not how prayer works.

If we want to be heard, we need to come humbly, quietly, and seek first his face. The first step is simply to be in his presence. We must regret that which distances us from him. We need to reject our sins and ask for forgiveness. Then we can await his response.

Father, forgive me for the times I approach you like an infant by wailing my needs without first acknowledging your greatness or asking to see your beautiful face. Forgive the sins I cling to and fail to confess. Hear my prayer, God, offered in love and reverence, and silence my cries.

*"If My people who are called by My name humble themselves
and pray and seek My face and turn from their wicked ways,
then I will hear from heaven, will forgive their sin
and will heal their land."*

2 Chronicles 7:14 esv

"My people who are called by My name…" What an
extraordinary thing to be called by the name of God. We
are children of the King, beloved of the Savior, and family
in Christ. As the Church, we are even his bride. When we
joined his family, he gave us his name. What confidence this
inspires, what hope!

He will always hear our prayers and, surely, as we come
humbly before him, there is nothing he won't do for us.

*God, I may have thought of myself as your child, or as the bride
of Christ, but I've not really considered what it means to be called
by your name. Oh, the power I have against darkness, and the
favor I have in your presence! What a blessing, God, to share your
beautiful name.*

Think of your last name. What does it mean to be part of your
family? Think of God's many names. What does it mean that
he gives this blessing to you?

Don't Be Troubled

"The Advocate, the Holy Spirit, whom the Father will send in my name, will teach you all things and will remind you of everything I have said to you."

JOHN 14:26 NIV

After his resurrection, before Jesus ascended into heaven, he left his disciples with something they'd never had before: peace. More specifically, he gave them his Holy Spirit that would guide them in his peace—a gift not of this world.

Whatever the world can offer us can also be taken from us. Any security, happiness, or temporary reprieve from suffering is just that: temporary. Only the things of heaven are permanent and cannot be taken away. Let the Holy Spirit remind you of those words of truth today.

Holy Spirit, let your words of life bring peace to my heart today.

"Do not let your hearts be troubled and do not be afraid."

JOHN 14:27 NIV

"Do not let your heart be troubled," Jesus tells us. This means we have a choice. Share the things with him that threaten your peace, and then remember they have no hold on you. You are his, and his peace is yours.

Why is it so hard to find peace in this world? Because we're looking in this world. True peace is found in Jesus. There will be a lot of things that may have taken away your sense of peace today. Allow the Holy Spirit to speak to you and help settle your heart and mind.

Thank you, Jesus, that I do not have to be afraid. Watch over me as I sleep and let your peace wash over me.

What have you been troubled about lately? Will you allow his peace to replace your fear?

Your Job

Ruth went out to gather grain behind the harvesters. And as it happened, she found herself working in a field that belonged to Boaz, the relative of her father-in-law, Elimelech. While she was there, Boaz arrived from Bethlehem and greeted the harvesters. "The LORD be with you!" he said. "The LORD bless you!" the harvesters replied.

RUTH 2:3-4 NLT

Let's face it, jobs are rarely glamorous. Ruth had to literally find food in the fields from the leftovers of the harvesters that had gone before. It can't have been easy out in the hot sun, and there was no pay.

Hopefully this makes you grateful for whatever type of job you are in. Whether you are looking after your children, working part-time for some extra cash, or heading into a full-blown career, it is all hard work. As you get started on your day job, hear Jesus calling out with his assurance and blessing.

Jesus, thank you for the job that I am in right now. Thank you for the opportunity to earn money and provide for my household. Help me to appreciate this job and to work hard, even when it doesn't feel rewarding. Thank you that you are with me along the way.

*Boaz asked his foreman, "Who is that young woman over there?
Who does she belong to?" And the foreman replied, "She is the
young woman from Moab who came back with Naomi. She asked
me this morning if she could gather grain behind the harvesters.
She has been hard at work ever since, except for a few minutes' rest
in the shelter."*

RUTH 2:5-7 NLT

When someone works hard, it gets noticed. The person in
charge of our workplace is usually very quick to see who is doing
well. Diligence paid off for Ruth, and it will pay off for you.

Did you see your place of work as an opportunity and blessing
today? It's easy to grumble about everything you have to do,
with little thanks, but be encouraged that God notices. He
cares that you have been hard at work, and he is ready to give
you rest and favor.

*God, I am thankful for the job that I have, as hard as it is. I can
get discouraged at times because it feels like I am not enjoying
every single moment. Give me perspective and remind me that your
loving eyes are on me the whole time, proud of the hard work that I
am putting in.*

What parts of your daily job do you love? What do you dislike?
Commit to being a diligent worker regardless of what you like
and do not like.

Overflow of Anger

You, O LORD, are a God full of compassion, and gracious,
Longsuffering and abundant in mercy and truth.

PSALM 86:15 NKJV

Where does the flashing overflow of anger come from? Or
the tendency to hold a grudge, or give the cold shoulder?
Shouting, huffing, slamming, seething… anger begins
somewhere deep inside of us where we've been offended. Or
disrespected. Or maybe mistreated.

Whatever the origin, anger is very difficult to control and the
enemy preys on our weak flesh and wounded ego to destroy
us. Prideful anger is an expression of our selfish desires: How
dare they make my life difficult? They should know better
than to get in the way of my ease and pleasure! Can you put
aside your angry thoughts today?

God, give me the patience as I deal with my friend, spouse,
children, or maybe that annoying drive to work. Help me to become
like you—full of compassion and grace.

You, O LORD, are a God merciful and gracious,
slow to anger and abounding in steadfast love and faithfulness.

PSALM 86:15 ESV

We are called to walk in the love and peace of Jesus Christ and to bear witness to his righteousness. When anger threatens to overcome your compassion, remember God's devotion to you and his unending love.

Despite your sin, God is long-suffering and gracious. If you submit your offenses to God and extend grace by his Holy Spirit, the harmful flames of anger are reduced to ash. His holy mercy washes them away, leaving your heart cleansed and your mind renewed.

Lord, thank you for giving me peace today. There are always going to be situations that test my patience and cause me to feel angry, but thank you that you give me grace to control my anger, or grace to forgive my angry actions!

Is there anything or anyone that you are angry with today? Ask God for his longsuffering, mercy, and truth.

Peaceful Tomorrow

"Do not worry about tomorrow, for tomorrow will worry about its own things. Sufficient for the day is its own trouble."

MATTHEW 6:34 NKJV

Many people today are overwhelmed and overbooked. Life is fast and it doesn't want to slow down for anyone. There are multiple assignments to complete, schedules to keep up with, meals to cook, chores to do, and relationships to foster. And if that's not enough, you may feel it all needs to be done with excellence.

Time out! When you are feeling stress creep into your life, it is important to get back to where God wants you to be—right next to him. He wants to gently walk with you and teach you how to overcome stress.

Father, you know all the things that stress me out. Help me to run to you before everything is overwhelming. Thank you for the peace you give me in place of my anxiety.

"Don't worry about tomorrow, for tomorrow will bring its own worries. Today's trouble is enough for today."

Matthew 6:34 NLT

All you can do is try your best and that is enough. Did you get that? Trying your best is enough! Nobody expects you to have super powers.

Often we put an unnecessary pressure on ourselves because we only see things through our own eyes. When we begin to spend more time with Jesus and ask him to help us see things as he sees them, we can begin to accept that trying our best is enough. Accept it tonight!

God, give me confidence to stand through the stress, knowing that doing my best is all that matters. I can have peace now knowing you will continue to take care of me through all my tomorrows.

What areas of your life are most stressful right now?

Toxic Thinking

This righteousness is given through faith in Jesus Christ to all who believe. There is no difference between Jew and Gentile, for all have sinned and fall short of the glory of God,

ROMANS 3:22-23 NIV

Sometimes while driving, little annoyances can spur us into a prideful mindset: we're the only ones driving at a safe speed, or signaling correctly, or paying attention to the rules of the road. Why doesn't anyone else know what they're doing?! Small things escalate quickly and suddenly we're out of control, figuratively speaking. It's pride, plain and simple. "I have it all figured out and everyone else needs to get with it." This kind of thinking is not only unpleasant for those around us, it's toxic to the soul. And it spreads quickly!

Think on this verse today whether you're on the road or not. Pray you'll arrive safely wherever you're going, and maybe try a pleasant wave to others on the way there.

God, I know that sometimes I am very judgmental of other people; yet, none of us can attain your standard. Give me a pleasant attitude toward those around me today.

We are made right with God by placing our faith in Jesus Christ. And this is true for everyone who believes, no matter who we are. For everyone has sinned; we all fall short of God's glorious standard.

ROMANS 3:22-23 NLT

It's best to set your mind on Christ and his reconciliation—and set it quickly before you start condemning friends and family too! In Christ, we're all just doing our best to get where we need to go. We're not superior to anyone, and we're not too terrible either because God created us and sent his Son to die for us. This makes us worthy.

Think about the wonderful, merciful gift of God tonight and thank him for making you right with him through that gift.

Lord, I have experienced your forgiveness, so I choose to forgive others who have hurt me. I know that you want me to be in right relationship with you, so give me graciousness as I deal with people tomorrow.

Do you need to experience reconciliation with God or others in your life?

No Temptation

> No temptation has overtaken you that is not common to man. God is faithful, and he will not let you be tempted beyond your ability, but with the temptation he will also provide the way of escape, that you may be able to endure it.
>
> 1 CORINTHIANS 10:13 ESV

Wouldn't life be so much easier without temptation? Temptation has this sneaky way of pressing in on every angle of our lives. It surrounds us. It can be relentless, and it is always unwelcome. Often it feels like we can't look left or right without it presenting itself.

A general misconception is that if we are tempted, then we must be weak in our faith. This is not true. No one is immune to temptation—even Jesus was tempted. The struggle was as real for him as it is for you. Go to him today with your struggle. He knows just what you need to do.

God, I need your help today. It's hard to share my temptation with you because I know you are perfect and you have never sinned. But you are full of grace. Help me bring my temptation into the light so it can't fester in the darkness.

The temptations in your life are no different from what others experience. And God is faithful. He will not allow the temptation to be more than you can stand. When you are tempted, he will show you a way out so that you can endure.

1 CORINTHIANS 10:13 NLT

We don't have to give into our temptation because in every moment of every day we are given choices. God's grace lies in those choices. We can bend a knee to our temptress and give up, or we can take up the shield of faith and fight.

When our temptation becomes too much for us to bear alone, we can go to the church, loved ones, or trusted family members and friends to help us. Shedding light on dark areas is a great way of escape. Those who really love us won't judge us; they will offer grace, compassion, and understanding. We don't have to battle temptation alone. God gives us others to battle with—we just have to be bold enough to ask them for help.

God help me to show humility by asking my trusted friends and family members for help in my area of weakness. I need your mercies that are new every morning. Thank you for your forgiveness and grace.

What temptation are you fighting? Don't attempt to battle it alone.

Dare to Hope

All the people were crying and feeling sad because the girl was dead, but Jesus said, "Stop crying. She is not dead, only asleep." The people laughed at Jesus because they knew the girl was dead. But Jesus took hold of her hand and called to her, "My child, stand up!" Her spirit came back into her, and she stood up at once. Then Jesus ordered that she be given something to eat.

LUKE 8:52-55 NCV

Do you know who you really belong to? Your father and mother rightly claim you as their child, but do you recognize Jesus as the one who also calls you his daughter? He knows your coming and going, and your every inner working. You are his.

God is faithful to the deepest needs of your heart; he knows you full well! Where is he directing you today? Are you a daughter in need of healing? Of hope? Hear his voice and let your spirit be renewed.

Father, thank you that you call me your daughter. I need to hear your voice as a loving father today. Speak to me as I wait on you.

*Now all wept and mourned for her; but He said, "Do not weep;
she is not dead, but sleeping." And they ridiculed Him,
knowing that she was dead.
But He put them all outside, took her by the hand and called,
saying, "Little girl, arise." Then her spirit returned, and she arose
immediately. And He commanded that she be given something to eat.*

Luke 8:52-55 NKJV

How difficult it is to put our needs into the hands of the
Father. Do we dare hope? Imagine watching a child die and
feeling the despair of her absence, as the father of the girl
in the story of Luke must have done. Then Jesus claims that
she is only asleep! Both the girl's father and Jesus love the
child, and both can claim her as their daughter, but only Jesus
commands her spirit and her life.

God's children hear his voice and obey his commands. Be
awakened to life this evening as you listen to the Father
calling sweet words of love to you.

*God, I am glad to know you as my Father. At times, I forget to bring
all my worries and fear to you. Help me to keep listening to you
and to learn to obey your commands.*

What do you need your Father to speak life into right now?
Ask him, knowing how much he cares for you.

Serving for Everyone

Your love must be real. Hate what is evil, and hold on to what is good.... Do not be lazy but work hard, serving the Lord with all your heart. Be joyful because you have hope. Be patient when trouble comes, and pray at all times. Share with God's people who need help.

ROMANS 12:9, 11-13 NCV

How many times a day do we see our hands but fail to recognize their potential, their power, their ability? Our hands can be used to bless many people around us. They can wipe away tears. They can work. They can comfort. They can serve!

There are many practical ways to serve those around us. We could give our time to a lonely friend, buy a meal for someone in need, spend an afternoon cleaning our elderly neighbor's home, or visit someone who is in the hospital. Think of how you can serve someone else today.

God, thank you that you made us to love each other and to give ourselves to each other. I know this might mean helping with jobs that don't seem rewarding or pleasant. But there is both joy and eternal blessing to be found in serving. I want to choose that today.

Don't just pretend to love others. Really love them. Hate what is wrong. Hold tightly to what is good. Never be lazy, but work hard and serve the Lord enthusiastically. Rejoice in our confident hope. Be patient in trouble, and keep on praying. When God's people are in need, be ready to help them. Always be eager to practice hospitality.

ROMANS 12:9, 11-13 NLT

We often think of serving others as a job for those in ministry: pastors serve, missionaries serve, humanitarians serve. But serving is something we can all do.

Think back to the last time you were served. Maybe someone finished a task that you were dreading or unknowingly provided for a great need. In an act of service, we not only receive a tangible gift, we also catch a glimpse of God's love for us. When we serve others, we are being used by God to show his love. Were you able to serve someone today? Could you serve again tomorrow, or tonight?

God, please show me who is in need of my time or resources. I want to love and serve the way you want me to. Give me clear instructions so I can be a blessing to those around me.

How can you serve someone today?

Enemy Tactic

Let all who take refuge in you rejoice;
let them ever sing for joy,
and spread your protection over them,
that those who love your name may exult in you.

PSALM 5:11 ESV

The more you dive into your relationship with the Lord, the more the enemy will want to pull you away. The more you begin to listen for God's voice, the more Satan will try to whisper in your ear. Allowing yourself to become closer to God is the last thing the enemy wants for you.

You're not good enough. Nothing is going right for you. You're making all the wrong decisions. These lies may play over and over again in your head until they start to sound like reality. Suddenly, you find yourself believing them. This isn't what the Lord wants for you! He wants you to be glad in him. Make sure you are listening to the right voice today.

Lord, guard my mind from thoughts that the enemy wants me to think. Help me to dwell on your goodness and what I know are words from you.

Let all who take refuge in you rejoice;
let them ever sing for joy.
Spread your protection over them,
so that those who love your name may exult in you.

PSALM 5:11 NRSV

There would have been many thoughts coming into your mind today. As you turn toward Scripture, are they words that give you joy and make you sing and rejoice? Those are the words that you need to hold on to.

Pray tonight for protection from the lies the enemy wants you to believe. Ask the Lord to speak in a voice that is loud enough to hear through the deception. He wants to rejoice with you; he wants what's best for you. Trust in that knowledge tonight as you spend time with him.

Lord, thank you that you give me wisdom to know what is truth and what are lies from the enemy. Continue to help me filter those thoughts and dwell on your words that make me glad and give me joy.

What thoughts have you been having that you need to get rid of? What thoughts do you need to treasure?

Praise Always

Let everything alive give praises to the LORD!
You praise him!
Hallelujah!

PSALM 150:6 TLB

We can praise God and weep at the same time. It sounds impossible, but with God it is not. Our hearts can feel heavy; yet, we can still praise God in our trials because he is good. He is good when things are hard. He is good when the future seems bleak. He is good when the rest of the world isn't. He is good all the time.

Praise God for his goodness today. Let everything praise him today!

Jesus, may I always glorify and praise you regardless of how my days are going. May my reaction to hard times be to speak of your goodness and your faithfulness. Let me never forget how worthy you are.

*Let everything that breathes sing praises to the L*ORD*!*
*Praise the L*ORD*!*

PSALM 150:6 NLT

Sometimes praising God when it's the last thing we want to do is actually the best thing we can do. When we praise God, we draw nearer to him. We can praise God with our actions, with our voices, and with our attitudes. Our praise confirms in our spirits that he is worthy, that he is holy, and that he is sovereign.

Praising God declares that he is the center of our lives, and that he has overcome every struggle we face.

God, I declare your faithfulness this evening. Everything in my life exists because of you. I want you to be at the center of my heart and my mind every day. You are so worthy of my praise.

Is God at the center of your life?

Application Accepted

Long ago, even before he made the world, God chose us to be his very own through what Christ would do for us; he decided then to make us holy in his eyes, without a single fault—we who stand before him covered with his love.

EPHESIANS 1:4 TLB

Applications are essential for gleaning the promising applicants from the inadequate. Fill out this form, and find out if you're approved for a home loan, for college admittance, for a credit card. We put our best qualities on paper, tweak our weaknesses, and hope for approval. But rejection is always a possibility.

With God, however, our acceptance has already been promised. We must only appeal to his Son, Jesus, who steps in on our behalf and petitions for our approval. There is no credit flaw, no failing grade, and no past default that his death on the cross doesn't redeem completely.

Thank you, Jesus, for redeeming all humanity so that we can live in this new life and hope that our sins are forgiven and we can walk closely with you. Help me to walk in holiness today, which is impossible without you, but possible with you!

In Christ, he chose us before the world was made so that we would be his holy people—people without blame before him.

EPHESIANS 1:4 NCV

Because we are covered with God's loving forgiveness, there is no flaw in us. We are accepted by him as part of his family and redeemed by his grace for his eternal kingdom.

Can you believe your acceptance? Stand on the promise that there is nothing in your history—no past or present sin—that can separate you from his love. Cast everything upon him and have faith; you are wholly accepted and abundantly loved!

Lord, your love amazes me every single day. I know that I am redeemed and no longer live in darkness, yet sometimes the drag of this life stops me from reflecting on this amazing acceptance. Thank you for taking me as I am and making me into your likeness.

What areas of your life have you seen completely transformed by Jesus?

He Is Real

He has given us his very great and precious promises, so that through them you may participate in the divine nature, having escaped the corruption in the world caused by evil desires.

2 PETER 1:4 NIV

The test for authenticity is often measured by applying some kind of force or foreign substance to that which is being tested. Determining whether something is made of real gold can be accomplished in a number of ways. Perhaps the most simple is by rubbing the gold on an unglazed ceramic plate. The color of the mark left on the plate determines the authenticity of the gold. Real gold will leave a gold mark. Fake gold will leave a black mark. You can see the analogy, can't you?

God is real, and he is good. He has given us an example of how to remain authentic in a world full of fraud and deception. If you have been hurt by someone you thought was being real with you, you are not alone.

God, I remember your great and precious promises today. I press on in your strength. Help me to be real with you and with others.

He has given us, through these things, his precious and very great promises, so that through them you may escape from the corruption that is in the world because of lust, and may become participants of the divine nature.

2 Peter 1:4 NRSV

At some time in our lives, we will undergo an authenticity test. We might be put through several—daily. What mark will we leave when we encounter those tests? When we brush up against difficulty? If we are authentic Christians, the mark we leave will be gold—the true mark of Christ.

Unfortunately, black marks and scars cover many people who have been hurt by fakes. Be authentic about who you are and share the true love of God with others.

Father, I want to be full of your real, authentic love. Help me to have grace for others' mistakes. I want to leave a mark that is golden—a mark that reflects your good character.

How can you continue to leave an authentic mark of gold when you brush up against difficult situations?

Like He Does

We love because he first loved us.

1 JOHN 4:19 NIV

God's greatest commandments are to love him and to love one another. Loving him may come easy; after all, he is patient and loving himself. But the second part of his command can be difficult because it means loving intrusive neighbors at the backyard barbecue, offensive cousins at Christmas dinners, rude cashiers at the grocery store check-out, and insufferable guests who have stayed one night too many in the guestroom.

Loving one another is only possible when we love like God does. When we love out of our humanity, sin gets in the way. Obeying the command to love begins with God's love. When we realize how great his love is for us—how undeserved, unending, and unconditional—we are humbled because we didn't earn it.

God, let me understand your love as much as my mind can grasp it, and then remind me to love others because of the great love that you have for me.

Our love for him comes as a result of his loving us first.

1 JOHN 4:19 TLB

God give his love even though we don't deserve it. He gives freely and abundantly, and this spurs us on to love others. We represent Jesus to the world through love.

If we know how high and wide and deep and long his love is for us, then we have no choice but to pour out that love on others. The intrusive becomes welcome, the offensive becomes peaceful, rudeness gives way to grace, and the insufferable is overshadowed by the cross and all that Jesus suffered there.

Jesus, I know that you love me and I am so grateful for your love, it fills my heart up. When I think about your love for me, it enables me to be more loving toward others. Thank you for a day of acknowledging your love. Let it shine through my deeds and words to others around me tomorrow.

In what situations are you finding it difficult to love others? What can you do to show love to these people tomorrow?

Stronger

Do you not know? Have you not heard?
The Lord is the everlasting God,
the Creator of the ends of the earth.
He will not grow tired or weary,
and his understanding no one can fathom.
He gives strength to the weary
and increases the power of the weak.
Even youths grow tired and weary,
and young men stumble and fall;
but those who hope in the Lord will renew their strength.
They will soar on wings like eagles;
they will run and not grow weary,
they will walk and not be faint.

Isaiah 40:28-31 niv

No matter how puny your muscles may seem to you, you are stronger than you know. You can do anything you set your mind to. And you'll do it because God gives you a supernatural strength to power through and endure.

God never wearies. He never gets too tired to make it through the worst the world can throw at you. Put your hope in him, and he will give you strength beyond your wildest imagination.

God, I simply put my hope in you today and ask for you to give me strength to run and not grow tired.

Surely you know. Surely you have heard.
*The L*ORD *is the God who lives forever, who created all the world.*
He does not become tired or need to rest.
No one can understand how great his wisdom is.
He gives strength to those who are tired
and more power to those who are weak.
Even children become tired and need to rest,
and young people trip and fall.
*But the people who trust the L*ORD *will become strong again.*
They will rise up as an eagle in the sky;
they will run and not need rest;
they will walk and not become tired.

ISAIAH 40:28-31 NCV

Others around you may stumble and fall, but not you! God gives you the tenacity to make it through your toughest of times when you just ask him. He wants to run with you until the very end.

Ask God for strength in each area where you feel weak. He loves it when you admit your need for him. It's when he gets to show off his strength the most!

God, I need your help tonight. There are many areas of weakness in my life and I want you to be shown strong through them.

In what areas do you feel weak right now?

Waiting for Dawn

The ransomed of the Lord shall return,
and come to Zion with singing;
everlasting joy shall be upon their heads;
they shall obtain joy and gladness,
and sorrow and sighing shall flee away.

ISAIAH 35:10 NRSV

The sin and sadness of life can make it seem like an endless night, where we are continually waiting for the dawn of Christ's return. In the darkest of nights, it doesn't always help to know that he will return someday, because this day is full of despair.

To you he gives comfort. Don't lose heart. He is coming for you. It can be hard because he seems to be taking a long time, but he is preparing a place for you. You are not forgotten in this long night; your pain is familiar to him. Keep your eyes fixed on him. Soon you will hear his voice. He is also longing for that moment.

God, sometimes I am afraid of eternity and other times I long for it. Help me to endure today and even to enjoy it, knowing that my eternity is secure in your hands.

The ransomed of the Lord will return
And come with joyful shouting to Zion,
With everlasting joy upon their heads.
They will find gladness and joy,
And sorrow and sighing will flee away.

ISAIAH 35:10 NASB

We live for the promise of his return. This promise overcomes our pain, our longing, our desperation, and our limits. All things become bearable and light under the assurance of seeing Jesus, embracing him, and gazing on his beauty!

We will be made into a pure and spotless bride. There is nothing more for us to marvel at him. Glorify him. Believe him. Love him. Thank him. Can you do that tonight?

Lord, I have been able to get through the day because I know that there is an end to sadness and suffering. Help me to bring your joy into my home, my work, and wherever else I may go. Give me peace as I sleep, knowing that I can face another day with the brightness of a future with you.

What suffering or sadness are you facing in this season? Thank God that there will one day be an end to it.

Sober and Alert

Think clearly and exercise self-control. Look forward to the gracious salvation that will come to you when Jesus Christ is revealed to the world.

1 PETER 1:13 NLT

Every day we face situations where we need to exercise self-control: in our attitudes toward others, especially when we disagree with them; with our friends when faced with conviction differences; with social media and maintaining healthy boundaries and time limits; with work commitments and making sure we try our best.

The wonderful news is that we don't have to be controlled by our own desires, whims, or strongholds. We are not weak; in fact, God has made us strong. We can be patient with our family, hold to our convictions, and develop healthy habits and boundaries. God's power lives within us!

God, thank you that your power lives in me, and that power gives me the ability to do what is right. Help me to remain sober and alert.

With minds that are alert and fully sober,
set your hope on the grace to be brought to you
when Jesus Christ is revealed at his coming.

1 PETER 1:13 NIV

Sometimes the pressure or expectation to have self-control can be overwhelming—especially when we are struggling with habits that are proving difficult to break free from. We might feel like we are at the mercy of our temptation.

There is no need to become frustrated with our sin. Instead, we can hold our heads high and defeat whatever habit enslaves us or temptation that entices us because God has given us self-control. There is hope to be free from old patterns. We don't have to let our sin patterns control our lives. We can take charge, make changes, and break bad habits.

Father, I don't want to forget that self-control isn't something I have to muster up; it is already in me! I want to take hold of it, and take back control today. Thank you for giving me the strength to do so.

In what areas of your life do you need to exercise more self-control?

Always There

As for God, His way is blameless;
The word of the LORD is tried;
He is a shield to all who take refuge in Him.
For who is God, but the LORD?
And who is a rock, except our God.

PSALM 18:30-31 NASB

From famous songs to television commercials to close friends, there's a promise that is often made and rarely kept. *I'm here for you; you can always count on me.* Most of us have been promised this sometime in our life, and most, if not all, have felt that sting of rejection or disappointment when things didn't quite turn out that way.

There is someone who you can always count on. You can tell him everything. He hears you. He'll wrap his arms around you and tell you everything is going to be all right. He is completely trustworthy.

Thank you, Jesus, that I don't have to be perfect. Thank you that you are perfect and that your promises are true. Help me to take comfort in the fact that you will be with me today and forevermore.

The ways of God are without fault.
The LORD's words are pure.
He is a shield to those who trust him.
Who is God? Only the LORD.
Who is the Rock? Only our God.

PSALM 18:30-31 NCV

In the midst of our trying circumstances, we call out to the people who promised to always be there, but they don't answer. They don't even call us back. Even the best friend, the closest sister, the doting parent will fail in their ability to be there for you.

The only one we can truly depend on in this life is God. He works in wonderful ways to show his faithfulness and love to us in our time of need. Thank him for always being with you tonight.

God, I have been disappointed by people. Some days feel more disappointing than others. Help me to have grace for those who have let me down, but also give me a new expectation that I can trust in you and that you are not like everyone else. No one is God but you!

Have you been disappointed or hurt by someone you love? Trust in the one who is dependable. God will always be there for you.

Encouraged

The humble will see their God at work and be glad.
Let all who seek God's help be encouraged.

PSALM 69:32 NLT

"Come on!" "You can do it!" "You're almost there!" Strings of praise and faces filled with expectant wonder look on. If you were standing outside the door, you'd think someone was about to accomplish something extremely difficult. You might rush into the room to examine for yourself what momentous occasion was taking place. And you'd perhaps be perplexed at the scene in front of you. The adults in the room are crouched down on the floor looking intently at… an infant rocking back and forth on hands and knees. It's an amusing picture, but one we can learn from.

Even when you feel your daunting milestone is somewhat pathetic—like moving and arm and a leg—God wants to be your constant source of encouragement. Ask for his help, and acknowledge his work in your life as you move from stalling to crawling.

God, sometimes I need encouragement just to move from one place to another. Thank you for your patience and constant encouragement.

The poor will see and be glad—
you who seek God, may your hearts live!

PSALM 69:32 NIV

Obstacles in life come our way, and sometimes we feel like we have to figure them out all on our own. We rock forward in faith and then back as doubt creeps in. Forward again as emotions propel us, and back once more as they overwhelm.

What we fail to recognize is that our Father delights in seeing us make that first move forward. He looks on in excitement as we lift an arm and then a leg. Ever encouraging, our God beckons us: Come to me. You can make it. You're almost there.

Father, this evening I choose to move toward you. I want to be closer.
I want to be with you. Thank you for helping me to press on even
when you could have given up long ago. You are a wonderful Father.

What do you need encouragement for today?

Trusting the Rock

Through Christ you have come to trust in God. And you have placed your faith and hope in God because he raised Christ from the dead and gave him great glory.

1 PETER 1:21 NLT

Balancing at the edge of the cliff, a climber clutches the ropes. Far below, waves crash against the rocks, the spray reaching up toward her toes. She looks up at the guide, firmly gripping the rope, and then beyond his firm stance to the anchor hammered into the cliff side. With a firm push, her legs propel her beyond the ledge and out into space, dropping toward the sea.

Of course she trusts the guide. His strong grip, years of experience, skill, and familiarity with the landscape go a long way in convincing her that she will belay safely to the bottom of the cliff. But it's the rock, pierced by the anchor, which gains her deepest faith. The rock will not fail, will not crumble, and will never falter under her weight. Sound familiar?

God, you are my rock. I depend on you for strength today.

Through Him believe in God, who raised Him from the dead and gave Him glory, so that your faith and hope are in God.

1 PETER 1:21 NKJV

As we leap, sometimes stumbling, along the cliffs of life, who can we trust? God our Father offers us an anchor in Jesus Christ, who overcame death and is the only hope we have. We can jump with ease from any height, knowing that his strong arms of love will surround us and that our destiny is sure.

Our faith grows stronger in this truth: we share in the glory of Jesus through his death and resurrection. Have you had to really trust God lately? How did you place your faith and hope in him?

Father God, thank you for being so trustworthy. Thank you that I never have to doubt you. You have anchored me in your Son, and your strong arms of love surround me tonight.

Are you willing to jump, knowing that God is your anchoring rock?

He Is Faithful

Your lovingkindness, O Lord, extends to the heavens,
Your faithfulness reaches to the skies.

PSALM 36:5 NASB

Few love stories demonstrate a higher level of faithfulness than that depicted by the life of Hosea the prophet. He was given what seemed to be a very unfair task—to take a prostitute as a wife and commit to loving her. He would watch as his wife and the mother of his children chose to leave the family and return to her life of prostitution. But it didn't end there. Hosea went in search of his wife, and finding her in her debauchery, he paid to bring her back home with him—guilty, broken, and dirty.

It would seem a romantic tale of undying love had it happened naturally. However, this story is even more inconceivable when considering that Hosea walked into it with his eyes wide open. Hosea's choice to obey God in spite of what he would suffer is beyond admirable.

God, I want to display my faithfulness to you like Hosea demonstrated. Help me not to chase after things of the world, but to remain faithful to you and your purpose for me instead.

LORD, your love reaches to the heavens,
your loyalty to the skies.

PSALM 36:5 NCV

The loyal story of Hosea sounds oddly familiar, doesn't it? Jesus, commissioned by the Father, pursued us until we decided to become his. But we just can't seem to keep ourselves out of the mess of this world.

Jesus doesn't quit. He comes for us again. The price he paid to restore our relationship was his life. He gave up everything to bring us home. That is faithfulness in its fullest measure. Do you know how precious you are to the Father? His faithfulness toward you cannot be exhausted. Let yourself believe it this evening.

Jesus, thank you for coming to rescue me time and time again. You have paid for me and yet still I struggle. Thank you for your grace and patience. You are my wonderful, merciful God.

How does your unfaithfulness cause you to doubt the faithfulness of God?

His Ways

*When David's time to die drew near, he commanded Solomon
his son, saying, "I am about to go the way of all the earth. Be
strong, and show yourself a man, and keep the charge of the
LORD your God, walking in his ways and keeping his statutes, his
commandments, his rules, and his testimonies, as it is written
in the Law of Moses, that you may prosper in all that you do and
wherever you turn."*

1 KINGS 2:1-3 ESV

We don't need books or inspirational speakers to tell us how
to be successful: we just need to heed the advice of David to
his son, Solomon. Be strong and walk in God's ways, and then
you will prosper in all that you do.

As you get ready for today's activities, think about what it
means to be strong and walk in God's ways. Strength doesn't
have to mean that you can withstand anything that comes your
way, it simply means that you continue to trust God despite
everything you face.

*Father, I choose to stay strong and unwavering when it comes
to what I know your Word says. Thank you that I have the holy
Scriptures to dwell on. Give me greater understanding of your Word
so I can discern your direction for my life.*

If your sons pay close attention to their way, to walk before me in faithfulness with all their heart and with all their soul, you shall not lack a man on the throne of Israel.

1 Kings 2:4, esv

There were a lot of successors to David's throne that did not walk before God with faithfulness of heart. Leaders seem to face particular challenges when it comes to pride, greed, wealth, and fame.

Having a great position of power can often be a temptation to stray from God's ways of humility and justice. If you are a leader in any area, remember these temptations and choose to follow God's ways above your own ideas and motivation.

Holy Spirit, be my guide as I try to walk in your ways. I don't always know which way is right and I am confounded by my own motivations. Give me strength of character to hold fast to the path of righteousness that you have set before me.

What area do you recognize as a weakness in your own life? How can you submit these areas to God's ways?

Seek Him Out

Seek more of his strength! Seek more of him!
Let's always be seeking the light of his face.

PSALM 105:4, TPT

If only we could carry the feeling we get from a great church service, Bible study, concert or conference everywhere we go. When we are filled with the Spirit, God's strength is our strength. When we are inspired by praise, we see the world through the Lord's eyes. When open to his amazing power, our wounds can be healed.

Life tends to make continual basking impossible, though. We have bills to pay, tests to study for, and things to clean. We are worn down by stress and struggle. These all distract us from seeking God. Having wandered from that wonderful place, the place we felt him closer than our own skin, we are reminded of how much we crave it—how much we need it. We're reminded to seek, to search, to pursue his presence. When we can't feel his light, we need only turn toward his face. Arms open, he's right where we left him.

God, sometimes I forget it's I who wander away. I find you in the obvious places, in church, in Christian fellowship, in songs that glorify you, and I expect you to follow me into the dark places. You remain in the light, loving me, reminding me, I need only seek your beautiful face.

Seek the L<small>ORD</small> and His strength;
seek His face evermore!

P<small>SALM</small> 105:4 <small>NKJV</small>

When separated from our companions in a crowd, we scan each face, looking for one that is familiar. Once we see the eyes we know, or the smile we love, we feel at ease. No matter where we are, their face can us home.

This is what our Lord wants from us. "Seek my face," he tells us. Look for the eyes that love you more than life. Search out the smile he's reserved just for you. Come home.

God, I spend most of time seeking things for myself: my purpose, my possessions, or my comfort. Remind me, God, that nothing matters more than seeking you. With your strength, I am strong. In this light of your loving gaze, I am home.

When you seek him, where do you look?

Discernment

*"Your servant is in the midst of Your people which You have chosen,
a great people who are too many to be numbered or counted. So
give Your servant an understanding heart to judge Your people to
discern between good and evil. For who is able to judge this great
people of Yours?"*

1 KINGS 3:8-9 NASB

Whether you are still studying, at home with children, or
working in a full-time career, the decisions that you have to
make get more complicated as your responsibilities increase.

It may have seemed like a simple thing for Solomon to have
asked for discernment, but in reality a whole nation relied on
him for his answers. You need discernment in your decision-
making even as you go about your day-to-day business. Let
God show you wisdom every step of the way.

*God, give me an understanding heart today, to make decisions
and discern between good and evil. I cannot do this on my own
and need your wisdom. Thank you for the presence of your Holy
Spirit to guide me.*

It was pleasing in the sight of the Lord that Solomon had asked this thing. God said to him, "Because you have asked this thing and have not asked for yourself long life, nor have asked riches for yourself, nor have you asked for the life of your enemies, but have asked for yourself discernment to understand justice, behold, I have done according to your words. Behold, I have given you a wise and discerning heart, so that there has been no one like you before you, nor shall one like you arise after you."

1 Kings 3:10-12 NASB

God wants us to acknowledge him in everything we do. He is ready and willing to provide us with wisdom and direction in our decisions, but we need to be ready to ask. Sometimes we are consumed with asking God for things like health and provision.

As you spend some time with your heavenly Father this evening, remember that a wise and discerning heart will lead to greater blessing than money or fame.

God, I am humbled that I am a child in your kingdom. Thank you for the privilege of being an heir to all that you have. Help me to focus tonight on what you require of me in the area of justice, that I would have a wise a discerning heart to display your love to the world.

What do you truly desire from God?

True Love Abides

As you received Christ Jesus the Lord, so continue to live in him.
COLOSSIANS 2:6 NCV

Few feelings can compare to new love. The anticipation, the discovery, and the excitement are overwhelming. It's hard to think of anything else. Whether a romance, a puppy, or a new friend, as the days go by, excitement is replaced by routine. Discovery gives way to familiarity. If we treasure the love, these feelings, though less intense, will grow deep and remain strong. A good routine takes hold. True love abides.

Falling in love with Jesus can be similar. The overwhelming joy of first finding him in your heart settles into the quiet peace of knowing he's always going to be there. Let us take care to treasure the love, allowing it to grow deep and abide.

Dearest Jesus, I love remembering the way I felt the first time you made yourself known to me, the first time I was certain of your abiding love. Sometimes I long to feel again the intensity of brand new love. And yet, I wouldn't trade the day-to-day joy of knowing you are with me for anything. I thank you for both the thrill of the beginning and the peace of the permanence.

As you received Christ Jesus the Lord, so walk in him,
COLOSSIANS 2:6 ESV

How did you receive Christ? With happiness, relief, or joyful dancing? Whichever way your love began, live it out with equal fervor!

If he gave you peace, walk in peace. If he brought you joy, jump, twirl, and sway in it. Whatever gift he gave your heart, let that gift define your walk with him.

Precious God, remind my heart how it felt to discover you. Inspire my steps with gratitude; move me to the rhythm of your grace. Let your joy be the song I dance to. Let the peace you gave me be the path I walk.

What gifts will define your walk if you determine to live this verse out?

The Answer

"The LORD said to my father David, 'Because it was in your heart to build a house for My name, you did well that it was in your heart. Nevertheless you shall not build the house, but your son who will be born to you, he will build the house for My name.'"

1 KINGS 8:18-19 NASB

We might ask things of God with all the right intentions, yet sometimes God just needs to say no. It is hard to accept no as an answer, but we need to trust that God has the bigger picture in mind. He is the one that is ultimately in control of his plan and although he is pleased with us, it doesn't always mean we get what we want.

Today, as you go about your tasks, be encouraged that God is pleased with you, and trust that he will figure out the rest.

God, give me humility and grace to accept that even some of my best intentions will not be answered in the way that I want them to be. Help me to recognize when your greater plan is at work and give me a thankful heart that I can trust you.

"The Lord has fulfilled His word which He spoke; for I have risen in place of my father David and sit on the throne of Israel, as the Lord promised, and have built the house for the name of the Lord, the God of Israel."

1 Kings 8:20 nasb

Even when God says no to a good intention, he still works out his plan for good. David didn't see the temple that he had in his heart to build, yet it was still built. Solomon likely built the temple even better than his father would have because of his great wisdom. The new temple was built out of the best material with the best workmanship known to man.

You might have to accept that your good intentions are the start of something incredible, but someone else may get the chance to do the thing you had been wanting to do. God is always on the throne, and he will prevail.

God, I pray for the people who may finish the work or the plan I have started. Thank you that you have used me and that you can use others. Help some of these dreams that I have that are a part of your will to be even bigger and more beautiful than I could have imagined.

What dream could God be saying no to you about? Can you accept that he might make this happen through someone else?

Tell Him

Nothing in all creation is hidden from God's sight.
Everything is uncovered and laid bare
before the eyes of him to whom we must give account.

HEBREWS 4:13 NIV

Face smeared with chocolate, and t-shirt covered in crumbs, the toddler insists she doesn't know what happened to the rest of the cookies. We can clearly see what she doesn't want us to know. It's almost humorous, the way she thinks that if she denies it, we won't see it.

Perhaps God is similarly amused when we try to keep him from knowing something us. It is quite silly to imagine we can keep secrets from our omniscient Lord. Yet we often act like it's possible to. We think that because we're pretending to have fun, he won't know we are in pain. Because we are denying the problem, he won't see the way it's slowly taking us down. He knows, dear one. He sees. And he adores you. Tell him the truth and see the love with which he responds.

God, I don't know why I try to keep anything from you, why I hide my pain or try to cover up my sin. I know you don't condemn or judge me. I know you find me precious. Please give me the strength to tell you what you already know, so I can have the peace that will follow when I do.

There is no creature hidden from His sight, but all things are naked and open to the eyes of Him to whom we must give account.

HEBREWS 4:13 NKJV

In the mid-1990's, a delightful book called Naked Babies was released. It featured, as you might expect, a series of black and white photographs of naked babies in all their roly-poly glory. It was absolutely precious.

We tend to think of our nakedness before God as exposure or weakness, but what if he sees us more like those darling, undressed little ones? No need for shame and nothing to hide, because our Papa thinks we are absolutely precious.

God, thank you that you see everything I do, and you still find me precious. I don't need to live in shame or hide anything from you. Help me to share everything with you, knowing that you already know and you love me unconditionally.

Spend a few minutes searching yourself for anything you are trying to keep hidden and ask God for the faith to lay it bare.

Listen to Your Heart

My heart has heard you say, "Come and talk with me."
And my heart responds, "LORD, I am coming."

PSALM 27:8 NLT

Faced with a crucial decision, a friend will often advise us to listen to our heart. The theory behind this advice is that the deepest part of us already knows what to do. Where we connect with our longing is where the answer awaits.

As a Christ-follower, the Holy Spirit is an active part of your life. Because of this active relationship, your heart will often be directed toward the Lord, to his will, and his way. When your mind has a question, listen to your heart and talk with your God.

God, listening to my heart should always result in hearing from you. I am blessed by your wisdom; you never guide me the wrong way. No matter what I must decide, whether it's major or mundane, may I turn toward you, and hear the words your Spirit speaks to my heart.

My heart said of you, "Go, worship him."
*So I come to worship you, L*ORD.
PSALM 27:8 NCV

We all have moments where we just need to honor God.
Sometimes it's a breathtaking sunset, or a sweet moment
with the ones you love the most. It may even be when you're
alone in the dark, uninspired by anything seen or felt, but
drawn to give him praise.

Awe, gratitude, or longing, to worship him is all the heart
wants to do. And when we do worship him? Oh, the sweet,
sweet communion we share with our glorious King!

Father God, my heart longs to sing of your greatness forever.
Because I will never truly be home until I am in heaven,
worshipping you for all eternity, this heart-longing never leaves
me. No song or prayer expresses all you are and all you've done.
Today, and every day, I worship you.

What is your favorite way to worship God? When do you feel
him draw near in response to your praise?

Fools for Him

The message of the cross is foolishness to those who are perishing,
but to us who are being saved it is the power of God.

1 CORINTHIANS 1:18 NKJV

Have you ever watched a television program with the sound
turned off? When we don't hear what is going on and don't
recognize the context, people's actions look strange and
might be hard to figure out. Unfortunately, many people won't
hear the message of the cross as good news because their eyes
have not yet seen the truth.

Be encouraged today that although some will fail to accept
the good news of Jesus Christ, others' eyes can be opened to
the truth within you. Rely on the wisdom of God and not the
wisdom of men.

God, as I think of the people I will come across today, many of
whom do not know you and seem to not want to know about you,
I pray that my life would be a wonderful witness to the reality of
your hope and love.

It is written: "I will destroy the wisdom of the wise,
and bring to nothing the understanding of the prudent."

1 CORINTHIANS 1:19 NKJV

At the end of the day we may feel like we have not made a significant impact on anything or anyone.

Be encouraged that today you were an example of the living God and that your life shares good news whether you feel like you have or not. Each day that you continue to have faith in Jesus Christ, you are carrying the good news.

God, thank you that I carry you with me each day. I pray that you would give me opportunities tomorrow to share the good news. Give me the right words at the right time.

What will you be able to share about the good news with someone tomorrow?

True Home

Our homeland is in heaven, and we are waiting for our Savior,
the Lord Jesus Christ, to come from heaven.

PHILIPPIANS 3:20 NCV

Where is home? Some will always think of the house or town they grew up in, while others have found home is where they chose to settle and raise their own families. Still others may feel most at home with a certain person, regardless of geography. Home feels right. Home feels secure.

Wherever we feel at home on earth, the Lord wants us to remember our true home is with him. All the warmth and love "home" provides us here is just a glimpse of what awaits us in heaven. No person or place can come close to providing the joy and security we will feel when we are united with Jesus.

Lord Jesus, as much as I love my earthly home, and as grateful as I am for it, I long for the day I am home with you. Eagerly, I wait for heaven, and for you, my true home.

*We are a colony of heaven on earth as we cling tightly
to our life-giver, the Lord Jesus Christ,*

Philippians 3:20 tpt

A trip to Italy won't make us Italian. Regardless of where we visit, we are citizens of where we are from. A piece of our hearts remains where it was planted. We eventually grow homesick, no matter how lovely our surroundings.

We may not remember heaven, but heaven remembers us. The piece of our hearts that remains there grows homesick and calls us to our true home.

Father God, I don't remember heaven, but my heart does. I love where I am, but I can't wait to be where you are—to come home.

Where is home the place for you? Who is home the person? What is it that gives you that feeling of rightness?

Train to Win

Don't you realize that in a race everyone runs, but only one person gets the prize? So run to win! All athletes are disciplined in their training. They do it to win a prize that will fade away, but we do it for an eternal prize. So I run with purpose in every step. I am not just shadowboxing.

1 CORINTHIANS 9:24-26 NLT

Apathy is a very real struggle. It can be hard to get motivated for work, cleaning up the house, or getting your assignments done. God doesn't want us to be apathetic in our faith. We can easily become distracted by things in life that don't matter as much as eternity.

Paul is suggesting here that we run to win, not just to endure life but to do the very best that we can. It's not about competition; it is about enthusiasm.

God, thank you for the day that you've given me. I pray that I would see the value of eternity in the little things that I do for you. Give me energy each day to run this race of faith.

I discipline my body like an athlete, training it to do what it should. Otherwise, I fear that after preaching to others I myself might be disqualified.

1 Corinthians 9:27 NLT

It can be exhausting even thinking about the amount of training a professional athlete puts into their particular sport. It feels almost impossible that we could get ourselves into that kind of shape.

Paul was using this analogy to describe the hard work it takes to maintain our faith in this life. This world needs us to be an example of a life lived with purpose.

God, thank you that I do have purpose in life. I pray where I am dragging my feet that you would help me to lift my eyes toward you and find inspiration to continue running with purpose toward the goal of eternity. Let my life be an inspiration to others.

Where are you struggling to see purpose in your life? Ask God to breathe new inspiration into this area.

Spiritual Guide

I have gone astray like a lost sheep;
seek Your servant, for I do not forget Your commandments.

PSALM 119:176 NASB

It's rare to find ourselves truly lost these days. A GPS points the way almost infallibly when we need directions, and our smartphones keep this technology within easy reach. Yet, occasionally, we find ourselves out of range, or with a map that is out of date. Maybe we made one too many wrong turns and are too muddled up to get back on track. Occasionally, we need more assistance than technology can give. We need someone to show us the way.

This same thing can happen on our faith walk. Despite the guidance from study, prayer and mentors, we may wander off the path and find ourselves lost. When we experience spiritual disorientation, we need God to show us the way. Wonderfully, the Lord's guidance is always infallible. He is never out of range, and his omniscience is never out of date. We can trust his guidance.

God, you are my spiritual GPS. Each time I lose my way, you find me. You hear when I call, and you light the proper path. I remember your highest command—to love you with all I am—and the way becomes familiar again. As I share your love with others, again I am found.

I have wandered away like a lost sheep;
come and find me, for I have not forgotten your commands.

PSALM 119:176 NLT

God hears the tender, humble pleas of his lost sheep. Whether from distraction or disobedience, when they realize they are lost, he hears their bleating and comes to their rescue. He always hears the cries of those who belong to him. He stays connected to the souls who love their Lord.

Even if getting geographically lost is rare, getting metaphorically lost is still quite common. As we progress along our faith journey, we get distracted, or we stumble, and wander off the path. What a blessing it is to know that the moment we recognize our predicament, we can call, and he will come.

Jesus, you are the Good Shepherd. You see me wander. You know when I have lost my way. Rather than scoop me up and carry me back, you let me learn. You let me remember how much better everything is with you. You wait for me to ask, and then you come.

Together with the Holy Spirit, search your heart. Where have you gotten a little lost? If you are ready, ask your Shepherd to come and find you. If not, pray for the will to call to him soon.

Embracing Difference

There are different kinds of spiritual gifts,
but the same Spirit is the source of them all.
There are different kinds of service,
but we serve the same Lord.

1 CORINTHIANS 12:4-5 NLT

We live in a world that still values certain things over others. This makes us believe that some things we do have more importance than others. We often apply this way of thinking to the way that we see ourselves within the context of our Christian family.

At church, we make certain gifts seem more important than our own. It's critical to understand that there are differences in the way people think, act, and feel. These differences all are used by the Spirit to do something great. We serve God in different ways but the point is that we serve the same God.

Jesus, I am sorry where I have placed certain gifts and talents in some kind of hierarchy. Help me to recognize my own worth in the body of believers that I'm part of, and help me to see the worth of every single person who contributes toward your church.

God works in different ways,
but it is the same God
who does the work in all of us.

1 CORINTHIANS 12:6 NLT

We are all guilty of expecting God to work in a certain way and then feeling disappointed when he doesn't. Sometimes we are quick to judge whether God is or isn't working in other people. It's not our place to judge what God is doing, we are each accountable for our own thoughts, actions, and feelings.

Be encouraged that God has given you something unique, and that he wants you to be a part of his greater work. Be aware that he may work in a way that is different from your own opinions and thoughts.

God, thank you for today and for giving me the opportunity to be myself. Help me to recognize the gifts that you've given me and to know that you value them and want me to use them to further your kingdom.

What are the different kinds of spiritual gifts that God has given you? How are you using these within the church?

He Knows

When I thought, "My foot slips,"
your steadfast love, O LORD, held me up.
PSALM 94:18 ESV

A practiced assistant knows which instrument the surgeon, mechanic, or chef needs before they even have to ask. An attentive mother spots the first signs of sickness, whether in the body or the heart. She offers the right kind of remedy or comfort instinctively. She knows her child.

As you are his child, the Lord is completely in tune with your needs. Before you even have to ask, he offers just what you need. He sees the slip before it happens, and his arms are waiting to catch you. Before your heart breaks, he prepares to comfort it. He knows his child.

God, I am humbled by your attentiveness to me. The moment I slip, I feel your arm steadying me. If I fail to grab it, you reach down to cushion my fall. As suddenly as sadness and disappointment come upon me, so too does the certainty of your unfailing support and comfort. You are steadfast, God, and I am grateful.

If I say, "My foot slips,"
Your mercy, O LORD, will hold me up.

PSALM 94:18 NKJV

How very close he must be, to respond the same moment we ask. Whether we call aloud or think our plea, he hears it and comes. No matter if we call to him the second we slip, or after a lifetime of free-falling, he is always anxious and eager to lift us up.

Thank you, Lord, for holding us up with your mercy.

God, what patience you have. You could prevent my slips and falls, but instead, you let me come to you. Knowing I must recognize my need before I can comprehend your mercy, you wait. How closely you remain, though it must be hard to watch at times. Thank you, Father, for sticking so close and for giving so much.

Do you tend to recognize your need for help the moment you slip, or do you need to fall for a while, maybe even hitting the bottom first? Invite the Spirit to speak to you each time you approach a slippery spot.

Heavenly Bodies

Let me reveal to you a wonderful secret. We will not all die, but we will all be transformed! It will happen in a moment, in the blink of an eye, when the last trumpet is blown. For when the trumpet sounds, those who have died will be raised to live forever. And we who are living will also be transformed.

1 CORINTHIANS 15:51-52 NLT

The concept of eternal life in Paul's day was a hard one for people to get their heads around. Now we are excited by the hope of eternity because we know with certainty that Jesus died and rose again. This means that we share in the same experience as Jesus: we will one day rise again and have our eternal life still to live.

This isn't the end and that should give you wonderful hope as you go about your day. Know that you are being transformed into his glory day by day.

Jesus, thank you that you died for me. Thank you for showing me death was defeated for good. Help me to live today in the knowledge that this is not the end and one day all things will be made new.

Our dying bodies must be transformed into bodies that will never die; our mortal bodies must be transformed into immortal bodies.

1 CORINTHIANS 15:53 NLT

When we get home from a day we often want to sit down and relax. This is because our bodies having been active and can become weary.

Won't it be wonderful when we realize that our new bodies are not perishing and we will not feel the weariness of the day? In the meantime, look after your body and allow yourself to rest and trust in the hope of the future glorious body.

God, I thank you for creating my whole person and that this body matters as well as my soul. Help me to be kind to my body. Thank you that one day I will be transformed with an eternal human form.

In what ways can you honor the body that God has given you? How can you give yourself the rest that you need?

Consolation

When my anxious thoughts multiply within me,
Your consolations delight my soul.

PSALM 94:19 NASB

How often do we experience anxiety like this? Like mold, one worry builds upon another until a fuzzy, foul surface completely obscures our peace. This is a verse to memorize, dear friend! When stress leads to worry, worry to anxiety, and anxiety threatens to give way to panic, God consoles us. Call to him. Remember him. In the midst of all that swirling chaos, he won't just soothe you, he will delight your soul.

Try this out. Turn to him. The situation may not change, but your perspective will. Watch his loveliness repel the things that try to steal your peace. Remembering his promises will bring you joy and delight right where you are.

God, thank you for showing me how easy it is to obliterate the overgrown anxieties of my thoughts. Your face, your light, and your goodness drown them out the moment I turn my attention to you. Delight replaces doubt, and my worry is overtaken by worship. How wonderful you are!

Whenever my busy thoughts were out of control,
the soothing comfort of your presence calmed me down
and overwhelmed me with delight.

PSALM 94:19 TPT

It would be enough, wouldn't it, if the Father were to stop at comforting us? If all he did was take away our fear and quiet our anxiety, our gratitude would still run deep. But he doesn't stop.

Loving Father that he is, he doesn't leave us simply feeling better. He takes our wringing hands and raises them up. He silences fear by overwhelming us with delight.

Father, how often I feel like a child before you. You hear my cry and replace it with laughter. First you soothe me by drying every tear, and then you make me laugh. First you comfort me, then you invite me to dance.

See how easy it is for your Father to turn your thoughts to wonderful things by trying it now. Surrender every anxiety to him, and see the way he ushers in peace, laughter and joy.

Choose His Way

"Take My yoke upon you and learn from Me,
for I am gentle and humble in heart,
and you will find rest for your souls.
For My yoke is easy and My burden is light."

MATTHEW 11:29-30 NASB

Imagine you're volunteering to work on a farm for a few days, and you get to choose your job. Would you like to break up and move boulders to prepare the field for plowing and planting, or would you prefer to walk behind the plow scattering seeds? Which is more appealing: the back-breaking heavy lifting or the steady purposeful stroll?

Unless we're trying hard to impress someone, or are gluttons for punishment, we're going to choose the seeds, right? This is exactly what it's like to walk with Christ. We can choose his way, and find rest for our souls, or we can go our own way and try to lift those heavy boulders. Which will we choose?

God, here and now, the choice to do life your way is easy. It's only when I get to the field—when I think it has to be hard in order for it to count—that I am tempted to take the harder way. I ask myself, "Am I spiritual enough, working hard enough, and sacrificing enough?" In these moments, remind me of your gentle way, and invite me, again, to choose it.

"Accept my teachings and learn from me,
because I am gentle and humble in spirit,
and you will find rest for your lives.
The burden that I ask you to accept is easy;
the load I give you to carry is light."

MATTHEW 11:29-30 NCV

Throughout our lives we seek to learn from those who know more than us. We seek teachers and experts we can trust. We rely on the truth of their knowledge. We are open to their instruction especially when we feel like they have a method that would make things easier for us.

How much better our lives would be if were as open to Jesus' teaching and instruction. Though humble and gentle, he is superior to any earthly expert. If we choose his way, not only will he offer us the best advice and insight, we are also promised a burden that is easy and a load that is light.

God, help me to accept your yoke. help me learn what you teach. You offer protection, grace, and rest. I sometimes eschew these gifts in favor of struggle and burdens. I take on things that are far too heavy. Humble me, God, to accept your peaceful rest.

Are you choosing the hard way over Jesus' way in any areas of your life? What might it feel like to bear his yoke instead?

Determine the Problem

The people of the city said to Elisha, "Look, our lord, this town is well situated, as you can see, but the water is bad and the land is unproductive." "Bring me a new bowl," he said, "and put salt in it." So they brought it to him. Then he went out to the spring and threw the salt into it, saying, "This is what the LORD says: 'I have healed this water. Never again will it cause death or make the land unproductive.'"

2 KINGS 2:19-21 NIV

It is in our human nature to be able to discern the positive and negatives of different situations. When you are making important decisions, you will often think about the pros and cons of that decision. The people of this city knew that they had a good thing with their location, but something needed to change about their water supply or it would be the end of them.

Perhaps you can apply this principle to a project you are working on, a relationship that needs working out, or simply something going on in your heart and mind. Figure out what needs healing and ask God to help right the wrong.

God, I need your wisdom to figure out some of the situations I am facing at the moment. Please help me to clarify what the problem is and then help me to trust you to heal and restore the things that are broken. I surrender to your work in my life today.

The water has remained pure to this day,
according to the word Elisha had spoken.

2 KINGS 2:22 NIV

Have you been able to gain insight into some of the difficult situations you are facing? Remember that the people brought their problems to Elisha, who asked and believed God to sort it all out.

You might have a trusted family member, friend, or leader who you can talk through your problems with. Perhaps you just need to go straight to Jesus and lean on his advice. Remember that having faith is just as important as knowing what is wrong. Be encouraged to hand over the problem to God and trust that he can make things whole.

God, thank you that you can bring healing into all kinds of situations. I need your help tonight. I ask for your peace as I leave my burdens and frustrations in your hands.

What problems have you been able to identify in your circumstances? Communicate these to God and let him provide the solution.

Fathom His Glory

The heavens proclaim the glory of God.
The skies display his craftsmanship.
Day after day they continue to speak;
night after night they make him known.

PSALM 19:1-2 NLT

If you want to be amazed, go outside and look up. Our sky is an endless, ever-changing canvas of awesome. How many shades of blue can there be? How many shapes of cloud? Even on a gray day, how incredible is it that all that vastness is so perfectly hidden? Sunrise and sunset? Breathtaking. Glorious.

When is the last time you stopped to marvel at God's incredible creativity? Take some time, right now, to notice something glorious. Go study a spring bloom. Go read about the miracle that is the human eye. Go look at photos you've taken of beautiful scenery. Try to fathom God's glory. What a craftsman God is!

God, I'm looking up and I am amazed. One day may be gray and dark, but the next is rich in color and light. Your sky is the most glorious painting I've ever seen. Sometimes I want to keep it as it is, to freeze time and remain staring at what you've created. Then I remember you are infinitely creative and I look forward to tomorrow, when you do it again.

The heavens declare the glory of God;
the skies proclaim the work of his hands.
Day after day they pour forth speech;
night after night they reveal knowledge.

PSALM 19:1–2 NIV

The night sky has its own mysterious beauty. Swathes of darkest blue and black are punctuated by pricks of light. How far away are the heavens seem. How large, up close, is that tiny, shimmering star? What the day proclaims out loud, the night whispers:

Look at this world! How vast, how lovely. How immeasurable are the stars, like the glory of the God who made it all.

God, you are truly awesome. One look at the night sky shows me how much I don't know. Stars that were there all day long are visible, glimmering symbols of your infinite creativity. As many stars as are visible on the clearest of nights, more are the ways you amaze me.

How have you been amazed by God lately?

Surrounded

When an attendant of the man of God rose early in the morning and went out, an army with horses and chariots was all around the city. His servant said, "Alas, master! What shall we do?" He replied, "Do not be afraid, for there are more with us than there are with them."

2 KINGS 6:15-16 NRSV

At times we wake up in the morning and feel dread or anxiety about the day ahead. We might feel as though there is a great army of trouble surrounding us as we look out.

If this is how you are feeling, ask God what to do. Give yourself time to still yourself before your Creator, the one who knows all things. He knows you better than anyone else. Hear him say back to you, "Do not be afraid, there are more on your side than against you."

Lord God, thank you that when I feel overwhelmed, you stand beside me and cause me to see that with you, I can conquer everything that I am facing today. Give me courage as I face battles, knowing that good is far greater than evil.

Elisha prayed: "O Lord, please open his eyes that he may see." So the Lord opened the eyes of the servant, and he saw; the mountain was full of horses and chariots of fire all around Elisha.

2 Kings 6:17 NRSV

If you have faced a lot of challenging issues today, remember to ask God, as Elisha did, to open your eyes so you can see what is really going on.

Be encouraged that while you may feel alone or with little strength, you actually have a whole army of angels from God standing with you in battle. God's spiritual forces are much more than the enemies you come up against.

Father God, open my eyes so I can see how strong the army is that is fighting with me. Thank you that you always give me strength to get through the challenging times. Let this time that I have set aside now, be a time where I receive strength and renewal from your ministering angels.

What emotional, physical, or spiritual battle feels too overwhelming for you right now? Allow God to open your eyes to see all the help that you have in him.

By God

With your help I can attack an army.
With God's help I can jump over a wall.

PSALM 18:29 NCV

Scriptures like this one remind us of God's unlimited power. There is truly nothing he can't do. Things we could never do without him—like attack armies and jump over walls—are possible with his help. This verse is very encouraging, and very easy to misinterpret.

Possible and probable are two different words. It's possible that God will give you super strength and the ability to fly but it's not very probable. Just because God can, doesn't mean he will. And the reason lies right there in the word will. The five accomplished, articulate Christian women praying to be chosen as the keynote speaker at an upcoming conference will not all be selected. The two teams ardently praying for a win will not both go home as victors. While the Lord wants us to take confidence in his limitless ability, he also wants us to pray unceasingly to know and do his will.

Father God, I love knowing that within your will, there is truly nothing I can't do. Which walls should I scale, and which should I turn from, Lord? Help me to lean in closely, so I'll hear as you reveal your will.

> *By you I can crush a troop,*
> *and by my God I can leap over a wall.*

PSALM 18:29 NRSV

Having covered the difference between possible and probable, let us now go ahead and embrace the boldness of this verse.

What enemy of your peace needs crushing? By God, you can knock it flat. What wall needs scaling? By your Savior, you can sail right over. Be empowered, friend. By your God, you've got this.

God, I believe you. I believe I can do anything—even scary, impossible things—by you. It is your strength, your might, your courage in me. By you, those enemy troops are going down.

Which aspect of today's verse did you need to lay claim of more: being in his will, or standing in his might?

Unmeasurable Joy

Our light affliction, which is but for a moment,
is working for us a far more exceeding and eternal weight of glory.

2 CORINTHIANS 4:17 NKJV

Think of an Olympic diver, sprinter, or swimmer. The short time they spend competing at the Games takes thousands upon thousands of hours to prepare for, and yet it's over in a moment. But think now of what isn't over: the remembered glory of that moment. For the rest of their lives, those athletes can recall the joy they felt achieving their goal—the moment all the pain, sacrifice, and preparation paid off.

This beautiful verse reveals something similar about eternity. What seems hard and is causing us pain now, is just a training session for what's to come. We're getting strong, preparing to hold a glory we can't even comprehend. We'll live with a joy that cannot be measured and, unlike a brief Olympic performance, it will never, ever end.

God, life is heavy sometimes. Please help me remember these are training days to strengthen my soul for the weight of eternal glory. Remind me on the days I want to buckle under the weight that one day, I'll stand in more joy than I can measure.

We view our slight, short-lived troubles in the light of eternity.
We see our difficulties as the substance that produces for us an
eternal, weighty glory far beyond all comparison.

2 CORINTHIANS 4:17 TPT

If we were to paddle up next to an iceberg while kayaking, we'd probably be impressed by its size. If we were to dive below the surface, though, we'd find ourselves overwhelmed by its true mass. Thanks to Titanic, most people know the part of the iceberg that is visible from the surface is only a fraction of the whole, or the tip of the iceberg.

Measuring our daily struggles in light of eternity is akin to seeing the whole iceberg. The tip may look imposing, but as part of our whole story, it's nothing we can't handle.

Father God, up against your perfect, eternal plan, this earthly
life is just the tip of the tip of the iceberg. I know the vastness,
depth, and goodness of what you have prepared for me. rom that
knowledge, I draw courage.

Think of a problem from your past that seemed gigantic at the time, only to be looked back upon as a small bump in the road.

Unveiled

Whenever anyone turns to the Lord, the veil is taken away.
Now the Lord is the Spirit,
and where the Spirit of the Lord is, there is freedom.

2 CORINTHIANS 3:16-17 NIV

It can be helpful to understand that those who haven't accepted Jesus are not seeing life clearly. What a difference it makes when that veil is taken away and life becomes full of meaning and possibility.

You experience freedom because you know the truth. Today, you will see many people who still have that veil over their face. Be gracious toward them and pray that they would turn to God so they can also experience freedom.

God, I pray for those people in my life who still have not turned toward you. Holy Spirit, reveal your truth so they may also walk in freedom.

We all, who with unveiled faces contemplate the Lord's glory,
are being transformed into his image with ever-increasing glory,
which comes from the Lord, who is the Spirit.

2 CORINTHIANS 3:18 NIV

Transformation in the natural world doesn't happen instantly in the way that a superhero goes from normal to amazing. Seeds become flowers slowly, babies become adults slowly.

This is like the transformation taking place in your heart. Your veil was taken off to see what Christ has done for you, and now you are in the process of being transformed to be like him.

God, thank you that a future glory awaits me. I am blessed to have a wonderful future of life in you. Help me to approach tomorrow with the perspective that I am heading toward glory.

What transformation have you seen in your own life that has glorified God?

Every Sweet Moment

*People should eat and drink
and enjoy the fruits of their labor,
for these are gifts from God.*

ECCLESIASTES 3:13 NLT

Do you savor your breakfast smoothie, grateful for the gift of year-round berries and the invention of blenders? Do you settle into your desk chair or work space and look around, grateful for a way to earn a living? How often, during a normal day, do you take time to enjoy your day, and to pause and acknowledge that life is a sweet, sweet gift from God?

Every moment is a gift. It's easy to lose sight of this, especially when hurry and worry are at the top of the to-do list. Take a second, right now in your mind, to add "enjoy" above them on the list.

God, thank you for the sweet, simple gifts in my life. I love the smells, tastes, conversations, and experiences you place on my path each day. Thank you, Holy Spirit, for helping me slow down enough to really enjoy them, and to see them for the gifts they are.

It is God's gift that all should eat and drink
and take pleasure in all their toil.

ECCLESIASTES 3:13 NRSV

Read the verse again. God wants you to enjoy your life. This means not just the mountaintop moments, but also the ordinary pleasures in your day.

Breakfast with an over-scheduled teenager is a blessing. Enjoy it! Coffee with a girlfriend is a gift. Open it with gladness. Lunch with your love, birthday cake with coworkers, and even quiet dinners with no one but your favorite furry friend are meant to be pleasures, so take pleasure in them.

God, when I think of all the times I rush through my meals, failing to really taste what I am eating or engage with who is with me, I realize all the blessings I've missed, all the gifts I've left unwrapped. Help me to savor these ordinary moments, God, and see them for the blessings that they are.

Do you find it easy, or more of a challenge, to take pleasure in the ordinary moments of life? Invite the Lord to keep you attentive to these sweet blessings.

Look at Eternity

We do not lose heart. Though outwardly we are wasting away, yet inwardly we are being renewed day by day. For our light and momentary troubles are achieving for us an eternal glory that far outweighs them all.

2 Corinthians 4:16-17 NIV

When our bodies start to fail us, either with sickness or just getting older, we can begin to feel down. It's hard to see that we are being transformed to greatness when we seem to be confronted with more trouble as life goes on.

Discouragement starts with fixating on the problem rather than the truth of the future. If you are feeling down on life right now, remember that one day all will be made right. Let yourself look toward Jesus instead of your daily troubles.

God, keep my eyes above any trouble that may come into my day. Help me to set aside worry, anxiety, and other stresses, knowing that they are only temporary.

No wonder we don't give up. For even though our outer person gradually wears out, our inner being is renewed every single day. We view our slight, short-lived troubles in the light of eternity. We see our difficulties as the substance that produces for us an eternal, weighty glory far beyond all comparison.

2 CORINTHIANS 4:16-17 TPT

It's in our nature to review and replay things of the day in our minds. Sometimes we remember the things someone said to make us laugh, or we replay an argument or some advice we gave.

It may take a bit of effort, but try looking at your day with the thoughts of the things that went on that were unseen. Think of the joy you experienced when laughing, think of the life you brought to someone else's day with your kind words. These are the things of eternity, and they are worth fixing your eyes on.

Father, I am grateful for the life that you have given me. Open my eyes to see the things of this world that do not matter, and allow me to dwell on things that are part of your lasting goodness.

In what ways can you see God's eternal goodness in your day-to-day life?

Only the Beginning

We do not look at the things which are seen, but at the things which are not seen. For the things which are seen are temporary, but the things which are not seen are eternal.

2 CORINTHIANS 4:18 NKJV

We need only recall any high or any low to realize how temporary things here really are. That day you thought you'd never smile again gave way to millions of smiles as your heart mended. The euphoria you felt upon first falling in love turned into a familiar, quieter rhythm, punctuated by occasional moments that felt distinctly not like love.

God really wants us to understand that this world is not our forever home, and this life is only the beginning of an eternity too wonderful to fathom. Our broken hearts will be utterly forgotten, and our deepest loves will be heightened and eclipsed beyond all imagining when we are united with him in heaven.

Father God, on the days I feel the weight of this world is too much to bear, remind me of all that awaits me. Remind me that I won't even recall these moments of pain. And, on the days I am convinced nothing could be better than the joy I'm feeling right then, flood me with the understanding that with you, I will feel all this and more—forever.

We don't look at the troubles we can see now; rather, we fix our gaze on things that cannot be seen. For the things we see now will soon be gone, but the things we cannot see will last forever.

2 CORINTHIANS 4:18 NLT

When is soon? Do you remember asking your parents that, knowing there wasn't a concrete answer? How long will I be waiting? Because the answer can't be known, the Lord invites us to shift our gaze. Past the current situation, past even our hope for the future, we are encouraged to look up.

Whatever has you asking, fix your focus on heaven, and see what hopefulness and light flood your heart.

Thank you, God, for reminding me I can always shift my gaze. Whenever I feel like I can't wait, can't endure, and can't hope, I can look up. Every promise of heaven is in my heart. Fixed upon eternity with you, there is nothing too burdensome for me to bear.

Does this encouragement feel easier said than done to you? Release your worries and let eternity flood your heart.

Equal Pay

Whatever you give is acceptable if you give it eagerly. And give according to what you have, not what you don't have. Of course, I don't mean your giving should make life easy for others and hard for yourselves. I only mean that there should be some equality.

2 CORINTHIANS 8:12-13 NLT

Most of us hold on to our hard-earned money because we live at the edge of our means. When you look at your spending, you may be able to identify a few things that could be given up for the sake of being able to save a little more for times when you and others are in need.

God doesn't ask you to give so you make yourself poor, but he does want you to be part of helping those who do not have as much as you do. Is there something that you can hold back from spending your money on today so you can give to a greater cause?

God, thank you for providing me with all that I need. Give me wisdom to know how to spend well so I can have a little extra to give when you show me someone in need. Help me to be a good steward of your money.

Right now you have plenty and can help those who are in need. Later, they will have plenty and can share with you when you need it. In this way, things will be equal.

2 CORINTHIANS 8:14 NLT

God's system of equality is always the best system. When you have plenty, make sure to give, so when you are in need, others will be generous to you. It's a bit of a "pay it forward" situation and it makes sense that our generosity will someday come back to us.

God doesn't want us to have divisions because some are poor and others are rich. Instead, he longs for us all to have what we need.

God, help me to be generous even when I am the one in need. I know you want a heart that is motivated by love and equality for all people. I pray you would use me to be a part of this wonderful proficiency of giving and receiving.

Do you need to be more generous, or do you need to pray for some generosity to be extended your way?

As We Hope

Rejoice in hope,
be patient in tribulation,
be constant in prayer.

ROMANS 12:12 ESV

If you really think about it, are we ever not waiting? Is there not always a blessing, healing or milestone in the distance? What a wonderful encouragement this is from Paul to make the most of these seasons!

While you hope, rejoice. In expectation of the thing you hope for, celebrate now. While you suffer, find patience. Relax, rest, and lean in to the promise that this too will pass. Pray, remain constant, and be faithful. Believing God's willingness and desire for you to have your heart's desire, bring it continually to him.

It's true, God, I am always waiting. Thank you for reminding me that as I wait, I have reason to hope, patience to persevere, and the privilege of coming to you with all my heart longs for. Because of how you flood my heart with hope, joy, and patience as I pray, waiting is a gift.

Be joyful because you have hope.
Be patient when trouble comes,
and pray at all times.

ROMANS 12:12 NCV

God makes everything better. Waiting ushers in hope when we surrender our concerns to him. Troubles produce patience, giving us peace and serenity that defy our situation. Even in the midst of a crisis, our heartfelt prayers can deliver us beyond our circumstances, to a place of certainty.

As we trust him, as we come before him, and as we hope in him, he fills us with joy.

Jesus, I need you. Without you, I can barely handle an unanswered message, let alone endure wondering about and waiting for an uncertain future. With you, all is certain. I don't need to know when or how. The hope in my heart is enough. The patience you provide is sustaining. The way you meet me when I pray is everything. If this joy is how it feels to hope, I can only imagine what awaits me when the answers come.

Which of these three encouragements comes the most naturally to you? With which do you most need the Spirit's help?

Thorns

Concerning this thing I pleaded with the Lord three times that it might depart from me. And He said to me, "My grace is sufficient for you, for My strength is made perfect in weakness." Therefore most gladly I will rather boast in my infirmities, that the power of Christ may rest upon me.

2 CORINTHIANS 12:8-9 NKJV

We are quick to plead for God to take away the things we are struggling with like ill health, weak will power, or faltering relationships.

God can move powerfully in these situations because, instead of relying on your own strengths, you realize your dependency on him. This speaks volumes to people around you who see that you have made the most out of your struggles.

Father God, thank you that you care enough about me to make sure that I have everything that I really need. Help me to stop complaining about the struggles in my life and to see them as blessings because they prove your strength and power in my life.

*I take pleasure in infirmities, in reproaches, in needs,
in persecutions, in distresses, for Christ's sake.
For when I am weak, then I am strong.*

2 CORINTHIANS 12:10 NKJV

Has your day had reproach, need, persecution, or distress? Rejoice! It may not feel like a time to be happy, yet you can be encouraged that God is at work in you, perhaps even more powerfully than if you had a victorious day.

God takes over when you are weak, so you can boast in his greatness and glorify his name. Consider it a privilege to go through hard times for the sake of the good news of Jesus.

God, thank you for my weakness. I know that nobody is perfect so I choose to acknowledge that I need your help. As you guide me, let your power of change be evident to those around me.

What are your weaknesses? How can you see God working through your imperfections?

Eternal Throne

"It shall be, when your days are fulfilled, when you must go to be with your fathers, that I will set up your seed after you, who will be of your sons; and I will establish his kingdom. He shall build Me a house, and I will establish his throne forever."

1 CHRONICLES 17:11–12 NKJV

David wanted to build another house for the Lord to dwell in, just as Israel had done time and time again with the ark, tents, and other tabernacles. God, however, had his plan through Jesus. The houses or temples that the people built for the Almighty were always pointing toward the house that God would dwell in once and for all, that is, Jesus Christ.

This was a kingdom that would never again be defeated or need to move; this is an eternal kingdom with the eternal king. Today, remember that you are a part of that new kingdom.

God, thank you that you always made a way for your presence to be with your people. Thank you that through Jesus Christ, I have you with me all the time. Let me draw near to you in all circumstances today.

"I will be his Father, and he shall be My son; and I will not take My mercy away from him, as I took it from him who was before you. And I will establish him in My house and in My kingdom forever; and his throne shall be established forever."

1 Chronicles 17:13–14, NKJV

David would probably not have known that God was talking about sending his Son from heaven into the world to save all humanity. We have the benefit of looking at Scripture after Jesus and realizing the master plan that God was setting up through his people.

David had a big part to play in the master plan. We are a bit like David now, waiting for Jesus to return and set up his kingdom forever. We don't know exactly what this is going to look like, but be assured that God is using you to achieve this wonderful restoration of the world.

God, I don't understand what the future holds, but I know that it will be great. Help me to approach life with hope and not fear. I choose tonight, to be confident that your kingdom will one day be fully present.

How do you think God is using you to help bring his kingdom on earth?

With Us

> *"Do do not fear, for I am with you; do not be dismayed,*
> *for I am your God. I will strengthen you and help you;*
> *I will uphold you with my righteous right hand."*

ISAIAH 41:10 NIV

"Don't be mad, but…" When a conversation begins this way, we automatically brace ourselves for bad news. We know what's about to follow is likely to make us mad. Just as, "Don't laugh…" means what's coming is bound to be funny. What the speaker is trying to tell us is that they hope we'll listen to what they have to say without jumping to an emotional response.

The Bible often tells us to set aside natural instincts like fear and sadness and urges us to instead take courage and consolation from God. How beautiful it is to know he wants to replace our worry and heal our heartbreak. Imagine him coming close, whispering to you: "My darling child, I know this is hard, but it breaks my heart to see you like this. Let me take it from you."

Oh, precious God, how comforting it is to know you want my fear, my sadness, and my pain. Every worry of mine brings you closer, longing to take it away. Help me hear you, God, when anxiety strikes or heartbreak comes. help me let go of my feelings and take on your loving comfort and strength.

> *"Do not fear, for I am with you, do not be afraid,*
> *for I am your God; I will strengthen you, I will help you,*
> *I will uphold you with my victorious right hand."*

ISAIAH 41:10 NRSV

Few things are harder to endure than being alone and afraid.
God knows this. That's why he encourages us again and again
to remember we are not alone. We are never alone. When the
bad news comes, he is with us. When the waiting gets long,
he is with us. When our knees grow weak, he is with us. When
we fall to the ground too exhausted to keep fighting, still, he
is with us.

He will lift us. He will strengthen us. He will never leave. He
is with us.

God, why is it so hard for me to remember I am never alone?
I sometimes think no one understands my quiet pain, but you
understand. I think no one sees this nagging fear, but you see.
I feel utterly alone in my weakness, but you are here. Especially
on the days I am certain no one will hold me up, thank you, God,
for proving me wrong.

How often do you feel lonely? Invite the Lord to flood your
heart, knowing you need never feel lonely again.

Make Me Gracious

"Judge not, and you will not be judged; condemn not, and you will not be condemned; forgive, and you will be forgiven."

LUKE 6:37 ESV

Have you ever made a mistake? Of course, you have – everyone has. Maybe after making a choice you quickly learned it was the wrong one? Or perhaps you spoke without thinking, and, even as the words left your mouth, you wished you hadn't said what you did. Did these bad choices make you a bad person? Of course not. They made you human, in need of compassion, forgiveness and grace.

When someone does us wrong, God gives us the ability to quickly trade places with them in our hearts. How we would want them to respond to us, he invites us to respond to them. Would you want to be forgiven? Forgive. Would you desire the benefit of the doubt? Extend it. As we become known for our compassion, forgiveness, and grace, we become the kind of people who can expect those gifts returned when we need them.

God, only you are perfect, yet I find myself holding others up to your standards. I judge for things I myself am guilty of. I withhold forgiveness, though I know how healing it would be for everyone. Make me gracious, God, that grace would be given back to me.

Jesus said, "Forsake the habit of criticizing and judging others, and then you will not be criticized and judged in return. Don't look at others and pronounce them guilty, and you will not experience guilty accusations yourself. Forgive over and over and you will be forgiven over and over."

LUKE 6:37 TPT

Is there a habit you are proud of overcoming? How did you do it? Conscious, willful attention is vital when we want to change our behavior. We may think we have no control over our thoughts, but we do. Just as we can stop reaching for the phone the second we are bored, or the bag of chips each time we are frustrated, so too can we ditch our critical spirits.

Give up judgement. Embrace forgiveness. Adopt a habit of grace.

God, can it really be this simple? Not that overcoming a time-worn habit is ever easy, but can I decide to be less judgmental, or more forgiving, and have it be so? With your help, I believe I can. Starting tonight, I will to be the gracious, forgiving, and compassionate person you would have me be, Lord. I forsake the habit of criticism and adopt the habit of grace.

How comfortable are you acknowledging and laying down your negative habits before God?

Uncomplicated Freedom

> *"I have swept away your offenses like a cloud,*
> *your sins like the morning mist.*
> *Return to me,*
> *for I have redeemed you."*
>
> ISAIAH 44:22 NIV

We over-complicate freedom in the Christian life. Through our legalisms, we try to find a way to humanize the redeeming work of the cross because we simply can't wrap our minds around the supernatural character of God.

Freedom is truly that simple. The beauty of the Gospel can be summed up in this single concept—grace, though undeserved, given without restraint. Accept it today. Walk in complete grace without question.

Jesus, I am so grateful that you treat my wrongdoing as a cloud to be swept away. Get rid of the sin in my life, let it disappear like this morning's mist. I walk into my day in the knowledge of my redemption.

"I have swept away your sins like a big cloud;
I have removed your sins like a cloud that disappears into the air.
Come back to me because I saved you."

ISAIAH 44:22 NCV

It can be hard to understand the complete grace offered at Calvary because we are incapable of giving that kind of grace. But when God says that he has forgotten our sin, and that he has made us new, he really means it.

God is love, and love keeps no record of wrongs. Nothing can keep us from his love. Salvation tore the veil that separated us from the holiness of God. That complete work cannot be diminished or erased by anything we do.

Jesus, let the things of this day grow dim as I bask in the warmth of your love. It is so good to be free from my sin and to feel as light as a cloud. Let your peace wash over me as I sleep.

What sin are you holding onto that you know you need to let go of? Let Jesus sweep it away like a cloud!

Hiding Place

*Wherever I am, though far away at the ends of the earth,
I will cry to you for help. When my heart is faint and overwhelmed,
lead me to the mighty, towering Rock of safety. For you are my
refuge, a high tower where my enemies can never reach me.*

PSALM 61:2-3 TLB

When emotional injuries—insecurities, anxieties, memories
of abuse, conflict, or pain—that were buried long ago come
to the surface of life, they transform from past scars to raw,
gaping wounds, brand new and scorching.

Earthly bandages cannot completely heal the pain. We need
God's touch, the balm of his tenderness, upon us. It aches,
but he is a safe hiding place—a refuge when we are afraid to
walk through the pain.

Do you believe that you are precious to him? That he loves you
with a fiercely protective, eternally faithful, inescapable love?
Well, he does.

*God, I submit my wounds to your careful attention. Thank you for
being my hiding place today.*

From the end of the earth I call to you
when my heart is faint.
Lead me to the rock
that is higher than I,
for you have been my refuge,
a strong tower against the enemy.

PSALM 61:2-3 ESV

Abiding in his safety and leaving a wound open is hard. We have to see it, feel it, and let God walk us through the healing process. And that might take time. But he is a loving, worthy, compassionate Father, whose treatment roots out all infection and disease so that the scars can remain healed. We are safe when we are in his care, and he promises to protect us.

He is true and worthy and invites you to bring him all of your hurts, pains, regrets, and brokenness so he can put it back together.

Father, thank you for being a safe place for me to rest in. I come to you tonight ready to walk through the healing process.

Will you take refuge in God's arms tonight?

Give Me Liberty

You are free from the power of sin and have become slaves of God.
Now you do those things that lead to holiness
and result in eternal life.

ROMANS 6:22 NLT

Freedom is a place without obligations. Freedom is to live exempt from debts, constraints, and bonds. Our obligation for the sins we've committed is to satisfy justice. Our souls cannot be free without a release from our debt of sin, and the currency demanded for a soul is death.

When our debt was paid by the death of Jesus, the truest form of freedom was declared over our soul. Our chains were broken, and our liberty was granted. When Jesus returned to heaven, he left his Spirit with us because where his Spirit is, there is freedom.

Holy Spirit, help me to live like a free person. I am no longer bound by sin and I am no longer a slave to darkness. Let your light shine brightly from my life today.

You are free from sin and have become slaves of God.
This brings you a life that is only for God,
and this gives you life forever.

ROMANS 6:22 NCV

There is a freedom waiting for you that will challenge any preconceived notions you've had of freedom. There is liberty in the presence of the Spirit of God that is unprecedented.

God wants you to walk forward out of sin and into the life of freedom that he intended for you. Leave your obligation at his feet—it's taken care of.

Jesus, you have paid my debt and I am therefore no longer in darkness. Help me to be faithful in my freedom and to show others your love so that they, too, can be set free.

What is your biggest challenge to freedom? Ask God for his strength to overcome this.

Sweet and Lovely

O my dove, in the clefts of the rock,
in the crannies of the cliff,
let me see your face,
let me hear your voice,
for your voice is sweet,
and your face is lovely.

SONG OF SOLOMON 2:14 ESV

Stress threatens to get the better of us, and sometimes we just want to hide. Remembering that secret bar of chocolate in the pantry, we may scurry off to do just that: bury ourselves away with the temporary but sweet comfort that helps the world slow down, if only for a moment.

We cannot outrun God's love for us, nor should we try. Instead, let's leave the false safety of the clefts and crannies and pantries with hidden chocolate and feel the pleasure of his friendship.

God, how can it be that you see me as beautiful and lovely? I am in awe of your gentle and perfect love. Help me to remember this throughout my day.

My beloved is like a dove hiding in the cracks of the rock,
in the secret places of the cliff.
Show me your face,
and let me hear your voice.
Your voice is sweet,
and your face is lovely.

SONG OF SOLOMON 2:14, NCV

Sometimes we want to scurry away from God. We get overwhelmed by his ministry, overdue for his forgiveness, or out of touch with his Word and we lose track of who he is. Instead of running toward him, we hide from him and look for other ways to meet our needs. We cannot hide from him, and in love he calls out to us.

God wants to hear your voice and see your face because he finds them sweet and lovely. Give him that pleasure this evening.

Father, I turn my face to you tonight. Thank you for looking at me with eyes of love and mercy. Thank you for finding me sweet and lovely. It is beyond what I can fathom.

Is there anyone else who can satisfy you so perfectly?

Healing Words

Careless words stab like a sword,
but wise words bring healing.

PROVERBS 12:18 NCV

Words can cut deeply. Isn't it amazing how many of us struggle to remember a phone number, but we can perfectly recall a string of harsh words spoken to us years ago?

Throughout the Bible, God characterizes a person of wisdom as one of few words. Perhaps this is because a careless word can do so much damage. None of us can deny that words carry power. They can easily leave a mark that is not quickly erased. Do our words bring damage or healing to those around us?

Holy Spirit, I am going to need your help as I speak today. I know that I don't always carefully watch what I say, so please remind me instantly when I am about to say something that is not good. Let wise and kind words come from my mouth today.

The words of the reckless pierce like swords,
but the tongue of the wise brings healing.

PROVERBS 12:18 NIV

We can't underestimate the power of our words. The beautiful thing about this verse is that it reminds us that wise words bring healing.

If you have spoken careless words today, you have the power to bring healing with new words of wisdom. If you have been pained by someone else's words, turn to the wisest words ever written—the Scriptures—to bring healing to the scars in your own heart.

Jesus, heal those wounds that have come from hurtful words. Forgive me when I have said wrong things, and give me the boldness to make things right. Heal me from recent words that have cut me to the heart.

Are you hurt from unkind words? Do you need to be forgiven for saying something unkind? Bring it all to Jesus in heartfelt prayer.

Great Counselor

Do not be anxious about anything, but in every situation, by prayer and petition, with thanksgiving, present your requests to God. And the peace of God, which transcends all understanding, will guard your hearts and your minds in Christ Jesus.

PHILIPPIANS 4:6-7 NIV

The counselor's suggestion box overflowed with ideas from the school's young students, varying from inventive and reasonable (replacing fluorescent lights with tons of twinkling Christmas lights) to imaginative but impractical (covering the hallways with giant slip n' slides). But each one was read aloud during weekly staff meetings. The children's ideas never decreased in volume or zeal; they believed that their school could be greater than any other, and that their school counselor not only respected but valued their input.

God bends his ear to our anxieties, our longings, our frustrations, and our worship. And we trust him because we want to be better than ever, to be more and more like him. We trust that our Counselor values our petitions. Bring him your requests this morning.

God, you are always in control. You don't worry about my fears or anxieties because you know what you have planned for me. Thank you for listening to my requests and always wanting the best for me.

Do not worry about anything, but pray and ask God for everything you need, always giving thanks. And God's peace, which is so great we cannot understand it, will keep your hearts and minds in Christ Jesus.

PHILIPPIANS 4:6–7 NCV

Students approached their favorite counselor with their personal troubles; he heard about failures on the soccer field, fights with best friends, botched geometry quizzes, and sibling rivalries. His door was always open, and the seats weren't empty for long. What did he offer the young hearts and minds? What was the secret to giving them serenity in the midst of those tumultuous years? He mimicked the example set by God, our great Counselor, who hears our worries and protects us with his peace.

It may seem difficult to give thanks in the midst of trouble and fear, but when we do, God replaces our worries with peace. He listens to our petitions and answers with what he knows is best for us. That is someone you can trust to share your heart with.

Good Counselor, thank you for your listening ear, your loving heart, your kind words of encouragement, and your arms of comfort. I am blessed to be able to seek advice from you.

Will you fill the suggestion box of your wonderful Counselor?

Make-Believe

I know that there is nothing better for people than to be happy and to do good while they live. That each of them may eat and drink, and find satisfaction in all their toil—this is the gift of God.

ECCLESIASTES 3:12-13 NIV

We all played our fair share of make-believe as children, twirling around the room in a fancy dress-up gown or running through the fields with a wild tale alive in our minds. Every child probably had those long summer evenings of chasing fireflies and catching dreams, or playing hide-and-go seek and finding destiny. Our starry-eyed youth took our imaginations on the wildest of journeys as our hearts pounded with the creations of our souls.

Pretending we are someone else, or somewhere else, begins early in childhood and more subtly continues as we age. We still allow imagination to transport us to other places, and other circumstances. Somehow it is easier for us to embrace the wonder of "what if" than the reality of "what is."

Father, as I look back on some of my childhood dreams, I realize that it was nice to dream and it made me feel happy. But today is my reality and I pray that you would help me to see my life as a gift. Stir joy in my heart once again.

There is nothing better than to be happy and enjoy ourselves as long as we can. And people should eat and drink and enjoy the fruits of their labor, for these are gifts from God.

ECCLESIASTES 3:12-13 NLT

It cannot be put more clearly. There is nothing better than to be happy in your life. Your life is made up of now. Each moment you live, each breath you take, it's right this very second.

To find happiness in your life is to find the best thing. And to find satisfaction in your effort is to find the gift of God. Treasure your life! Be satisfied with where you are. Satisfaction is living each day as if it were the dream.

Lord, I want to be content with where I am at in life. Even more than that, I want to be happy. Thank you that you still care about my dreams, and thank you that life is a journey and process of shaping and re-shaping those dreams. Thank you for every moment including right now.

What dreams are you still holding on to? Enjoy the process of getting to those dreams and remember that God wants your happiness.

Surrender

*"In the same way, those of you who do not give up
everything you have cannot be my disciples."*

LUKE 14:33 NIV

Surrender is offering what you have to someone else without reservation. Once you surrender something, you give up your ownership and your rights along with it. What does a life fully-surrendered to Christ look like? It's holding nothing back from God, and surrendering every single part to him.

Full surrender to a holy God cannot be fabricated. God, the omniscient one, cannot be fooled by eloquent words or false commitment. Complete surrender to him can be nothing less than sincere, legitimate, full abandonment.

God, I don't know how to fully surrender myself to you, so instead hear my heart behind the words. I really want to have a life that is dedicated to you and even though I fail, I still want to give it all up for you. Give me a chance to show you that today.

"Any one of you who does not renounce all that he has cannot be my disciple."

LUKE 14:33 ESV

Being a disciple of Christ requires complete and total surrender of everything you have and everything you are. He is not asking you to give up anything that he wasn't willing to give for you.

When Jesus gave up the glory and rights of his heavenly throne, he surrendered more for you than you ever could for him. Jesus never sold this life as being casual, simple, or inexpensive. But he did promise that the reward would be great.

Jesus, let me remember the rewards that I have for a life surrendered to you far outweighs any earthly treasure. I choose to serve you today and every day. Give me the strength and grace to pursue you with all my heart.

What is God asking you to surrender? Trust that he knows what is best for you.

Firm Foundation

Let your roots grow down into him,
and let your lives be built on him.

COLOSSIANS 2:7 NLT

His brothers laughed at his heavy laboring, day in and day out, while they lounged around. Their homes had taken no time at all to complete, and they liked them just fine. Until the wolf came, with his gusting huffs and puffs and then… The story is as familiar as its lesson: take the time to do things right so when trouble comes you will be safe. Build with worthy materials, and you'll have something that lasts through the fiercest of storms.

The third brother must've been a God-fearing little pig, as he took the advice that Jesus gave to his followers. Build on the rock and your house will not fall. Build on something shifting, like sand, grass, or sticks, and watch it fall when the rains, floods, and winds come. God is the rock on which we can build with confidence.

God, I am so grateful for your wisdom. You prepare me for the storms of life and you give me a place to seek refuge. Thank you for being my steady rock.

Keep your roots deep in him and have your lives built on him.
Be strong in the faith, just as you were taught,
and always be thankful.

COLOSSIANS 2:7 NCV

Not only can we have assurance in God's firm foundation, but he promises to bless us as we dwell with him. Rains, flooding, gusting wind will come, but he will see us through every storm with truth which will strengthen our faith. We will see him triumph over sin and darkness and we will overflow with thankfulness!

In the midst of the storms, you can rejoice! As the winds howl around you, your faith will grow strong. Nothing will come against you that can blow your house down when you build it on the strong foundation of Jesus.

Father, your foundation is secure. I want to build my life on you. Thank you for sheltering me from the storm, for being a steady place to rest when the storms come.

How have you seen Jesus as your stronghold recently?

Idolatry

Do not turn aside; for then you would go after empty things which cannot profit or deliver, for they are nothing.

1 SAMUEL 12:21 NKJV

It's easy to think of idolatry as a distant issue, defined by people in foreign clothing bowing before intricately carved literal idols. But idolatry isn't limited to a physical, obvious idol. Idolatry is extreme devotion to something or someone.

We can be consumed with admiration for many things. Idolatry can take a million forms in our lives. Idols are simply things that take the number one place in our hearts that should belong to God alone.

God, help me to be aware of the things that are becoming idols in my life. Give me a good strategy for getting rid of these idols so that I have you at the center of my life again.

Do not turn away after useless idols.
They can do you no good, nor can they rescue you,
because they are useless.

1 SAMUEL 12:21 NIV

Idols—whether money, a person, a career, or a dream—cannot deliver us. Only the God of the universe, who saved us with his great love, is worthy of our extreme admiration. Only he deserves our love and our reverence. Other things that we may be tempted to chase after won't give us a return or profit.

Ask God to reveal idols in your life tonight. Then trust that he will help you begin to get rid of those idols so you can refocus your time and energy on him.

Father, thank you for revealing things that are idols in my life. I realize that I have made things more important than you. I am spending time with you now, reflecting on your Word, and I know this counts more than those other things. Help me to keep this time a discipline so that I can draw nearer to you.

Examine your heart and ask yourself the hard questions. Is God sitting exclusively on the throne of your heart? Or are there other things there that have taken his place as the object of your most extreme passion and affection?

Temptation

Great is our Lord and abundant in strength;
His understanding is infinite.

PSALM 147:5 NASB

When you approach God to ask for help in resisting temptation, or for forgiveness for a sin you've given into, do you feel ashamed? Do you feel like God couldn't possibly understand how you fell into that sin once again?

We know that Jesus was tempted to sin while he was here on earth, but we also know that he never gave in. Because he experienced temptation, he has great compassion toward us when we struggle with the desire to sin.

I am so glad that you understand what I am going through, Lord. At times I feel like nobody understands or cares, but I am reminded today that you have infinite understanding of my complicated heart.

*Great is our L*ORD*, and abundant in power;*
his understanding is beyond measure.

PSALM 147:5 ESV

Jesus understands your temptation to sin because he was tempted in the same ways. You have an advocate with Jesus—one who understands just how difficult it is to resist temptation because he has faced it.

You can have confidence when you approach God to ask for forgiveness. He gives mercy and grace freely to those who earnestly seek it.

Jesus, I am so glad that you are my friend. More than that, you are a strong friend in whom I can confide. Thank you for understanding me, listening to me, and being my strength. You are so great.

What do you need Jesus to understand in your life? Tell him all about it.

Scars of Brokenness

He will take our weak mortal bodies and change them into glorious bodies like his own, using the same power with which he will bring everything under his control.

PHILIPPIANS 3:21 NLT

When a flower pot crashes to the pavement or a vase shatters to the floor, we consider the damage in hopes that it can be repaired. What is left? Dangerously tiny shards of glass, too small to piece back together? Or simple, bulky pieces, like those of a puzzle, needing only glue and patience? One thing is certain: we will work harder to fix something that has great value to us.

Hold everything up to God, who fully covers everything and in the process makes you whole.

Father, thank you for picking me up and putting me back together again. You will make me glorious as I continue to submit to your work in my life.

Who, by the power that enables him to bring everything
under his control, will transform our lowly bodies
so that they will be like his glorious body.

PHILIPPIANS 3:21 NIV

Just like broken pottery, we are broken vessels in need
of extensive repair. No elaborate doctoring is required,
however, just the humblest of procedures. We hold out
our hands and give our broken, desperate, painful, sinful,
prideful selves over to the one who mends us into wholeness
without a single remaining scar or crack.

How can God do this? Because he is both holy and whole, and
we are his creation. We were always meant to be perfect, but
sin got in the way. Now, we can only submit to the one whose
healing work never leaves a scar and whose abiding love
makes us whole forever.

Thank you, Creator God, for knowing me so well, and for bringing
me complete healing and wholeness. I rest in that thought tonight.

Do you have scars of brokenness that need healing?

Covering Offense

Whoever covers an offense seeks love,
but he who repeats a matter separates close friends.

PROVERBS 17:9 ESV

When a close friend does something that offends us, our hurt can cause us to look for validation from someone completely outside the issue. We feel the need to process our pain, so we find a listening ear who will confirm our feelings.

Next time someone offends you, instead of finding someone to commiserate with you, run to God and ask him for the strength to forgive. Choose to forgive the fault and protect your friendship rather than extending the pain by sharing it with others.

Lord, I know I need to be wiser about who I choose to share my heart with. I know that sometimes I indulge in gossip, even if it is about myself. Give me a really good conscience when I know I am overstepping the boundary. Help me to keep my integrity intact.

He who covers a transgression seeks love,
But he who repeats a matter separates friends.

PROVERBS 17:9 NKJV

By mulling a matter over both in our minds and with our words, we allow our anger to build. And the more we repeat the offense to listeners who validate us based on our side of the story, the further we travel from reconciliation.

In order for love to prosper in our relationships, we must choose forgiveness over offense. We have to lay down whatever rights we felt we had in the situation and put love first—because love is of God.

Jesus, I know that you chose love to cover all our sins. Help me to choose love instead of retribution when I have been wronged. Guard my heart, my mind, and especially my mouth. Keep wisdom and peace forever on my lips.

What offense are you holding on to? Bring it to God and leave it there.

Too Simple

If you confess with your mouth that Jesus is Lord and believe in your heart that God raised him from the dead, you will be saved. For with the heart one believes and is justified, and with the mouth one confesses and is saved.

ROMANS 10:9-10 ESV

How can it be that a humble prayer, a simple and yet astounding desire to lay down one's life and take up a life like Jesus Christ, establishes our eternity in the kingdom of heaven? Is it possible that such an act can really guarantee salvation? Our acceptance into God's family begins with this one act, yet it can feel too simplistic, too easy. We live in a world where, more often than not, we get what we deserve and nothing comes easy.

Paul emphasized how simple the path to salvation really is in his letter to the Roman church: if you believe it, say it. There is no other way. Believe that your simple and earnest prayer assures your acceptance. And it is this simple. God's Word promises that it is.

God, I see all the extra things I try to do to gain your approval. Help me to understand your simple acceptance of me and walk confidently in that.

If you confess with your lips that Jesus is Lord and believe in your heart that God raised him from the dead, you will be saved. For one believes with the heart and so is justified, and one confesses with the mouth and so is saved.

<small>ROMANS 10:9-10 NRSV</small>

Sometimes, because we can't believe that acceptance can come from such a simple act, we reconstruct the gospel. We want to feel like we deserve God's grace, or that we have earned it, or that we've traded fairly. We build another set of requirements: more praying, more giving, more reading, more serving. Quiet time. Worship team. Children's ministry. Bible study. All of these habits are good and Christ-like, but they don't guarantee more acceptance. Not from God, anyway.

Trust that God's gift of salvation is really as simple as confessing and believing.

God, I thank you for the simplicity of your gift. I know that Jesus is Lord and I know you raised him from the dead. Thank you that I am saved and accepted because I deeply believe these statements to be true.

Do you find it difficult to believe in the simplicity of God's requirement for acceptance?

Stubborn Hearts

"I am the LORD your God,
who brought you up out of the land of Egypt.
Open your mouth wide, and I will fill it.
But my people did not listen to my voice;
Israel would not submit to me.
So I gave them over to their stubborn hearts,
to follow their own counsels."

PSALM 81:10-12 ESV

Stubbornness is a tricky attribute. There is often no opening for conversation with a stubborn person. They have their own idea about how things should be done, and they aren't usually willing to listen to the advice of others.

We can all be stubborn in certain ways. Unfortunately, our stubbornness sometimes comes out toward God. We feel his Spirit gently advising us, but we rationalize it away in our heads instead of allowing it to guide our hearts. God can do more in a month with a life fully surrendered to him than he can do in years with a life that's holding back.

God, I am sorry for holding back from the things that you have asked me to do. I am afraid, embarrassed, and just a bit stubborn, like the people of Israel. I don't want to let my stubborn heart get in the way, so help me to trust you and let go so you can do what you want with my life.

> *"I, the LORD, am your God,*
> *Who brought you up from the land of Egypt;*
> *Open your mouth wide and I will fill it.*
> *But My people did not listen to My voice,*
> *And Israel did not obey Me.*
> *So I gave them over to the stubbornness of their heart,*
> *To walk in their own devices."*

PSALM 81:10-12 NASB

Did you hear the gentle voice of God, today? Don't forget what he has done for you. God wants to fill your mouth and use your life, but you have to open it up to him.

Don't hold back. Give God every part of you tonight, and follow his counsel rather than your own. Surrender your stubborn heart to him completely.

God, I hear you, even as I read this Scripture. I know that you have done great things for me, and that you want me to listen to your voice. I know that you have my best in mind. I choose to submit to you in this moment so I can follow your wise counsel and bring glory to your name.

Is there any area of your life in which you have a stubborn heart toward God?

The Unknown

"Thus says the LORD who made it,
the Lord who formed it to establish it the LORD is His name:
'Call to Me, and I will answer you,
and show you great and mighty things,
which you do not know.'"

JEREMIAH 33:2-3 NKJV

"If you're there God, give me a sign!" People have screamed this into the heavens many times throughout the years. We want to see something that will tell us that God is real—and not just real, but also present. We want that experience that will bring heaven to earth and expel our doubt with a single lightning bolt.

God is more than able to give us those miraculous signs as we have seen countless times throughout the Bible and throughout history. But he is so much more than experience. We mistakenly think experience is the peak of his power. Other gods can perform miracles and deliver experiences, but the one true God continues to show his power in the valley. He is even in the valley of the shadow of death where miracles seem non-existent. Those other gods have nothing to offer us in despair.

God, thank you for showing your power and goodness in my life and your continued work in this world.

*"Thus says the L*ord *who made the earth,*
*the Lord who formed it to establish it—the L*ord *is his name:*
'Call to me and I will answer you, and will tell you great
and hidden things that you have not known.'"

Jeremiah 33:2-3 esv

God was present with you today and will show himself to you
in different ways tomorrow. God will show us things we aren't
even expecting. Sometimes we limit him to our experience
and what we presently know of both him and of life. He wants
to show us great and mighty things.

God is not limited by time, space, or human understanding.
Put your hope and faith in the God who knows everything.

Show yourself to me, tonight, Lord Jesus. I know you are with me,
and I don't need any signs or wonders, but fill me with knowledge
of your presence and the peace of your nearness.

How has God shown himself to you in the small things today?

Sustained

I lay down and slept;
I awoke, for the LORD sustains me.

PSALM 3:5 NASB

There is always something to worry about, isn't there? Whether it's health, finances, relationships, or details, there are many unknowns in life that can easily keep us worrying. But what if we stopped worrying? What if we stopped questioning and decided instead to feel peace? What if we could trust completely that God would take care of us and our loved ones. God is our rock and he alone will sustain us.

There will be many unknowns in your life. There will be moments when the rug feels as though it's been pulled out from under you, and there is nothing to do but despair. In those moments that you can't control, you can trust. You can rest your soul, your mind, and your body in the hands of the one who has the power to sustain you.

Lord, today I face the unknown. Let me rest in the knowledge that you will sustain me.

I lie down and sleep;
I wake again, for the LORD sustains me.

PSALM 3:5 NRSV

The words in Psalm 3 can bring us comfort and peace when we are fearful. It speaks volumes about the grace of God: the protection and safety of his hand. But the verse goes beyond peace and comfort to the power of God. We only wake up because of his sustaining power.

When we trust and believe in this God who possesses the power of life and death, what do we have to fear? Our entire lives are in his hands. We can't change that fact, so we might as well rest in it.

God, tonight I need that rest. I need to rest my body and I need to rest my soul. I believe you have the power of life and death, so I ask that as I sleep, you will sustain me.

What is interfering with your ability to rest right now? Ask God to give you a solution so you can rest physically and spiritually.

Exceptional Fruit

*The fruit of the Spirit is love, joy, peace, patience, kindness,
goodness, faithfulness, gentleness, self-control;
against such things there is no law.*

GALATIANS 5:22-23 ESV

Making applesauce with autumn's abundant apple harvest is
a beloved pastime across northern parts of America. Experts
have developed award-winning recipes whose secret, they
say, is combining multiple varieties of apples to produce a
complex flavor profile. The result is a balance of the tart,
sweet, crisp, mellow, and bold flavors for which apples
are so well-loved. Each variety of apple is essential to the
applesauce; their distinct flavors mesh into a delicious thing
of beauty.

In the applesauce of God's ministry, each believer's spiritual
fruit flavor-profile is essential. The fruit of the Spirit looks,
tastes, feels, smells, and sounds different for each of us.
In some, joy is a loud shout of excitement; in others it is
quiet worship. One believer's kindness might feel soft while
another's is firm. Peace can be expressed in as many ways as
there are to use an apple.

*God, I can see how we are all made with a distinct flavor to benefit
the whole of your body. Help me to remember that I am unique and
needed.*

The fruit of the Spirit is love, joy, peace, patience, kindness, generosity, faithfulness, gentleness, and self-control. There is no law against such things.

GALATIANS 5:22-23 NRSV

When we compare the evidence of our fruit against other believers, lies are whispered to our flesh: your fruit isn't as shiny, your fruit isn't as fragrant, your fruit is too mushy and flavorless. A lie is born in thinking that all trees produce the same fruit. That just isn't true.

Your relationship with Jesus Christ is unique. He produces, between you and the Holy Spirit, an exceptional fruit that only grows from your branches. You can be who God made you to be. We are all capable and expected to grow fruit that exhibits the fruit of the Holy Spirit. When we come together, according to God's perfect recipe, for his glory, it is truly delicious.

Thank you, Lord, for your perfect recipe. You know how to make exceptional fruit. Help me to listen to your guidance so I can play my part just right.

In the past, how have you compared your fruit to others?

Generosity

Give freely and become more wealthy;
be stingy and lose everything.
The generous will prosper;
those who refresh others will themselves be refreshed.

PROVERBS 11:24-25 NLT

There is need everywhere we look. Families who need homes, missionaries who need support, food shelves that need donations, and non-profit organizations that need finances. But how can we even begin to meet those needs? How could we possibly give enough to make a difference?

Generosity can be scary. Giving might mean that we will have to do without. Giving costs us something. We think that we have to have less in order to do more. But in God's economy, he who gives generously will be repaid lavishly. He who holds nothing back will inherit everything.

God, give me an opportunity to be generous, today. It feels a little scary for me to say that, but I know that you want me to be a generous giver, and I know that it will be good for me to give, and good for someone to receive.

One person gives freely, yet gains even more;
another withholds unduly, but comes to poverty.
A generous person will prosper;
whoever refreshes others will be refreshed.

PROVERBS 11:24-25 NIV

Were you able to give to someone, today? Remember that God will provide for your every need, no matter how much you give to others.

God doesn't measure wealth the way we do. He doesn't operate on our economic system. He gives with rewards that will last forever, and wealth that will never run out.

Lord, give me another chance to give to someone. Thank you that each new day brings another opportunity to serve you and to serve others. I look forward to whoever I might meet tomorrow that has a need.

What or who is God asking you to be generous toward?

What Is True

"Sanctify them by the truth; your word is truth."

JOHN 17:17 NIV

Where does belief originate? We can look to scientific evidence of the earth's creation by an intelligent designer, and there are many scientific specialists who can discuss the details passionately and convincingly. We can read the prophecies from Scripture that also point to the truth of God's power, presence, and passion. Then there are scholars, preachers, and authorities who tell you about the prophecies. The historic evidence of the existence of Jesus Christ comes with another set of experts who can explain the proof and compelling evidence.

God created the earth. He spoke the planets, oceans, and trees into being. He imparted to the prophets details of the coming Messiah, and Jesus came and fulfilled those promises in perfect detail. But our very testimonies—our transformation from death to life—are the simple and powerful proof that what we believe is true.

God, I am so convinced that what I believe is the truth because you have shown yourself to me in so many ways. Help me not to be swayed by the philosophies of this world. You are truth.

*"Make them holy by your truth;
teach them your word, which is truth."*

JOHN 17:17 NLT

The humble followers of Jesus who have experienced his saving grace also give us reason to believe. We were blind, but now we can see. We were lost, and now we are found. We were dead in our sins, but now we are alive in Jesus Christ! This is all we can know for certain.

We may not be scientists, theologians, or experts in apologetics, but we know that we were blind and God enlightened us. We were lost and God gave us a home. We were dead and he raised us from our graves and gave us hope. By faith, we know that what we believe is true.

Father, thank you for your saving grace. You are truth and life. I believe in you because you have always shown yourself to be faithful and true.

Take a moment to reflect on the undeniable truth that you are different today than you were before you knew God.

Stumbling in the Dark

*The Word gave life to everything that was created,
and his life brought light to everyone.
The light shines in the darkness,
and the darkness can never extinguish it.*

JOHN 1:4-5 NLT

Have you ever walked somewhere in the pitch black? You bump into things, knock stuff over, and often can't even place where you are or where you're going. Everything becomes muddled in the darkness. Without light to guide us, we can't see where we're going, or what we're running into.

Many times throughout the Bible, God likens being in sin to being in darkness. When we immerse ourselves in sin, thus rejecting the light of the truth, we can no longer see what we are running into.

Lord, shine your light into my heart. Illuminate my sin so that I can repent and be free of the darkness. I want to walk without stumbling today.

In him was life, and the life was the light of men.
The light shines in the darkness,
and the darkness has not overcome it.

JOHN 1:4–5 ESV

Darkness of sin will cloud our thinking and our rationale, and we won't even be able to determine what other sins are coming our way when we leave our sin unchecked. By allowing sinful messages to enter our souls through different avenues, we lose our ability to navigate our lives.

When wickedness begins to overtake your life, you lose the ability to recognize what is making you sin. Strive to keep your soul sensitive to the truth. Keep sight of the light by spending time in God's Word.

I thank you, God, that darkness cannot stand up to light. Now that I know the truth of your ways, the darkness has been expelled and my faith in you will never be extinguished. Help me to shine the light into other people around me so that they will be exposed to your truth.

Who can you share the light of Christ with this week?

I Am Alive

Such love has no fear, because perfect love expels all fear.
If we are afraid, it is for fear of punishment,
and this shows that we have not fully experienced his perfect love.

1 JOHN 4:18 NLT

Fear rears its ugly head in lots of ugly ways; the spider waiting in your bathtub, the high bridge you pass going to your favorite park, the loud noise outside your bedroom window in the middle of the night. Fear can be gripping, paralyzing, or terrifying for some. For others, it is motivation to conquer weakness. Those fears are mostly related to phobias, which, one could argue, stem from basic human defense instincts. What about the fears that keep us awake at night? The worries and anxieties that cannot be brushed aside?

Jesus' followers had one such worry: what would happen on Judgment Day? Was Jesus' death enough to cover their sins completely and guarantee their eternity in heaven? John points out their fear as one of punishment. But there isn't room for fear alongside perfect love, and if we are abiding in the love of Jesus, then we have perfect love in us. Fear must surrender.

God, thank you that there is no fear in love. I embrace your perfect love today and walk without fear.

There is no fear in love. But perfect love drives out fear,
because fear has to do with punishment.
The one who fears is not made perfect in love.

1 JOHN 4:18 NIV

We must surrender to the truth that sets us free: Jesus died
and is now alive—so our sin is dead and we are alive. We are
alive! Death, sin, and fear are overcome! Jesus has overcome!

You can choose not to be fearful, instead living with the
resurrection in mind. Jesus has overcome it all; we have
nothing to fear and no more debt to pay. Heights and spiders
and enclosed spaces might still quicken your heart, but you
can rest easy in his perfect love, now and for all eternity. Are
you alive with this truth? Fear cannot remain in the presence
of perfect love.

Father, I surrender to your truth. You have set me free from fear
because you are perfect in your love for me.

How can you train yourself to bask in the love of God?

Victory

*Thank God! He gives us victory over sin and death
through our Lord Jesus Christ.
So, my dear brothers and sisters,
be strong and immovable.*

1 CORINTHIANS 15:57-58 NLT

Have you ever watched one of those movie battle scenes where the good guys are grossly outnumbered? You wince as the evil army swoops in with thousands of troops carrying sophisticated weapons. While the good army has a lot of heart, you know they don't stand much of a chance. But when it all seems lost, there is that moment when, out of nowhere, reinforcements arrive in a surge of hope to assist the good army. Suddenly, they go from losing terribly to winning victoriously!

Daily, we are engaged in our own battle against sin. Left to ourselves, we don't have the strength necessary to win the fight. But when it seems all hope is lost, our reinforcement—Jesus Christ—arrives, and we gain the strength to boldly obtain the victory over sin.

Jesus, forgive my sins and help me to gain the victory over any darkness that would try and creep back into my life today.

Thanks be to God, who gives us the victory
through our Lord Jesus Christ.
Therefore, my beloved, be steadfast, immovable,
always excelling in the work of the Lord,
because you know that in the Lord
your labor is not in vain.

1 CORINTHIANS 15:57–58 NRSV

You may go through seasons in your life when you feel like sin has you outnumbered. Temptation is great, and you don't feel that you have the strength to overcome it. But know that you don't have to fight alone. You have the power of God on your side, and he has already won against sin and death.

Embrace victory over sin tonight as you thank Jesus for his work on the cross.

Lord, I feel like I am confessing sin to you time and time again, and yet I know you want me to recognize that I already have the victory. You won this victory on the cross and I no longer have to live in the guilt and shame because you have set me free!

Where do you need to see the victorious Christ reign in your life again?

No Compromise

When troubles of any kind come your way,
consider it an opportunity for great joy.

JAMES 1:2 NLT

The best products are built using the best ingredients. Some companies compromise, and when trouble inevitably comes, their products suffer and they lose money. But organizations dedicated to quality without compromise build things that endure. Oh, beloved, that our faith would be strengthened for endurance! What are we made of? Can we stand the test? Trouble is on the horizon, but we are advised to see it as an opportunity for great joy.

Built with quality, we can have great joy. Our endurance grows and we are proven perfect and complete, needing nothing. We will not compromise. We want more opportunities for great joy! Bring the tests! Grow our endurance! When the final product is revealed, we will shine like pure gold.

God, help me to endure through the testing so I will be found lacking nothing.

Consider it pure joy, my brothers and sisters,
whenever you face trials of many kinds.

JAMES 1:2 NIV

This isn't easy advice to follow, but in his wisdom, God gave his Word for our benefit. What would we expect him to say? Dear children, when troubles of any kind come your way, curl up into a ball of despair for all hope is probably lost. Of course not! God is building us to last!

We would not gain blessing through hopelessness. No, he builds our faith with the highest-quality parts: hope in the promises of God's Word, humility from the grace that he has given us, and love for God who first loved us.

Lord, help me to find joy in the trials that come my way. You know my future and you are building me to last!

In what areas do you find it easiest to compromise?

People of Truth

This Book of the Law shall not depart from your mouth, but you shall meditate in it day and night, that you may observe to do according to all that is written in it. For then you will make your way prosperous, and then you will have good success.

JOSHUA 1:8 NKJV

Have you ever met someone who speaks hard-hitting truth every time you talk to them? They seem to be soaked in the presence of God, and you know that when you hear them speak, you will be ministered to by the power of the Holy Spirit through them. These people echo the heart of God because they study the Word of God.

If you are constantly in the Word—inundating your soul, your spirit, and your mind with the power of God—then the power of God is what will resurface when you open your mouth and speak to others. His goodness, kindness, mercy, and grace will flow out of you, and you will become a person of truth.

Lord, I want to only speak truth about you and about other people. Help me today, to speak only good things.

Study this Book of Instruction continually. Meditate on it day and night so you will be sure to obey everything written in it. Only then will you prosper and succeed in all you do.

JOSHUA 1:8 NLT

If we meditate on truth, we will become people of truth. If we read the Bible constantly, truth will flow out of us—along with joy, peace and wisdom. Even in our normal conversations we will find ourselves using phrases that are directly from Scripture.

God wants his praise and his words to be continually on our lips—a never-ending worship service to him as we speak.

Father, I worship you this evening. It is so refreshing to stop and dwell on you. Thank you that you receive my praise. Receive my words of worship to you, Almighty God.

What other words of praise do you have for the Father right now?

Faithful Servant

*"The servant to whom he had entrusted the five bags of silver came
forward with five more and said, 'Master, you gave me five bags
of silver to invest, and I have earned five more.'
The master was full of praise. 'Well done, my good and faithful
servant. You have been faithful in handling this small amount,
so now I will give you many more responsibilities.
Let's celebrate together!'"*

MATTHEW 25:20-21 NLT

By committing our lives to serving Jesus Christ, we commit
to investing the treasure he has given us and growing it to an
even greater value for his kingdom. When our Master returns,
we should have something to show for our years of serving
him and proclaiming his name on earth. By faith, we make
good on our commitment to Jesus by sharing the gospel, and
serving widows, orphans, and refugees in our land. We love
as Jesus loved.

Yes, we will make mistakes, and of course God's grace is
sufficient for us. Do what you say you will do; after all, God
has kept his promises to you. Look forward to the day when
you will hear the fulfilment of your commitment: "Well done,
my good and faithful servant. Let's celebrate together!"

*Oh God, how I desire to hear those words, "Well done." I want to be
a good and faithful servant. Give me strength to do that, please.*

"Then the one who had received the five talents came forward, bringing five more talents, saying, 'Master, you handed over to me five talents; see, I have made five more talents.' His master said to him, 'Well done, good and trustworthy slave; you have been trustworthy in a few things, I will put you in charge of many things; enter into the joy of your master.'"

MATTHEW 25:20-21 NRSV

We commit to being faithful, honest, and diligent, just as God is. Our lives are a representation of Jesus, and our ability to make good on our commitments illustrates God's faithfulness. We are modeling godliness to a godless world. We demonstrate his truth, love, integrity, and mercy to a world lost in sin. Make good on your commitments to the world in order to shine the light of Jesus in the darkness.

Spend some time reflecting on the faithfulness and dependability of God, and let that be your motivation!

Help me, Father, to be a faithful servant. I want to use the talents you have given me wisely.

What do you find to be the hardest part of keeping your promises?

Unpredictable Life

A furious squall came up, and the waves broke over the boat, so that it was nearly swamped. Jesus was in the stern, sleeping on a cushion. The disciples woke him and said to him, "Teacher, don't you care if we drown?"
He got up, rebuked the wind and said to the waves, "Quiet! Be still!" Then the wind died down and it was completely calm. He said to his disciples, "Why are you so afraid? Do you still have no faith?"

MARK 4:37-40 NIV

It takes time to adjust to changing situations. Sailors need time to get their "sea legs," mountain climbers rest in order to adjust their lungs to altitude changes, and scuba divers surface slowly to regulate pressure. Even adjusting to daylight-savings can take some time.

As his child, you are always in his presence. No matter what you are facing, you can walk confidently. It may take some time, but he is prepared for everything and will prepare you, too.

God, thank you that you can prepare me for life's storms. Help me to listen to your voice and heed your warnings so I am ready for difficulties as they come along. You are faithful to me and I know you will be with me through everything I face.

A great windstorm arose, and the waves beat into the boat, so that the boat was already being swamped. But he was in the stern, asleep on the cushion; and they woke him up and said to him, "Teacher, do you not care that we are perishing?" He woke up and rebuked the wind, and said to the sea, "Peace! Be still!" Then the wind ceased, and there was a dead calm. He said to them, "Why are you afraid? Have you still no faith?"

MARK 4:37-40 NRSV

During their time with Jesus in his ministry on earth, the disciples had to adjust quickly to radical situations. A daughter was raised from the dead, a boy's meager lunch multiplied to feed a crowd of 5,000, a demon was cast into a herd of pigs that threw themselves off a cliff. Could they have woken up in the morning and sufficiently prepared for such things? Then one day, they get in a boat and their limited faith is tested.

It seems as though the disciples never really adjusted to the unpredictability of life with Jesus. Have you? If they struggled while in his very presence, how can we have faith to walk confidently into the unknown? We have his Word and the assurance that his presence is all we need; he is constant in the face of change.

God, I trust that you are steady in the storm and you will not leave me.

What changes are you going through that make you feel uneasy?

Don't Give Up

"We built the wall and the whole wall was joined together to half its height, for the people had a mind to work. Now when Sanballat, Tobiah, the Arabs, the Ammonites and the Ashdodites heard that the repair of the walls of Jerusalem went on, and that the breaches began to be closed, they were very angry. All of them conspired together to come and fight against Jerusalem and to cause a disturbance in it. But we prayed to our God, and because of them we set up a guard against them day and night."

NEHEMIAH 4:6-9 NASB

There were so many reasons for Nehemiah to give up on rebuilding the wall. They were insulted from every angle, they were threatened with attacks, and there was so much rubble that the workers were getting exhausted and their strength was giving out. Nehemiah continued to pray and figured out how to cover each of these problems.

You will have dreams for your future; God doesn't want to give up on your heart's desires. Figure out the things that are going come against you and discover a strategy for how to work through those.

Father, thank you for the promises that you made to me. There are still dreams and hopes that I have for the future, but I don't really know how they're going to happen. Give me the strategy and strength of character to never give up.

"Half of my servants carried on the work while half of them held the spears, the shields, the bows and the breastplates; and the captains were behind the whole house of Judah. Those who were rebuilding the wall and those who carried burdens took their load with one hand doing the work and the other holding a weapon."

NEHEMIAH 4:16-17 NASB

Nehemiah had to be prepared for everything, so he had his people multi-task. They would build with one hand and hold weapons and shields in the other.

We don't always get to the final dream without all the other necessary parts of life. We have other jobs to do while we are working toward the bigger things.

God, help me to see the value in the day-to-day tasks of life. I know that you want me to be prepared for everything as I work toward my dreams and aspirations. Thank you for equipping me to be someone who can do a lot of things at the same time.

What is the spear or shield that you are holding in your hand that you need to give more value to? Recognize the significance in multi-tasking.

Great Faith

The LORD was with Joseph and showed him steadfast love and gave him favor in the sight of the keeper of the prison. The keeper of the prison paid no attention to anything that was in Joseph's charge, because the LORD was with him. And whatever he did, the LORD made it succeed.

GENESIS 39:21,23 ESV

When looking for models of faith and perseverance, we needn't look farther than Joseph, son of Jacob, from the Old Testament. Stripped, thrown into a well and sold into slavery by his own brothers, then jailed for a crime he didn't commit, Joseph is a timeless example of how God's blessings can supersede our circumstances.

Because of his great faith, Joseph didn't just survive slavery and imprisonment, he thrived—so much so he became the second-highest official in Egypt. Joseph loved God so much, that he felt his presence everywhere he went. This allowed him to experience joy and success in the worst of circumstances and least likely of places.

God, thank you for reminding me that though many things are out of my control, I always have at least one choice: to love, trust and obey you. When I do this, you bless me with your presence. Because joy and favor accompany your presence, I am always free to choose them as well—no matter where I am.

The LORD was with Joseph and showed him steadfast love; he gave him favor in the sight of the chief jailer. The chief jailer paid no heed to anything that was in Joseph's care, because the LORD was with him; and whatever he did, the LORD made it prosper.

GENESIS 39:21,23 NRSV

Have you ever seen the joy of a young Haitian child, dancing for Jesus? Or the peace in the eyes of an African mother, lifting up a song of praise to her Savior?

The happiness that comes from those surrounded by poverty, disease, and devastation is from the Lord of their hearts, the One who lives with them. That kind of joy is a choice.

Jesus, I choose joy. I choose not to look around, but up instead— at the one who saves, sustains, and grants me peace in every circumstance. When things are bleak, I choose you and find hope. When things are great, I choose you and feel grateful.

As the day closes, bring your concerns and your thanks before the Lord. Be bold and ask for the joy that is consistently yours to take hold of—good days or bad.

Time to Feast

Nehemiah continued, "Go and celebrate with a feast of rich foods and sweet drinks, and share gifts of food with people who have nothing prepared. This is a sacred day before our LORD. Don't be dejected and sad, for the joy of the LORD is your strength!"

NEHEMIAH 8:10 NLT

When the words of the law were read out to the people of Israel they began to weep. It can be a sobering thing to realize your sin before the Lord. It is right to feel a sense of mourning for the things that we have done wrong and for the consequences of wrong, yet God does not want you to dwell on guilt. He wants you to celebrate because he is a God that gives mercy and restoration.

As you get up and get ready for your day, don't be dejected and sad, let God's joy in your heart be your strength.

God, there have been many times when I have turned away from you. At times I have pursued my own ways and I have regrets. Allow me to receive your mercy and to live in the joy of knowing that I am forgiven today and forever.

The Levites, too, quieted the people, telling them, "Hush! Don't weep! For this is a sacred day." So the people went away to eat and drink at a festive meal, to share gifts of food, and to celebrate with great joy because they had heard God's words and understood them.

NEHEMIAH 8:11-12 NLT

Understanding God's Word is a thing to be celebrated. When God's words confuse you, ask for discernment and clarity. Seek out wisdom about what the Scriptures say.

Your heart will rejoice when you understand the Word because you are beginning to understand the father heart of God. Let his love fill you tonight, and remember to celebrate his love with others.

God, thank you for giving me wisdom and discernment to understand your Word. Holy Spirit, thank you for helping me to understand and get life from what I read in Scripture. Guide me each day to know more of you and help me to celebrate those times when I see the truth of your Word.

How can you celebrate the joy of understanding the goodness of God?

Still Good

I say to the Lord, "You are my Lord;
I have no good apart from you."

PSALM 16:2 ESV

Is there something you used to enjoy that, when you look back on it now, has lost its appeal? Maybe it's your favorite sugary cereal from childhood, or a destructive habit you've overcome, or that girlhood crush you're so glad you didn't marry. With time comes wisdom and with wisdom, perspective.

Jesus brings perspective too. Once he's the most important part of our lives, everything in our lives gets better. Because of his kindness, we are kind and our relationships get better. Because of his patience we are patient and our worries become fewer. Now imagine him gone. Would anything, no matter how wonderful, still be good?

Jesus, you don't just make everything better; you are the reason anything is good. Because you are love, without you I'd have no love. You are the reason I see beauty; you are the source of all grace. I can't imagine life without you. Thank you, God, that I don't need to! Because I am yours, we will never be apart.

I said to the LORD God,
"You are my Maker, my Mediator, and my Master.
Any good thing you find in me has come from you."

PSALM 16:2 TPT

Jesus isn't just responsible for the good things in our lives; he's also the author of the good things in us. Your tenderness, humor, and talent? That's Jesus in you. Your faith, perseverance, and loyalty? All the Lord.

You are wonderful. He made you so because he wants you to show the world how wonderful he is. Just by being you, you can lead others closer to him.

God, I'm not always comfortable listing out the ways I'm special, but when I realize they are ways you are special, I see them in a new light. Magnify the things that make me attractive to others, Jesus, so I can reflect your goodness to them. Allow me to see the ways you shine in them as well, so I will know even more of the ways you are wonderful.

List out the ways the Lord has made you special. Ask the Spirit to reveal every single one, then thank him for using you to shine his light.

Love on the Increase

I pray that your love will overflow more and more, and that you will keep on growing in knowledge and understanding. For I want you to understand what really matters, so that you may live pure and blameless lives until the day of Christ's return.

PHILIPPIANS 1:9-10 NLT

The beauty of love is that it keeps growing. If we feed love with the right motivation, it will increase. As we understand more about love, we know the deep importance of sharing this love with all people.

Love gives us the purest lens in which to view other people. With it, we gain better insight and more grace into situations. If you come across a difficult situation with somebody today, remember the lens of love and let it guide you to do the right thing.

God, I thank you for the path that love leads me on. I pray that I would follow that path because I know that this is the way to have right relationships with people. Help my love for others to grow more today.

May you always be filled with the fruit of your salvation—
the righteous character produced in your life by Jesus Christ—
for this will bring much glory and praise to God.

PHILIPPIANS 1:11 NLT

Were you able to view people through the lens of Christ's love today? People can be hard to love sometimes, but the more we put it into practice, the easier it becomes.

When we practice love, we honor Jesus because we display exactly the kind of life that he showed on earth. You will begin to see the fruit of your love toward people as you allow it to increase.

God, I'm sorry I have failed to show love in situations where I needed to. Thank you that your love for me allows me to love others.

Who needs to experience your increasing love this week?

First

Do nothing from selfish ambition or conceit, but in humility regard others as better than yourselves. Let each of you look not to your own interests, but to the interests of others.

PHILIPPIANS 2:3-4 NRSV

Can we ever truly grasp what Jesus had to give up in order to become human and walk this earth with us? Scripture tells us that although Jesus had equality with God, he gave up his supreme entitlement to become human.

We may never quite understand this act, but we can accept that Jesus' birth and death on the cross was our ultimate example of sacrifice. Are you willing to sacrifice, as in the example of Jesus, regarding others before yourself?

God, today I choose to look out for the interest of others. Thank you that I can be confident in your love for me, and that this confidence can lead me to make others feel important and special.

Let the same mind be in you that was in Christ Jesus.

PHILIPPIANS 2:5 NRSV

Do you recognize selfish ambition in your life? Reflect on Jesus' sacrifice, and in your thankfulness, make a commitment to imitate him by seeing the good in others and pursuing their interests above your own.

This is not to attribute a higher worth based on superior authority or qualities, but to understand people's value in light of Christ.

God, sometimes I don't feel I have the energy to expend on others. Help me to relax tonight and be encouraged to look outside myself. I know you will present me with an opportunity to love outrageously and I ask for the strength to be up to that challenge.

What can you do to imitate Christ in his humility and sacrifice this week?

He Understands

The LORD looks down from heaven and sees the whole human race.
From his throne he observes all who live on the earth.
He made their hearts, so he understands everything they do.

PSALM 33:13-15 NLT

Do you remember how you first felt when you heard that God is always watching you and sees everything you do? Whether you were quite young, or it was just a few years ago, it likely made you a little self-conscious. Everything? What about all the things we'd rather not be seen?

Take heart. Yes, he sees all but remember, as the maker of your heart, he also knows exactly how it works. He understands you. Your Father knows the place your less-than-perfect moments come from and, out of love and tenderness, he forgives them. Immediately and completely, he forgives you.

Father God, I confess there are things I do that I'd rather you not see. But I don't need to fret over it. You made my heart, and you understand the reason for every regrettable word, thought, and action. You get me. You see, you forgive, and you set me free. Why would I ever want to hide?

The Lord looks over us from where he rules in heaven.
Gazing into every heart from his lofty dwelling place, he observes
all the peoples of the earth.
The Creator of our hearts considers and examines everything we do.

PSALM 33:13-15 TPT

"Watch me, Daddy!" Like a dad watches his little girl on a balance beam, what a comfort it is to know Abba watches your life. Every time you leap and land perfectly, you feel his beaming pride. When you lose your balance and fall off, it's his loving encouragement that bolsters your courage to get back up and try again.

He's watching. He sees. And he's very, very proud of you.

God, just like that little gymnast on the beam, I love to know you are watching me. I love making you proud and hearing you cheer as I land a new skill. Just as much, I love knowing you see my wobbles and falls. It changes nothing about how you feel about me, which makes me eager and confident to try again. Thank you, Abba, for seeing me.

Run through your day in your head, imagining your Father seeing it all. What made him proud? When was he encouraging you not to give up?

Against the Dark Sky

Do everything without complaining and arguing, so that no one can criticize you. Live clean, innocent lives as children of God, shining like bright lights in a world full of crooked and perverse people.

PHILIPPIANS 2:14–15 NLT

The temptation to complain or bicker can be overwhelming at times. Any discussion involving opinions and decision will have a certain amount of tension because we all want to be heard, and we all value our own opinions.

Our complaints are often valid and true, but we miss the joy that the Lord desires for us when we seek out only the negative. Choose to be positive and truthful today.

God, I often get pulled into the negativity of this world, so I ask that I would be sensitive to the prompting of the Holy Spirit when I start to head down that path. Keep my words full of life and love.

Hold firmly to the word of life; then, on the day of Christ's return, I will be proud that I did not run the race in vain and that my work was not useless.

PHILIPPIANS 2:14-15 NLT

Choosing to be positive and to speak positively is something that will make you stand out like the stars against a black sky—did you get a good sense of that today? If not tomorrow is another day.

This letter from Paul to the Philippians was written thousands of years ago, but it could just have easily been written today. We still live in a warped and crooked generation. Let's shine like stars against the dark sky. Let us hold firmly to his Word as we speak life to those around us.

God, as I reflect on my day and my words, I pray you would show me the times when my words were uplifting and helpful. Forgive me when I have had unkind words or a grumbling heart. Teach me to speak words of wisdom and to have a positive attitude toward life.

Are there people in your life who are causing you to be negative? What can you do to avoid negative conversations?

Garbage

I once thought these things were valuable, but now I consider them worthless because of what Christ has done. Yes, everything else is worthless when compared with the infinite value of knowing Christ Jesus my Lord. For his sake I have discarded everything else, counting it all as garbage, so that I could gain Christ and become one with him. I no longer count on my own righteousness through obeying the law; rather, I become righteous through faith in Christ. For God's way of making us right with himself depends on faith.

PHILIPPIANS 3:7-9 NLT

Once you've experienced the true beauty of a relationship with Christ, everything else becomes somehow insignificant. What you once held dear no longer seems important.

Compared to knowing Christ as your Savior, everything else the world values just pales in comparison.

God, as I get ready for a new day, I pray that I would be able to see the insignificance of some of the things that I pursue, and that I would see the significance of others. I ask that you give me discernment of what is garbage and what is treasure.

I want to know Christ and experience the mighty power that raised him from the dead. I want to suffer with him, sharing in his death, so that one way or another I will experience the resurrection from the dead!

PHILIPPIANS 3:10-11 NLT

Have you fully embraced the ways of God? Would you be willing to lose everything for him?

Grasp a hold of the beauty he's offering. Pray for a heart that's glad to be rid of earthly treasures and eager for what's in store for a true believer.

Jesus, I believe that not only did you die to restore humanity, but that you rose again to show us we have eternal life in you. This is an amazing truth about humanity that I want to share with the world. Give me the boldness to be a witness of what you have done for us.

What does the resurrection mean to you? How can you translate this meaning to an unbeliever?

Unmistakably Clear

"This command I give you today is not too hard for you; it is not beyond what you can do. It is not up in heaven. You do not have to ask, "Who will go up to heaven and get it for us so we can obey it and keep it?" It is not on the other side of the sea. You do not have to ask, "Who will go across the sea and get it? Who will tell it to us so we can keep it?" No, the word is very near you. It is in your mouth and in your heart so you may obey it."

DEUTERONOMY 30:11-14 NLT

A single, paved road through a dense forest is easy to follow. We don't stand on the road and worry about which way to go. The way is clear. It's obvious. Isn't this passage from Deuteronomy wonderful? It's almost amusing, isn't it? A modern translation might say, "It's basic addition people, not rocket science!"

Have you ever wondered how Jesus feels about love? Probably not, because he made himself perfectly, unmistakably clear on that front. When the Lord wants us to understand something, he makes sure we can.

Father God, though I love the way certain passages may take my whole life to understand, I also appreciate how simple you make the big things. When it comes to life, salvation, and eternity, you've made yourself unmistakably clear. Like a road through a forest, you show me exactly where to go.

"This commandment which I command you today is not too mysterious for you, nor is it far off. It is not in heaven, that you should say, 'Who will ascend into heaven for us and bring it to us, that we may hear it and do it?' Nor is it beyond the sea, that you should say, 'Who will go over the sea for us and bring it to us, that we may hear it and do it?' But the word is very near you, in your mouth and in your heart, that you may do it."

DEUTERONOMY 30:11-14 NKJV

I don't know how I know, I just know. I feel it in my heart. It's the right thing to do.

One of God's most beautiful gifts to us is our conscience. Innately, even before we ask Jesus into our hearts, a sense of right and wrong lives there. Once we have surrendered our hearts to Christ, his Holy Spirit gives us an even more powerful understanding of how he would have us speak, live, and be.

Lord Jesus, thank you for your Holy Spirit. Living in me is the knowledge and conviction of how to honor you with my life. I carry your commitment to love, grace, and service in my heart. These are the virtues you call me to live out.

What are the things you "just know"? Thank the Lord for your conscience and intuition.

Where You Live

*Lord, I love the house where you live,
he place where your glory dwells.*

PSALM 26:8 NIV

You know that house, the one where, every time you're in it you just feel good? It may be picture-perfect, without a pillow out of place or a stray crumb in sight, or it may be the messiest, most mismatched home you know. Decorations and dust bunnies have nothing to do with it - a house feels good when love lives there. When love lives there, so does the Lord.

A home where the Lord's presence is welcome is a home where we feel not just welcome but wanted. We feel at home. There needn't be devotionals on every table or Bible verses stenciled on the walls; his presence dwells in the presence of love—of those who love him.

God, I want my home to be that house. The moment someone walks in my door, whisper "welcome" to their hearts. Make my heart and table equally open, God, so every guest will love my home and recognize it the house where you live.

Lord, I love your home, this place of dazzling glory,
bathed in the splendor and light of your presence!
PSALM 26:8 TPT

Just as our homes don't need to be grand to hold his glory, neither does the place we go to be in the presence of our Lord. While it may be a beautiful church, with stained glass and worn hymnals, it may also be a coffee shop where you gather with girlfriends, trail you run on, or a lake you sit by.

The glory belongs to him, not the place. The light of his presence is the source of its splendor.

God, anywhere I find you becomes dazzling to me. Whether my church, my friend's table, or my own living room, everywhere takes on a dazzling warmth when you come to meet with me. I love your home, God, wherever I find it.

Where's your favorite place to meet with God?

Such a Time

When Esther's words were reported to Mordecai, he sent back this answer: "Do not think that because you are in the king's house you alone of all the Jews will escape. For if you remain silent at this time, relief and deliverance for the Jews will arise from another place, but you and your father's family will perish. And who knows but that you have come to your royal position for such a time as this?"

ESTHER 4:12-14 NIV

God never makes mistakes; his plans are intentional and he positions his people everywhere. Esther was a woman of noble and trustworthy character, and because of this, she was used to help God's people in one of their times of greatest need.

You may not know how you are a part of God's great plan, but if you remain true to God and keep your heart loyal to him, he is going to use you. As you go about your various duties today, remember that God has put you here for such a time as this.

Heavenly Father, I trust in the plan that you have for humanity and for my life. I want to be a part of doing your work on earth, so I pray you would give me the courage to do whatever you ask of me.

Esther sent this reply to Mordecai: "Go, gather together all the Jews who are in Susa, and fast for me. Do not eat or drink for three days, night or day. I and my attendants will fast as you do. When this is done, I will go to the king, even though it is against the law. And if I perish, I perish."

ESTHER 4:15-16 NIV

Esther did not act rashly. Instead she made it her intention to seek the Lord wholeheartedly.

At times, fasting is the right thing to do to gain clarity and focus when you need direction. For Esther, her life depended on approaching the king in the right way.

If you are facing some serious decisions in your life, consider fasting or doing something extreme that will allow you to be entirely dedicated to hearing God's voice.

God, I want to hear your voice in the times I really need your guidance. Give me a strategy to be able to focus on your words of truth and to understand the right way forward.

What big decisions are you facing at the moment? Commit these decisions to God tonight and choose to dedicate some time to asking for an answer.

Let Wisdom Pour

*"To those who listen to my teaching, more understanding will
be given. But for those who are not listening, even what little
understanding they have will be taken away from them."*

MARK 4:25 NLT

Imagine a runner who trains for a marathon, completes it,
then stops running. After a year has gone by, she remembers
how much fun she had on race day—how satisfying it felt to
cross the finish line feeling strong and accomplished. She
shows up to run the marathon the next year but, several miles
in, she realizes she won't make it. She's lost her base. To go
the distance, you can't just want to run; you need to train.

Following Christ is similar. You need to build—and maintain—
your base. If you want to follow Christ, you have to be a
Christ-follower. Read your Bible. Pray for understanding. Put
what you learn into practice every day.

*God, thank you for your Word. Every time I read it, I understand
more of who you are. From this solid base, more and more of the
world makes sense. I am strong. I can go the distance. Give me a
hunger to keep listening, God, because I want to grow as strong
and go as far as I can.*

"Those who listen with open hearts will receive more revelation. But those who don't listen with open hearts will lose what little they think they have!"

MARK 4:25 TPT

You have two water bottles. One has a lid on, the other does not. Both are half full. Held under the faucet, which bottle will be filled?

To be filled to the top with Jesus' wisdom, we must remain open. Closing our hearts to teaching that feels inconvenient, or makes us uncomfortable, leaves them closed to teaching that would help us grow.

Jesus, I give you permission to take the lid off my heart. Let your wisdom pour, let your knowledge fill me to the brim, and let your love overflow. I want to know you so well that everything you say becomes music to my ears.

Is there a teaching of Jesus' you struggle to embrace? Pray for an open mind, so you can understand the heart behind his words.

I Will See

> *"I know that my Redeemer lives,*
> *and he will stand upon the earth at last.*
> *And after my body has decayed,*
> *yet in my body I will see God!*
> *I will see him for myself."*

JOB 19:25-26 NLT

Job's faith has been weakened by the test, but he clutches desperately to the one promise that can sustain him: no matter what happens to Job in his earth-bound life, nothing can take away the joy he will share with God in his eternal life.

Everything on earth is a fleeting treasure, a momentary comfort that can be lost in a flash. But the assurance of your eternal place in his kingdom, if you have submitted your life to Jesus Christ, is indestructible.

Jesus, you are my redeemer, and I thank you that even though I have far less to complain about than Job did, I can still bring my troubles before you and know that one day you will take it all away. Let me find joy in that knowledge today.

"Yes, I will see him with my own eyes.
I am overwhelmed at the thought!"

JOB 19:27 NLT

Job went through all the emotions expected of someone who
has lost everything and is in deep pain. He mourns, and
laments, and weeps. He is confused, hopeless, and weak. Yet
even in his lament, Job speaks the truth about God. His heart
is driven toward something beyond his present circumstance
and as he lifts his eyes to the heavens, he exclaims, "Yes, I
will see him with my own eyes."

If your day has been discouraging, lift your eyes toward the
heavens and let your heart be confident that one day your
troubles will be gone and you will see Jesus with your own eyes.

God, thank you for your joy that sustains me every day. Thank you
that you have been good to me today, and that you will show your
goodness tomorrow especially when I ask for it.

What eternal values can you bring into your day tomorrow?

Welcome and Safe

"I am the door. If anyone enters by me,
he will be saved and will go in and out and find pasture."

JOHN 10:9 ESV

When you have a guest in your home, they come and go through the door. Were they to slip around back and shimmy in a window, you'd find their behavior odd, probably even untrustworthy. If you have a security system, they'd likely set it off. People who are where they are allowed to be don't need to find a back way in or sneak out. They don't set off the alarms and all is well.

When deciding what influences to allow in our lives, it helps to see Christ as a door. Anything welcome, safe, and helpful will come through the front door, while anything that needs an excuse or compromise, or that needs to be hidden, is likely to set off an alarm. The latter are things we are better off not letting in.

God, you keep me safe. Thank you for your presence as the door all influence must pass through. Anything looking to sneak in through a window, you sound the alarm for. Anything invited and safe is in agreement with your will for my life. It—or they—can come and go freely because they mean me no harm.

"I am the gate; whoever enters through me will be saved.
They will come in and go out, and find pasture."

JOHN 10:9 NIV

Whether we've always followed him, or he is new to our lives, there will come a time when we wonder if we can follow Jesus and still have fun. Is choosing Christ akin to surrendering our freedom? According to Jesus, the opposite is true.

Nothing is forbidden because no things have any power over us. His Holy Spirit stands at the gate and fills our hearts with a passion for that which will keep us safe and give us life. Because of our good gatekeeper, we have free reign to explore the whole pasture.

Again, Father, I find myself amazed by the freedom of surrender. When I give my heart to your Son, relinquishing all control, I am freed from the power of sin. I can move freely knowing his Spirit guards the gate. As long as I trust him, I will be saved.

Do you feel as free as Christ says you are? Spend some time praying about this with him.

Fountain of Youth

"Let their flesh be renewed like a child's;
let them be restored as in the days of their youth."

JOB 33:25 NIV

Think back to when you were a child. Do you remember what it was like caring only for the moment; moments of freedom and unpredictability, lost in make-believe and dreams? That was then, and this is now.

How do you feel about the past? What life has threatened to strip from you, God can restore and reshape. Forget today about the things which never really mattered all that much, and remember what it is to breathe life in your lungs.

God, restore to me the beauty of childlike faith. I want to find favor with you simply because I delight in being called your child.

> *"That person can pray to God and find favor with him,*
> *they will see God's face and shout for joy;*
> *he will restore them to full well-being."*

JOB 33:26 NIV

Responsibility eventually overtakes carefree spontaneity. Reality drowns out limitless dreams.

Restoration of full well-being can be ours. Doesn't that sound just like childhood? God can restore to you what's been lost.

God, I am so overcome with responsibility. Sometimes I want to go back to just relying and trusting on someone else to take care of everything. I thank you that there is also freedom that comes with responsibility. I ask you now for a simple restoration of a carefree heart.

Where do you need God to help you lighten the load? Let him release the burden on your heart and give you freedom in your spirit.

Be Certain

We are pressed on every side by troubles, but we are not crushed.
We are perplexed, but not driven to despair.
We are hunted down, but never abandoned by God.
We get knocked down, but we are not destroyed.

2 CORINTHIANS 4:8-9 NLT

If your life is really going well, especially if you find yourself amazed and wondering how it's all working out, this is a good indication that you are where God is and where he wants you to be. How did you manage to get everywhere you needed to be today? How does this month's bank balance have just enough, when only days ago you were unsure how you'd pay this month's bills?

If you want to be certain God is active in your life, just consider the astonishing fact that you are still standing, thriving, and rising to another day's challenges when you know, without a doubt, you can't possibly be doing it on your own.

God, the evidence of you in me is everywhere. thank you! I know I succeed because of you, I understand because of you, and I remain whole and strong because of you. Things can come at me, and they do, but they cannot break me, because of you.

We are hard pressed on every side, but not crushed;
perplexed, but not in despair; persecuted, but not abandoned;
struck down, but not destroyed.

2 CORINTHIANS 4:8-9 NIV

What did you overcome today? What pressures failed to crush you? What confusion failed to crush your hope? Were you mistreated or misjudged today? Did you still feel supported and loved by your Savior? Maybe you even got knocked down—hard.

How wonderful of our great God to pick you right back up.

God, even on the good days, as I look back on them later I see the many ways you kept me safe and whole. You are so good, God, so attentive! On the hard days, even on the worst ones, I see the ways you kept me here, believing. You are my hope, Lord. You keep me rising.

Sit with your thoughts until the Holy Spirit calls to mind at least one way the Lord kept you today. Marvel at his attentiveness and thank him for it.

True Philosophy

See to it that no one takes you captive through hollow and deceptive philosophy, which depends on human tradition and the elemental spiritual forces of this world rather than on Christ.

COLOSSIANS 2:8 NIV

There are plenty of theories and philosophies about our world: how it came to exist, what our purpose is, why we behave the way we do. We are intelligent beings, but we are not the supreme being who created the heavens and the earth.

The wisdom of God, shown through Jesus Christ, is the only truth and everything else should be understood through the message of his life, death, and resurrection. You will no doubt face various philosophies as you go through your day, but stand firm in your belief in God.

Jesus, when the world comes at me with a different truth to yours, help me to be discerning of right and wrong. Thank you for sending the Holy Spirit who can guide me with wisdom.

In Christ all the fullness of the Deity lives in bodily form,
and in Christ you have been brought to fullness.
He is the head over every power and authority.

COLOSSIANS 2:9-10 NIV

It is important to remember that Jesus was not only fully human but fully divine. This means that he had all the power given to him from above and that his words were not confused with the world's.

When you see Jesus, you see God. When Jesus took our sins to the cross, he defeated death. We are now on this side of that victory. Claim the power that is yours through Jesus.

Jesus, thank you for coming to earth so we could know about the Father. Thank you for redeeming me from my old life and giving me a new life, where I have been brought to fullness.

In which areas of your life do you need to claim the authority of Jesus?

Wise Steps

*Look carefully then how you walk, not as unwise but as wise,
making the best use of the time, because the days are evil.*

EPHESIANS 5:15-16 ESV

Have you ever been driving, particularly on a route you travel often, and realized you stopped paying attention some time ago? You've managed to miss your exit or pass your turn, and now you'll need to turn around. Depending on where you are and at what time of day, these mistakes can cost valuable time.

When Paul encouraged the Ephesians to look carefully how they walked, he undoubtedly had something similar in mind. Imagine a long journey by foot, and how disastrous a missed milestone could be. Our journey with Christ is an important one, and every step is valuable. We are wise to pay careful attention to how we walk it.

God, though I value my walk with you, it's amazingly easy for me to lose focus. Though my intention is to follow the path you set, I get distracted by my own thoughts, or something grabs my attention, and before I know it, I've missed the turn. Make me wise in my steps, Father, so every single one will count for good.

*Be careful how you walk, not as unwise men but as wise,
making the most of your time, because the days are evil.*

EPHESIANS 5:15-16 NASB

As easy as it is to lose our way, how much easier is it to lose
track of the time? Armed with good intentions and a plan, we
set out. Then the phone rings or the computer pings, and we
are pulled in another direction. Minutes or even hours later,
we wonder where the time went.

Our hours are finite, both in the day and on this earth. In
order to make the most of the time we've even given, we must
be wise in how we spend it.

*God, as the Eternal One, time means nothing to you and yet you
never waste a minute. I can't really comprehend it, as I am so
adept at losing track of the hours you've granted me. Forgive me,
God, for being unwise with this precious gift. I am grateful for it.
grant me the discipline to prove it by how I walk.*

How often do you lose track of time? Ask the Lord's help in
making the hours matter.

Wondering

I call to you, God,
and you answer me.
Listen to me now,
and hear what I say.

PSALM 17:6 NCV

If only answers to prayer came so simply or quickly. Perhaps you want to know what courses to study, what job offer to accept, what school your kids should go to.

God's Word encourages us again and again to come to him with our questions, concerns, and deepest longings. He does promise a reply, though not necessarily in the form of a check in a box.

God, I call to you now, asking for answers. At times I am unsure if I am asking the right thing, but I know it doesn't matter because you will hear me and you will answer, even if it isn't the answer that I want.

Show me the wonders of your great love,
you who save by your right hand
those who take refuge in you from their foes.

PSALM 17:7 NIV

As you come to the end of another day, are there things that your heart is aching for? Do you have concerns, fears, or hopes for this week, or this year?

God is waiting expectantly for your prayers, and he will answer you. It may not be today, or even for a long time, but keep asking. Keep waiting for his reply. He hears you.

Jesus, I feel full of questions that I'm not sure you are answering. Give me confidence in remembering that your Word says that you do hear me and that you do answer. Answer me, and help me to discern what you are saying.

What are you longing to know? Just ask God.

Mean Well

"You hypocrite, first take the log out of your own eye, and then you will see clearly to take the speck out of your brother's eye."

MATTHEW 7:5 NASB

Picturing a log protruding from your eye be a bit comical but it should also be convicting. If you aren't convicted, head to a mirror because there's something stuck in your eye. Instead of recalling all the times we felt victimized by a hypocrite, let's try to remember the times we were a hypocrite.

Jesus taught this same lesson another way. Remember the woman who was dragged from her house by an indignant mob prepared to stone her to death? Once Jesus invited them to examine their own sin, how many still threw a rock?

God, thank you for making sure I never get too comfortable with my own righteousness. If I'm spending more time thinking about other people's faults than my own, show me to a mirror. Keep my hands far from the eyes of my friends, Jesus, until the day my own are clear.

"You're being hypercritical and a hypocrite! First acknowledge your own 'blind spots' and deal with them, and then you'll be capable of dealing with the 'blind spot' of your friend."

MATTHEW 7:5 TPT

When we want to call out our friend on their sin, it's because we mean well, right? Seeing that friend mired in a sin, we want to help her out of it. Jesus knows this, and he gives us a way to do just that.

We can pray for her. Privately, just between us and the Lord, we can ask him to show her a better way. After that, it's time to trust him, and to be prepared for whatever he decides to show us about ourselves

I do mean well, Lord. It hurts me to see someone hurting themselves by a sin they don't recognize. What you help me remember is that I am not unique in this. Even as I pray for my friend, somewhere a friend is probably talking to you about me. Thank you, Jesus, for her well-meaning heart and for the humbling work you are doing in mine.

Be willing to sit with any discomfort this verse brought up today. Whether seeing something new about yourself or being willing to trust your friends' blind spots to Jesus, just sit with it until the Lord brings you peace.

What He Gives

"Don't be so concerned about perishable things like food. Spend your energy seeking the eternal life that the Son of Man can give you. For God the Father has given me the seal of his approval."

JOHN 6:27 NLT

It's easy to get caught up in this life, isn't it? After all, it's all we know. We want to live well and, in our desire to do so, we find ourselves chasing not just provision, but approval and even excess. Have goals, the world tells us, ones that can be realized here on earth.

Look up. Look to heaven and remember the real goal, the only one worthy of all your striving. In Jesus, our lives have meaning that goes far beyond paychecks and pleasures. What he gives us, no one can ever take away.

Jesus, you are the goal. Forgive me for taking my eyes of you, the real prize, and chasing after things that cannot last. Tilt my chin toward heaven, God, that I would strive only for that which is eternal.

"Do not work for the food which perishes, but for the food which endures to eternal life, which the Son of Man will give to you, for on Him the Father, God, has set His seal."

JOHN 6:27 NASB

Think about your work, and the reasons you do it. How many of them have eternal significance?

If you are working only for a paycheck, consider asking Jesus to infuse you with a greater purpose. You needn't necessarily change jobs; the enduring reward of working for the Lord is finding meaning right where we are.

God, the moment I rise, turn my thoughts to you. I want to live and work for the reward you offer. I want my eternal life to start right now, as you infuse my life with meaning because I've chosen to live it pursuing you.

How could a change in your perspective, or a new, more kingdom-minded goal, help you find more meaning in your current job?

He Knows

The Spirit helps us with our weakness. We do not know how to pray as we should. But the Spirit himself speaks to God for us, even begs God for us with deep feelings that words cannot explain.

ROMANS 8:26 NCV

There are days prayer feels like an unknown expression. We know we want something—we sense an ache or longing—but can't quite identify it. Other times, we're simply in too much pain to focus. We need, we need… but we can't get the words out.

"What do I want?" we cry. The Holy Spirit, because he lives inside us, knows us so intimately he can actually step in and pray on our behalf. He knows even when we don't.

Holy Spirit, let your presence wash over me right now. This morning I need you to pray for me because I just don't have the words. Thank you for knowing my heart.

The Spirit helps us in our weakness. For we do not know what to pray for as we ought, but the Spirit himself intercedes for us with groanings too deep for words.

ROMANS 8:26 ESV

If your day has been filled with stresses of all kinds, it can be overwhelming to know where to start with the time that you have dedicated right now to sit down with the Lord. That's why we have the Holy Spirit.

Sometimes we don't need to use words, we just need him. Rely on him tonight, to speak on your behalf.

Holy Spirit, I bring my entire day to you and ask that you filter what I really need from the Father right now. Please ask for these things for me.

What is your weakness right now? Thank the Holy Spirit for knowing your heart and expressing it when you can't.

Garment of Praise

Enter his gates with thanksgiving,
and his courts with praise.
Give thanks to him, bless his name.
For the LORD is good;
his steadfast love endures forever,
and his faithfulness to all generations.

PSALM 100:4-5 NRSV

Have you ever looked into a child's grumpy face and demanded that they don't smile? Even the most stubborn child can often be coaxed out of their funk by a few tickles or funny faces. Unfortunately, the same can't be said for adults. Imagine trying to change the attitude of a crotchety older woman with the same method. The picture is somewhat ridiculous.

God doesn't only deserve our praise when life is going well. He is worthy of our adoration every second of every day—no matter the situation. Living this out takes a good dose of faith. If you feel like today is going to be a tough one, decide now to smile.

God, this morning I choose to go about my day with a smile. You are always worthy of my praise and I want others to know that by my actions today.

Come into his city with songs of thanksgiving
and into his courtyards with songs of praise.
Thank him and praise his name.
The LORD is good. His love is forever,
and his loyalty goes on and on.

PSALM 100:4-5 NCV

When life's situations get us down, and all around us lie darkness and depression, it takes a great deal of faith to choose praise. But often that's the only thing that can really pull us out of those dark moments.

When you choose to thank God for his goodness and grace, you can't help but see life in a more positive light. As you praise God, your focus shifts from you to him.

Lord, thank you for walking with me today. I continue to choose a smile this evening and I thank you for all the good you have done in my life.

What does it look like for you to put on a garment of praise today?

Prepare Him Room

*"He must become greater and greater,
and I must become less and less."*

JOHN 3:30 NLT

Imagine your life if all you ever did was add to your possessions. Unless we want to be featured on a certain, very popular reality television show about people with far too much stuff, bringing new things in necessitates taking old things out. We don't build a bigger closet, we go through and select which items to donate. We don't build a bigger garage, we trade the aging sedan, SUV, or minivan for a newer, better model.

So too, when we accept Christ's sacrifice and the Holy Spirit takes up residence in our hearts, we must make room. Old habits must make way for fresh, inspired new ways of being. As his presence grows inside us, the old ways diminish.

Lord, help me push aside the old to create room for the new. Give me renewed joy today in knowing that you are becoming a bigger and better part of my life.

"He must increase, but I must decrease."

JOHN 3:30 NKJV

When we allow Jesus to increase in our lives, things like jealousy, bitterness, and insecurity need to be bagged up and taken out so that graciousness, forgiveness, and confidence Christ offers can move in.

Did you create room for Jesus, today? Perhaps you were focusing on other things – your work, your romantic life, or your social media. Jesus wants more of your energy, more of your life. If that sounds exhausting or impossible, share that with him. Allow your time with him tonight to build the desire to know him more.

Jesus, I don't know how to make room for you. I feel too busy to spend a lot of time in prayer or other spiritual things. Give me creative ways to pursue you so I can see you increase in my life.

How much space are you allowing the Holy Spirit right now, and how much are you holding onto for yourself?

Protection not Perfection

You have been a defense for the helpless,
a defense for the needy in his distress,
a refuge from the storm, a shade from the heat.

ISAIAH 25:4 NASB

In Christ, we are protected. We have a strong shield, a faithful defender, and a constant guardian. Many have mistaken this promise as a guarantee against pain, suffering, or hardship. When sorrows overwhelm us, can we stay faithful to our protector? Will we interpret adversity as betrayal, or embrace a protection that sometimes involves endurance, anguish, and pain?

God's security shelters us according to what we need, not necessarily from what pains us. His hand is upon you though, defending and sheltering you.

God, I see your hand of protection over my life even when things aren't going as I hope. Thank you.

You have been a refuge for the poor,
a refuge for the needy in their distress,
a shelter from the storm and a shade from the heat.
For the breath of the ruthless is like a storm driving against a wall.

ISAIAH 25:4 NIV

Protection does not mean perfection. Can we trust God only when our lives follow a path of ease? Faith gives depth to our expectations; we may not see through the dark clouds of the storm, but we know that God has prepared us for them. No matter how hard the rain falls or how fast the winds blow, we believe in his protection over us as we pass through it.

The storms will rage and the heat will blister, each in their turn and maybe for a long time. Can you believe that he is protecting you through it all? Let no storm shake your faith in this, beloved.

Father, help me to look to you in the storm. I choose to believe that you are protecting me even when the storms are raging.

How is your faith deepened when you recognize that he is with you in the storm?

Humility

If I must boast, I will boast of the things that show my weakness.

2 CORINTHIANS 11:30 NIV

"You did an incredible job; you're so talented!" Quick, how do you respond? Going beyond thank you and actually accepting—embracing—the kind words being spoken about us is difficult for many. As little girls, we're told it's rude not to say thank you when complimented, but society, and our peers, also send an opposing message: we'd best not be perceived as boastful. So what should we do?

Accept compliments, but acknowledge that your best qualities are gifts from God. Talk freely about the ways God made you special, and how infinitely special you find him.

Father God, you gave me many wonderful gifts. Help me to have humility with the things that I am good at because I know that they all come from you. Let me be a witness to your goodness.

If I have to boast, I will boast of what pertains to my weakness.

2 CORINTHIANS 11:30 NASB

It is freeing to learn that everything good about us is actually about Jesus. Every good gift, from beauty to a lovely singing voice to the ability to sink a three-pointer on the basketball court, is from him.

You're not full of yourself; you're full of him! Even better, every time we mess up is an opportunity to brag about his perfection. After all, we're only human. We can't do anything on our own.

Lord, let me be honest to others when I mess up. Let people see my weaknesses so they know that I am human and no different to anyone else. Allow your heart to shine through mine so I can lead others to you.

Where have you messed up lately? Can you allow your weakness to be exposed to others?

Redeemed

"Truly, truly, I say to you, whoever hears my word and believes him who sent me has eternal life. He does not come into judgment, but has passed from death to life. Truly, truly, I say to you, an hour is coming, and is now here, when the dead will hear the voice of the Son of God, and those who hear will live."

JOHN 5:24-25 ESV

Because of Jesus Christ, we get to start over. His grace covers us and we receive his mercies anew each morning. Because of Jesus Christ, we dipped into everlasting pools of healing, baptized by the cool and refreshing presence of the Holy Spirit. We approached the throne humble, expectant, and thirsty because we could no longer shoulder the weight of our sins. Burdens unloaded at the foot of the throne; we were redeemed for freedom and live now in the promise of life everlasting. We have passed from death to life.

Being redeemed means being reinvented, refurbished, and revitalized. Something broken, ugly, or useless is given purpose. We are given a purpose in our redemption: to plead with those still in bondage to break free from their chains. The hour is coming when it will be too late.

God, I believe that you have truly erased every sin I have confessed. Thank you.

> *"I tell you the truth, whoever hears what I say and believes in the One who sent me has eternal life. That person will not be judged guilty but has already left death and entered life. I tell you the truth, the time is coming and is already here when the dead will hear the voice of the Son of God, and those who hear will have life."*
>
> JOHN 5:24-25 NCV

We have the assurance of our redemption, but do we live like the redeemed every day? Do we rejoice like slaves who have been set free? Redeemed, we abandon the path once walked for the one navigated by God.

Slaves cannot determine their steps; they are ordered to walk. But children of God have been ransomed and set free. They must choose to run from the paths of materialism, pride, vanity, and idolatry that have been paved by the world. Choose the path of freedom this evening.

Father, you have redeemed me and set me free. Help me not to pursue things that lead me away from you. I want to walk in freedom and truth.

Spend some time expressing your thanks to God for the redemptive work of his Son in your life.

Being Known

You know what I long for, LORD;
you hear my every sigh.

PSALM 38:9 NLT

Think of the most perfect gift you've ever received. Not the most extravagant, but the one that was just so perfectly you that you realized the giver really knew you. They heard you, that one time, when you mentioned that one thing, perhaps in passing, and because they were listening with their heart, they saw into yours. They get you.

Spend some time this morning with the one who truly understands your every thought. God knows you better than you know yourself. Take comfort in that today.

Father, you know exactly where my heart is and how I am feeling right now. You understand me more than anyone in this life because you created me. Help me to know that I am understood today.

O Lᴏʀᴅ, all my longing is known to you;
my sighing is not hidden from you.

Psᴀʟᴍ 38:9 ɴʀsᴠ

We love to be understood, and we long to be seen. For many of us it's how we know we are loved. How much, then, must the Father love us? He who knows everything about us—who takes the time to listen to every longing and comfort every sigh—is waiting to give us his perfect gifts.

You are known and you are loved. Let that thought create peace in your heart and mind this evening as you get ready to finish your day.

God, there are a lot of things that I long for. I have a list that gets bigger and bigger by the day. Help me know what is just selfish desire, and what is really a heartfelt desire that comes from a heart after yours.

Share your longing with God today. Let him show you his great love by revealing how intimately he knows you. Let him give you a good and perfect gift.

Contend for Peace

Don't just pretend to love others. Really love them.
Hate what is wrong. Hold tightly to what is good.
Love each other with genuine affection,
and take delight in honoring each other.
Do all that you can to live in peace with everyone.

ROMANS 12:9-10, 18 NLT

These are very convicting directions from God's Word. Unless you have completely mastered loving everyone you meet, Paul's words to the Roman church might leave you feeling a little squeamish. How can we determine to really love each other? In the same breath we can hate what is wrong and then do what is wrong. We are holding tightly to what is good, but at the smallest distraction we let go and grab hold of something shinier. Someone we genuinely love and delight to honor can become an easy target for our criticism and jealousy.

Ask for God's love for others to overwhelm your heart so you can really love them. Ask for his mindset to replace yours, and cling tightly to his good Word.

God, give me your heart of love and forgiveness toward people
I need to make peace with today.

Your love must be real. Hate what is evil,
and hold on to what is good.
Love each other like brothers and sisters.
Give each other more honor than you want for yourselves.
Do your best to live in peace with everyone.

ROMANS 12:9-10, 18 NCV

We are flawed. Deeply and truly we are flawed, but not hopelessly. If God commands that we do all that we can to live at peace with everyone, we can believe that he has made a way for us to achieve it. Begin with confession and repentance. Cry out to God for his Holy Spirit to change you from the inside—your thoughts, your opinions, your outlook—so that your words and deeds will also be transformed.

Read and meditate on Scripture, day and night, so that it is painted on the walls of your mind. Contend for peace in all relationships by putting off old habits and adopting God's heart of love.

Father, start transformation in my heart so I can change from the inside out. I want to have your thoughts toward people and treat them with love. I need peace in my relationships, and you're the only one who can make it last.

Which relationships in your life need peace right now?

Other Opinions

Yes, the LORD is for me; he will help me.
I will look in triumph at those who hate me.
It is better to take refuge in the LORD
than to trust in people.

PSALM 118:7-8 NLT

God created you for relationship with him, just as he created Adam and Eve. He delights in your voice, your laughter, and your ideas. He longs to fellowship with you just as he did with his first son and daughter. But, like Adam and Eve, we are sometimes persuaded by the opinions of others instead of listening and obeying the commands of our Father and greatest friend.

When life gets difficult, we can run to him with our frustrations. When we're overwhelmed with sadness or grief, we can carry our pain to him. In the heat of anger or frustration, we can call on him for freedom. He is a friend that offers all of this—and more—in mercy and love, and he is worthy of our friendship.

Thank you for loving me so much, Father, that you want to share in my everyday moments. I ask you to walk with me throughout this day.

The LORD is with me to help me,
so I will see my enemies defeated.
It is better to trust the LORD
than to trust people.

PSALM 118:7-8 NCV

It is understandably tempting to share our grievances, triumphs, problems, or desires with friends and loved ones we can easily call on the phone or meet for coffee. God has given us wonderful relationships! But we run the risk of listening first to their opinions rather than God's, and this risk can trap us in sin.

Don't let others' opinions of you matter more than God's. Train your heart to run first to God with your pain, joy, frustration, and excitement. His friendship will never let you down!

God, what you think of me matters most. I want to remember this when I am sharing with others. I don't need to impress people or hide the truth from them because only your opinion truly matters.

How much value do you place on the opinions of others?

Our Strength

Though the fig tree should not blossom
And there be no fruit on the vines,
Though the yield of the olive should fail
And the fields produce no food,
Though the flock should be cut off from the fold
And there be no cattle in the stalls,
Yet I will exult in the Lord,
I will rejoice in the God of my salvation.

HABAKKUK 3:17-18 NASB

The pile of bills, the noise the car is making, the layoff rumors at work, the child who stayed home sick—again. Pressures can overwhelm us especially when they accumulate. Add in the stresses we put on ourselves—Am I good enough? Why did I say that? Other women's houses aren't this cluttered.—and you've got a potent recipe for insecurity.

When things seem impossible, and they often do, praise God that we have his promises and his power. It is not up to us to solve our problems; we need only to trust the Lord and accept his help.

God, give me assurance that I can rejoice in you even in my moments of deepest despair. Help me to see that spring will return once again.

Even though the fig trees have no blossoms,
and there are no grapes on the vines;
even though the olive crop fails,
and the fields lie empty and barren;
even though the flocks die in the fields,
and the cattle barns are empty,
yet I will rejoice in the Lord!
I will be joyful in the God of my salvation!

HABAKKUK 3:17-18 NLT

Has your day felt dry and unfruitful? Did everything seem to go wrong? Maybe you didn't finish your tasks, or you didn't react well to someone's request for you to do more work. You might have had an argument, or felt deflated by something somebody said to you.

Life can be hard and unfair at times. Praise God, anyway! He cares about your bad day, but he also cares about your heart and he is waiting to deposit some joy into a day of despair.

Lord, I guess things weren't so bad today. It might have felt like things didn't go my way, but I still have you. I still have your love, your grace, and an eternal life to look forward to. Bring me joy, tonight, as I sit here with you.

Where could you use a little, or a lot, of God's strength right now? Offer your worries to your Father.

Embracing Solitude

After sending them home, he went up into the hills by himself
to pray. Night fell while he was there alone.

MATTHEW 14:23 NLT

Everyone in the house is gone—for the entire weekend. How
did those words make you feel? Were you considering who to
call for a fun night out, or reveling in the thought of hours of
uninterrupted quiet time to read, relax, and restore? Perhaps
both ideas appeal to you: a little social time, and a little alone
time.

Imagine Jesus slipping off, unnoticed, and going to spend
time with his Father. What intimacy they must have shared;
how restorative those hours of prayer must have been.
Whatever your feelings about solitude, ask God to give you
Jesus' heart for alone-time with him.

Jesus, thank you that you know the importance of being alone.
Thank you for this moment of being alone with you before I head
into another day full of others. Help this time to refresh me for the
day ahead.

After he had dismissed the crowds, he went up on the mountain by himself to pray. When evening came, he was there alone.

MATTHEW 14:23 ESV

Jesus cherished his alone time. He guarded it. Amidst the stories of ministering to crowds, feeding thousands, and untold hours spent with the twelve he chose as apostles, it's easy to miss this fact. Studying the gospels, we see a pattern emerge: he healed, then he went off to pray alone; he taught, then he climbed the mountain to pray alone; the disciples went out on the boat, and Jesus remained on the shore—alone.

How do you feel in your alone time with God? Spend a small portion of this evening recharging your batteries by embracing solitude with your Creator.

God, I'm glad to spend just a little more time with you this evening. Thank you for the ability to slip away and feel refreshed by some encouraging words and your presence. Uplift me and rejuvenate me for another day.

Where can you go for some alone time? Give yourself some space even if only for a few short minutes.

Developing Maturity

We know how much God loves us, and we have put our trust in his love. God is love, and all who live in love live in God, and God lives in them. And as we live in God, our love grows more perfect. So we will not be afraid on the day of judgment, but we can face him with confidence because we live like Jesus here in this world.

1 JOHN 4:16-17 NLT

Responsibility is something that is sorely lacking in the world. We have excuses for everything. We even have excuses for excuses. Nothing is anyone's fault, and we are encouraged to live solely for ourselves.

As we work on developing love for others, we recognize God's heart and we begin to carry compassion and a desire to help. As we love God, we gain better understanding of his love for us, and we become more aware of our need for his grace. This is the maturity that he desires for us: closeness to him, and relationship with others.

Lord, give me your heart. Help me to become more aware of your maturing work in my life.

We know and rely on the love God has for us. God is love. Whoever lives in love lives in God, and God in them. This is how love is made complete among us so that we will have confidence on the day of judgment: In this world we are like Jesus.

1 JOHN 4:16-17 NIV

Without responsibility, how can we expect to grow in our relationship with God? We can't live oblivious to our fault or the needs around us. God calls us to a higher level of living. He asks us to love him first and our neighbor next. He tells us to respect each other, to consider others as more important than ourselves. It's so counter-culture that we have to really work at developing it.

Spend some time this evening pondering how you can grow in maturity in your relationship with the Lord. Begin thinking of ways you can show awareness of others' needs and set aside your own.

God, I know I think of myself far too often. It's what the world tells me to do. I don't want to listen to the advice and trends of the world, though. I want to consider others and love them well.

What areas in your life are lacking a sense of responsibility?

Discovering Beauty

Even those people at the ends of the earth fear your miracles.
You are praised from where the sun rises to where it sets.

PSALM 65:8 NCV

God's beauty is all around us; it includes the people he has put under our care. Beauty can be seen in the little girl with a darling lisp as well as the pierced and tattooed teen with purple hair and attitude. It emanates from every person God created.

All of us are wonders of God's creation. Sometimes we need to slow down a bit to look for the beauty and diversity of the world around us. Break your habit this evening and take time to appreciate the beauty of God's creation.

Father, I am in awe of your wonders. I want to see and appreciate the miracles you have placed right in front of me.

The whole earth is filled with awe at your wonders.

PSALM 65:8 NIV

Have you ever looked at a spider's web covered with dewdrops? What about the iridescence of a hummingbird wing, a glistening canyon covered in ferns, a breathtaking sunset, or a chubby-faced giggling baby? Our hearts soar overlooking the snowcapped mountains and listening to birdsongs on a summer's afternoon.

Each day we are presented with the beauty of God's world. You may be surprised to find it on your daily drive or by listening a little closer to one of your co-workers.

Lord God, help me to see the world around me with new eyes of amazement.

What beauty do you see as you look around this evening?

Our Destiny

There is still a vision for the appointed time;
it speaks of the end, and does not lie.
If it seems to tarry, wait for it;
it will surely come, it will not delay.

HABAKKUK 2:3 NRSV

As we listen to a talented singer, or watch a brilliant athlete, these people, so apparently effortless in their pursuits, seem born for just those things. This is their destiny, we think. What is my destiny? We may then wonder. What was I born to do?

You still have so much life ahead of you. Whether you are young or getting older, God has not forgotten you! He has gifted you with things that will bring him glory. Bring your talents to God, use them where you need to, and be patient for the fruitfulness.

Lord, show me what you want me to do with my talents. Help me to recognize my gifts in the things that I do from day to day. Let me think about your glory, not my own.

These things I plan won't happen right away. Slowly, steadily, surely, the time approaches when the vision will be fulfilled. If it seems slow, do not despair, for these things will surely come to pass. Just be patient! They will not be overdue a single day!

HABAKKUK 2:3 TLB

Whether or not you believe you have a specific purpose, God knows you do. And he knows just what it is, and how long—how many false starts and poor decisions—it will take you to fulfill it.

God is deeply interested in the destinies of those who call him Father, just as he is in the ultimate fate of the whole world. Talk to him tonight about your hopes and dreams.

Jesus, help me to be patient as I work out what talents you are calling me to use. I have failed in a few things and have lost confidence, so please show me what you are guiding me in, and then give me the boldness to keep going.

Are you waiting on God to fulfill—or reveal—your destiny? Take comfort in the passage above, and thank him for his perfect timing. If waiting is hard, ask for his help.

Times of Doubt

God you are near me always, so close to me;
every one of your commands reveals truth.
I've known all along how true and unchanging
is every word you speak, established forever!

PSALM 119:151-152 TPT

The sun will set tonight; it will rise tomorrow. This is truth. We have no reason to doubt what we've witnessed every day of our lives. But when experience tells us otherwise, or perhaps we have no experience to go on, doubts creep in. It's going to snow tomorrow. "I doubt that," we say.

Remember, today, that God's truth is unchanging. It is sure as the sun that rose this morning and will set tonight.

God, just as the Psalmist wrote, you are near me always; you are so close to me. Thank you that every one of your commands reveals truth. Let me trust in your truth as I go into my day.

You are near, O LORD,
and all your commandments are true.
Long have I known from your testimonies
that you have founded them forever.

PSALM 119:151-152 ESV

When someone we trust says they'll be there for us, we have faith in their words. Someone who has repeatedly let us down can make the same promise, but we remain uncertain until they've shown up and proven themselves.

Do you feel unsettled tonight? Are you doubting? God wants to erase that doubt and he will; you only need to have faith.

Lord God, I have faith in your words. Others may let me down. Sometimes I don't even keep true to my word. But your words are true and unchanging!

Examine your prayer life. Do you trust God, or do you doubt his promises to you? Why? Share your heart openly with him, and ask him for unwavering faith.

Stand on the Truth

Your words are true from the start,
and all your laws will be fair forever.
I am as happy over your promises
as if I had found a great treasure.

PSALM 119:160, 162 NCV

The world shouts, "Truth is relative!" "Truth is what I believe!" "Truth is what I want it to be!" We cannot entertain these lies. Truth is found in God's Word alone. Truth is absolute. It has not changed since the beginning of time and it will not change on into eternity.

Stand together with those who believe and declare that God's Word is the definition of truth itself.

Father, help me not to listen to the world's definition of truth. Only your Word is truth. You are truth.

The sum of your word is truth;
and every one of your righteous ordinances endures forever.
I rejoice at your word
like one who finds great spoil.

PSALM 119:160, 162 NASB

Because God's Word is true, we can believe everything it says. It's by far not the most popular thing to stake our morals, beliefs, and decisions on, and we can be sure to expect a good amount of opposition and ridicule when we do. This is why it's important to surround ourselves with others who also believe wholeheartedly in the absolute nature of God's Word.

Spend some time this evening in the truth. Absorb it and let it bring you life.

God, I stand on your Word tonight. I believe everything that is written in Scripture. I know it is truth. Help me to find others who believe the same.

What does it look like for you to stand on the truth of God's Word in this season of your life?

Renewal

Teach me your way, Lord,
that I may rely on your faithfulness;
give me an undivided heart,
that I may fear your name.

PSALM 86:11 NIV

It's hard to find someone who doesn't love fall. The gorgeous colors; the return of scarves, sleeves, and cute boots; the peaceful silence of a home where kids have returned to their classrooms—all invite a spirit of renewal.

As the outside air begins to change and leaves begin to fall, a clean slate seems entirely possible. Think of the amazing things you could achieve in God this year. It can start today!

Lord, teach me your ways. I am so hungry for you to refresh my heart and bring new things into my life. I pray that refreshing would begin this morning.

Teach me your ways, O LORD,
that I may live according to your truth!
Grant me purity of heart,
so that I may honor you.

PSALM 86:11 NLT

Even when life is humming along quite nicely, the idea of a fresh beginning is irresistible. For some of us, the transition from summer to fall feels more like New Year's Day than New Year's Day does.

Spend some time dreaming with God about what this fall might bring to you, and what you might bring to it.

God, give me a fresh perspective, this evening. As I think about this week, or the rest of this year, I ask that you show me new beginnings. Keep my heart pure so that I can clearly hear your direction.

If God were to purify your heart, where would he begin?

Every Situation

Then you will understand what is right, just, and fair,
and you will find the right way to go.
For wisdom will enter your heart,
and knowledge will fill you with joy.
Wise choices will watch over you.
Understanding will keep you safe.

PROVERBS 2:9-11 NLT

All of life is a test. As we live each day, the tests we face teach us valuable lessons. It may seem backwards: usually lessons are learned to prepare us for a test. But in life, the test often comes first. Through the lessons, God gives us the wisdom we need for the next test.

It's a safe bet that the tests will keep coming. Thankfully, our hearts gain understanding every time. Tension and uncertainty melt away; joy blossoms. Solomon's advice is that we listen to wisdom, apply it, and learn as we go. Then we will have understanding; we will find the right path with wisdom in our hearts and joy from knowledge.

Thank you, God, for giving me the opportunity to make wise choices.

Then you will understand righteousness and justice
and equity, every good path;
for wisdom will come into your heart,
and knowledge will be pleasant to your soul;
prudence will watch over you;
and understanding will guard you.

PROVERBS 2:9-11 NRSV

Gaining wisdom doesn't guarantee that you won't stumble and fall on your face or stick your foot in your mouth. You will still make mistakes, say the wrong thing at the wrong time, and wish you could go back in time and do it right. It stings.

Even when we fail the test, we learn a lesson and gain wisdom. If we humble ourselves, we can trust that God will give us wisdom in every situation. Another test is just around the corner, waiting for us to pass with flying colors!

Father, even though I fail your tests often, I thank you that I can take joy in the wisdom I gain from those tests. You don't expect me to get it right the first time, and you even have grace if I fail it the second time. Thank you for continuing to be patient with me while I learn.

What valuable lessons have you learned from life's tests?

Not My Power

We have this treasure in jars of clay,
to show that the surpassing power belongs to God and not to us.

2 CORINTHIANS 4:7 ESV

We've all heard a story: a 110–pound mother stops a moving car with her bare hands, or defeats a charging bear, to save her toddler. We love the image of the tiny defeating the mighty. The sheer unlikeliness of it is what makes it so compelling; love will make the impossible possible.

When we feel called to do something for God, our first instinct may be to list our shortcomings. We focus on our ability, our strength, forgetting the One who promises to equip us with all we need. We are like Esther, wondering, What if I fail? The fact we could easily fail is what makes it a great story.

God, I know you have called me to love you and love others. I know that you have given me specific gifts for a specific time. I rely on your power, not my own strength, to do these things for you.

We have this treasure in jars of clay to show that this all-surpassing power is from God and not from us.

2 Corinthians 4:7 NIV

Have you felt God prompting you to do something that seems impossible? What if all you had to do was agree to try? Maybe you dream of accomplishing something but don't believe you could. What if he gave you that dream, and he's just waiting for you to ask for his help?

As you rest this evening, reflect on those dreams. Ask for his power to accomplish them.

Lord, I take this time now to acknowledge the dreams that you have placed in my heart from so early on in my life. I know they are dreams that you have put there for a reason. Thank you that it is not in my strength to accomplish these, but it is with you that I can. Restore my hope in those dreams tonight.

What are the dreams that God wants to restore to your heart, tonight?

Greatest Comforter

You have given me many troubles and bad times,
but you will give me life again.
When I am almost dead,
you will keep me alive.
You will make me greater than ever,
and you will comfort me again.

PSALM 71:20-21 NCV

As Christians, we are never promised that we will go through life seeing no trouble. In fact, it's quite the opposite. We're told time and time again in the Bible that there will be tough times, that we will be persecuted for our beliefs, and we won't always have a life of ease.

But there is good news despite all that. We have someone we can always turn to in our times of pain. God is waiting for us to run to him. He is the greatest comforter we could ever find. He wants to restore us, refresh us, and bring us contentment amidst the darkness of our anguish.

Thank you, God, that there is hope and life in you. You are my Comforter.

You who have made me see many troubles and calamities
will revive me again;
from the depths of the earth
you will bring me up again.
You will increase my honor,
and comfort me once again.

PSALM 71:20-21 NRSV

You can always turn to Jesus during times of trial. He will open his arms and welcome you, helping you find your way through it all. If you feel burdened by what life has offered you, pray for his peace today. He will restore you over and over again.

Be encouraged by the Psalmist's response. In the midst of his trouble, he gave himself to the Lord. He knew that was the only way to life, comfort, and joy.

Father, you have kept me safe from myself. Help me to run to you for comfort when I need it most.

In what areas do you need God's comfort today?

Follow Through

You desired faithfulness even in the womb;
you taught me wisdom in that secret place.

PSALM 51:6 NIV

Commitment, follow-through, and faithfulness are all words
that mean about the same thing. They are character traits
that God desires in you. Some things we commit to because
they seem fun or easy. Other things deserve our commitment
because they are the right things to do. These are the
commitments that are often more difficult to stick with.

Faithfulness is one of the nine fruits of the spirit written in
Galatians 5:22-23. It holds great value before God. As his
child, you are an example and a light to many. When God calls
you to be faithful, it means that you do what you say you are
going to do even when it is inconvenient. You stick with it
because others are depending on you.

Thank you, Lord, for your commitment to me today.

You delight in truth in the inward being,
and you teach me wisdom in the secret heart.

PSALM 51:6 ESV

By learning to be a more faithful person, you will find that others trust and respect you deeply. Jesus was faithful to his Father in the most difficult commitment imaginable—being crucified on the cross for our sins.

Because of Jesus' faithfulness to his commitment, we are able to be in relationship with the Father. That is something to be extremely grateful for.

God, help me to go against the grain of my culture and begin following through on my commitments.

How can you show faithfulness in areas you have committed yourself to?

What You Need

*My God will use his wonderful riches in Christ Jesus
to give you everything you need.*

PHILIPPIANS 4:19 NCV

What do you need? The more you think about it, the smaller
the list becomes, and the easier it is to believe the Lord will
always make sure you have it. Because of his great love for
you, he will make a way to feed and clothe and keep you safe.
But beyond that, so far beyond that, he will supply you from
the riches of Christ.

This hints at a life of unspeakable joy. This suggests all the
patience we require, and the ability to be kind to everyone
we meet. This opens the way to an abundance of selfless love.
And what more could we possibly need?

*God, I get caught up in what I think I need, in this world's idea of
riches. But you offer riches in Christ, treasures beyond measure.
Make me rich in love, loaded with generosity. Give me a wealth of
wisdom, so I will know your riches are all I really need.*

My God will supply every need of yours
according to his riches in glory in Christ Jesus.

PHILIPPIANS 4:19 ESV

Have you ever wondered how it is that God always seems to know what you need? How wonderful it is too, that he never tires of supplying it. Even when material needs appear to go unmet, the tender, intimate way he loves us supplies us with a level of joy and peace we may not otherwise have experienced, and didn't know we needed.

The way the Lord ministers to us in our need often illuminates how much we actually have. His sustaining grace has a way of eclipsing suffering and want, giving us a joyful satisfaction in every circumstance.

Father God, you are such a wonderful provider! Some of the most joyful, contented people I've ever seen are those with little more than your love to sustain them. This inspires my heart to trust and fills it with gratitude for the amazing way you've supplied my life. I know I don't deserve it but that never stops you. Your provision is as endless as your love. Provide me now with a heart as grateful as this knowledge deserves.

Tell God what you really need tonight.

Clean It Up

Whoever conceals their sins does not prosper,
but the one who confesses and renounces them finds mercy.

PROVERBS 28:13 NIV

When we make a mess on the floor, the worse thing to do is to sweep it under the rug and leave it there. Dirt doesn't go away. It needs to be cleaned, or it will stain, stink, and create mold.

When we fail to examine our hearts in situations—even arguments where we think we are right—we allow some buildup that isn't healthy for anyone. We need to search out our sin and clean it up. Mercy will always follow the humble.

God, give me the humility to admit when I am wrong today.

Blessed is the one who always trembles before God,
but whoever hardens their heart falls into trouble.

PROVERBS 28:14, NIV

Have you had an argument recently, perhaps even today, and left convinced that the other person was the one in the wrong? Consider what part of it you could have done better: there are always two sides to a fight.

Even if it is small, confess your wrongdoing, and be prepared to forgive. Don't let your heart be hardened. Let God's mercy toward you become your strength to forgive.

God, I thank you that there is great blessing in humility. I forgive those who have wronged me today and ask for you to continue to soften my heart.

Who needs to experience your forgiveness right now?

The Well

He gives strength to those who are tired
and more power to those who are weak.

ISAIAH 40:29 NCV

He knows you are tired; he has strength and more strength to give you. He knows when you feel weak; his power is yours for the asking. How encouraging! And how true. Test him in this; he wants you to.

On a morning that feels like you haven't rested at all, ask confidently for strength. On a day that is simply too heavy, when your burdens have left you weak, call out boldly for power. Expect it. Be ready for it. Because he will supply it.

God, you are my power supply. This is good because my own reserves run continually low. Forgive me for forgetting to rely on you sometimes, for getting far more exhausted than I need to before calling out to you. I call and you supply; it's amazing. How generous you are and how very strong.

He gives power to the faint,
and strengthens the powerless.

ISAIAH 40:29 NRSV

Have you had a day that just drained you, maybe even this one? It's tempting to wonder if the Lord is paying attention, to wonder why he didn't come in and plug the drain, especially if we asked him to.

One of the reasons our Father allows us to become depleted is so we'll remember he is our source. For power, strength, courage, hope, and more, he is the well.

God, your strength can move mountains, and I've got one I could use your help with. Because I know how intimately you attend to me, I know you are aware of my burden. I know you won't allow it to crush me, but there are days it brings me quite low. I need you. Is that why you allow me to bear it, so I'll remember? Remember I need you, remember I have you, always, remember I am never alone.

Pour your heart out to God regarding where you are feeling faint, where the weight grows heavy.

Spiritual Fitness

Bodily exercise profits a little,
but godliness is profitable for all things,
having promise of the life that now is and of
that which is to come.

1 TIMOTHY 4:8 NKJV

We know the value of exercise; it benefits the body and the mind. We also know that exercise requires determination and discipline. There is, however, exercise that is more beneficial than physical exercise. Scripture compares godliness with bodily exercise.

Godliness is not just something that we instantly receive when we accept Christ as our Savior. Godliness is a work in progress. It requires discipline and commitment to understanding what it means to be like Jesus.

Father, I need that discipline in my life. I don't just want to make a plan, I want to have the strength and stamina to carry through on that plan. I look toward the higher goal of eternity.

This is a faithful saying and worthy of all acceptance.
For to this end we both labor and suffer reproach,
because we trust in the living God,
who is the Savior of all men,
especially of those who believe.

1 TIMOTHY 4:9-10 NKJV

Do you accept that you are going to have to put in the time and effort to prioritize spiritual practices in the same way you try to with physical exercise?

Godliness has benefit beyond this life. Be encouraged that you will be rewarded in both this life and the life to come.

Jesus, I want to be spiritually fit. I know the benefits of having you in my life daily. Thank you that I have had the opportunity to read a Scripture this morning and now this evening. Help me to keep this discipline of spending time with you.

Where do you need extra spiritual training? Ask the Holy Spirit to be your personal trainer.

Paid

> *"Beware of practicing your righteousness before other people in order to be seen by them, for then you will have no reward from your Father who is in heaven."*
>
> MATTHEW 6:1 ESV

Awards, recognition, promotion, and accolades feel great—even more so when they are unexpected. It's one kind of thrill to enter a contest and come out on top, and a whole other to receive a surprise thank you, celebration, or shout-out. There you were, just doing you, and boom! You didn't even know anyone was watching.

This is the kind of service that is pleasing to the Lord. We give because we are able, help because we are moved. Our hearts are on the giving, on the helping, not on the attention we will receive for doing it. And Jesus' heart is bursting with love for ours.

Holy Spirit, give me this kind of heart. I want to be so focused on what I can give, how I can help, and who I can serve, I don't even begin to notice who sees. I want my goodness to please you. I don't need accolades and awards, just a heart that loves to help.

"Be careful! When you do good things, don't do them in front of people to be seen by them. If you do that, you will have no reward from your Father in heaven."

MATTHEW 6:1 NCV

If you performed a job for your neighbors, you wouldn't expect to be paid by both the husband and the wife. One job equals one payday, right? This is a helpful way to consider what Jesus is saying about our good deeds.

If we work for the attention and approval of people, we've been paid when they notice us, when they tell us how good we are. Why expect the Lord to pay us again?

God, search my heart. You know my motives better than I. Am I volunteering my time to impress my friends, or to please my Father? Do I donate so I can feel good about myself, or so that I can help assure your children are being fed? I want to work for you, God, and for your glory alone.

It's okay to enjoy being appreciated. The Lord encourages us to recognize one another. Approval is a wonderful reward; just let him search your heart, to make sure it's not your motivation.

Show Respect

All who are under the yoke of slavery should consider their masters worthy of full respect, so that God's name and our teaching may not be slandered

1 TIMOTHY 6:1 NIV

While we don't like to think of ourselves as servants, many of us are involved in employment or some type of service. The Bible says much about those who have shown diligence and respect to those who are in authority.

We don't want to give people an opportunity to think of us as lazy or uncaring. When we work hard, we represent the servant nature of Christ. Show people that you are capable of putting others first today.

God, as I think about getting on with my usual day-to-day tasks, I pray that you would give me renewed energy to respect people who I work for, or those who have a position of authority.

Those who have believing masters should not show them disrespect just because they are fellow believers. Instead, they should serve them even better because their masters are dear to them as fellow believers and are devoted to the welfare of their slaves.

1 TIMOTHY 6:2 NIV

There is a higher purpose to us respecting our employers. When we show diligence, commitment, and effort, we are honoring God's name as a witness of Christian living.

Be encouraged as you go into your place of work (whether home, study, or employment), knowing that as you show good service, you are positively representing the name of Jesus.

Jesus, thank you for this time of rest tonight. Give me the will to do a really great job tomorrow and to show respect for those who are in leadership.

Who can you pray for tonight who is in a position of authority over you?

There Is Nothing

Do not throw away your confidence, which has a great reward.

HEBREWS 10:35 NASB

We'd never throw money in the trash, or an exquisitely prepared meal down the disposal. Our most treasured heirlooms are not in danger of being tossed into the ocean. We hold on to things of value, which is what makes this admonishment from Hebrews so intriguing. Throw away confidence? Why would we do that?

Usually, if something of value is cast aside, it's by accident. Haste, or distraction, causes us not to notice what is happening. Perhaps we set our confidence down when we pick up worry. Perhaps we throw it off to catch a flying load of shame. However, it could happen, let's do all we can to hold on to our confidence like the treasure it is.

Lord Jesus, you give me the gift of confidence. It is the reason I can come before you with my needs, the reason I can fall asleep at night knowing they will be met. It is what allows me to stand apart from a world that tells me to want the world. Don't let me throw it away. Let me hold onto it as I hold onto you.

Do not throw away this confident trust in the Lord.
Remember the great reward it brings you!

HEBREWS 10:35 NLT

Who do you trust? Is it because they've given you no reason to doubt you, they have filled you with confidence in their integrity, ability, and commitment?

This person you trust, can you imagine willingly giving up the closeness you share? It's unthinkable. Equally unimaginable would be to give up on the Lord. The awesome rewards of a life spent loving and trusting Christ are simply too great to throw away.

Jesus, what could be worth giving you up, throwing away my trust in you, placing my confidence elsewhere? There is nothing, there is no one, who could possibly care for me, understand me, and empower me the way you do. Whatever else I hold onto, let none of it come before you.

For as many seconds as you can bear it, imagine your life without the confident hope you have in the Lord. Thank him that this will never, ever be.

Obeying God

Peter and the other apostles replied:
"We must obey God rather than human beings!"

ACTS 5:29 NIV

The boldness of the apostles in Acts is amazing. Over and over, they refuse to stop teaching, healing, and proclaiming in the name of Jesus. Jail, beatings, and even shipwrecks don't deter them from their God-given mission. It really didn't matter what people wanted them to do; they needed to do what God wanted them to do.

Somewhere in the world, right this very moment, a missionary is doing the same. Despite the illegality of Christianity, they are holding a Bible study in their living room. They are speaking of Jesus on the subway. They are praying in a sidewalk café. Their freedom and even their lives are at risk, but they can't stop to care about that; they need to do what God has called them to do.

Awesome. The call you place on some who love you, and the obedience with which they respond, is awesome, God. I'm listening in case you want to ask more of me. Compelled by love to obey you, may the example of my brothers and sisters inspire me to be as brave as you call me to be.

Peter and the apostles answered,
"We must obey God rather than any human authority."
ACTS 5:29 NRSV

Obeying God means walking in light, living in love, and speaking the truth. Why would we resist? And yet we do. The pull of the world is strong, and we want to fit in. We want to be liked. We hate to offend. And yet we must.

To walk in light, we must leave darkness behind. Living in love means turning from hate. Speaking the truth requires a willingness to offend in the name of love.

Holy Spirit, I need your help. Compel me to the light, draw me toward love, plant me in truth. I must obey you. Not because you demand it, but because it's all I want from life.

In the absence of a cross necklace or a Bible in your hand, how long would it take for a person to recognize you as a Christ follower? Pray honestly about this, asking the Holy Spirit to speak to your heart.

A Kind of Rich

Teach those who are rich in this world not to be proud and not to trust in their money, which is so unreliable. Their trust should be in God, who richly gives us all we need for our enjoyment.

1 TIMOTHY 6:17 NLT

We think that more money will get us what we want, and sometimes it does, momentarily. All too often, when we finally buy that thing we have been waiting for, we don't feel that much better and we begin to look at the next thing.

Wealth in this life won't give us what our heart really desires. We won't find lasting peace or lasting joy. God is the one who fulfills these desires because he brings a better kind of richness to our relationships and situations. Ask his for love, not money, today.

God, let me be generous today, but not just with money. Challenge me to be generous with my time, energy, or a kind word.

Tell them to use their money to do good.
They should be rich in good works and generous to those in need,
always being ready to share with others.

1 TIMOTHY 6:18 NLT

Have you fallen into the trap of thinking that spending will give you enjoyment? The Scripture says that God is the source for our enjoyment. He would rather we use our money to do good.

Gifts are wonderful, but allow yourself to dwell on the goodness that you can share with others, particularly those in need.

God, give me an opportunity to give to someone in need. I pray that you will give me a more generous heart and expose the times when I am buying something of little value.

Have you felt challenged to spend wisely lately? Who can you be generous to this week?

You Are New

> If anyone is in Christ, there is a new creation:
> everything old has passed away;
> see, everything has become new!
>
> 2 CORINTHIANS 5:17 NRSV

The Lord makes all things new. The moment you chose to love him, he began transforming you. He washed you clean. Years of sin, guilt, regret and grime are gone. It's hard to grasp, isn't it? You're a whole new you. So how well are you grasping it? Do you really believe you are forgiven? Can it be true that you are new?

You may need help understanding that the old self, the one who needed defenses, regrets, grudges, and contention is truly gone. You may go looking for her. You may try to dig her up. You don't need her anymore. You never did.

Perfect Father, can this be true? Can this bright, joyful, gracious, peaceful person be me? Help me believe it, and help me accept this gift of transformation. Help me leave the old self where she lies and bask in the beauty of my newness in you.

Anyone who belongs to Christ has become a new person.
The old life is gone; a new life has begun!

2 CORINTHIANS 5:17 NLT

There are periods, whether of hours or days, where the newness we have in Christ can feel like a pair of new jeans: a little stiff, a little scratchy. We may long for the worn, frayed familiarity of our old selves.

God understands. He knows newness takes getting used to. That's why we have his Spirit with us, to listen, encourage, and uplift us as we settle in.

Thank you, God, for your endless patience. You don't judge me for reaching back toward the familiar; you love me, then and now, and you understand that newness, even when it's so much better, takes time to settle into. While I find my way to comfort, let me settle into you.

Regardless of how long ago he made you new, do you find yourself looking for—digging up—your old self? Take your thoughts before him and let him set you free from any old chains.

Gods Inspiration

Continue in what you have learned and have become convinced of, because you know those from whom you learned it, and how from infancy you have known the Holy Scriptures, which are able to make you wise for salvation through faith in Christ Jesus.

2 TIMOTHY 4:14-15 NIV

We don't just stop at salvation—there is so much more to learn about God. While you may be assured of the message of the gospel, it is important to continue to incorporate the Scripture into your daily life so it is always on your heart and ready to guide you in all your situations.

In the days of this Scripture, people had to rely on their memory and public readings of the Scripture. Our job is really much easier as we have the Scripture available at the touch of a button. Use this to your advantage, and soak yourself in the Word today.

God, give me creative ways to incorporate Scripture into my daily life. I don't want to stop at just being saved, I want to learn how to live a life that is wholly guided by your principles.

All Scripture is God-breathed and is useful for teaching, rebuking,
correcting and training in righteousness, so that the servant of God
may be thoroughly equipped for every good work.

2 TIMOTHY 4:16–17 NIV

Were you able to read a bit more Scripture today or have there
been too many things on your to-do list? Remember that
reading Scripture isn't about completing a task, it's there
because God wants you to be inspired by the words that he
has breathed life into.

God's Word is living, which means that he can speak into your
situations and heart at the moments when you need it the
most. Let him encourage you tonight, so you are equipped for
the day ahead.

Holy God, your Word really is a lamp to my feet and a light to my
path. Thank you for your incredible words that can help to correct,
train, and equip me to continue to do life with your guidance.
Holy Spirit, encourage my heart each day to remember these words
of life.

What is God speaking to you through his Word this evening?

Waiting for Perfect

Farmers who wait for perfect weather never plant. If they watch every cloud, they never harvest. Just as you cannot understand the path of the wind or the mystery of a tiny baby growing in its mother's womb, so you cannot understand the activity of God, who does all things.

ECCLESIASTES 11:4-5 NLT

Even in our modern age with all our scientific advantages, our weather still remains one of the most unpredictable phenomena. There are many unknowns when we set about to make decisions that we can often paralyze ourselves from doing anything. We try to wait for everything to line up and make sense, but how often are circumstances ideal? How often do we think we need to wait until they are?

We cannot control or predict much in life, but God can. Instead of putting trust in your ideas, trust in God's direction for you today.

God, sometimes I wait too long for the perfect timing. Help me to be realistic that there hardly ever is a "best time" to do things. Help me to do my very best today.

*Plant your seed in the morning and keep busy all afternoon,
for you don't know if profit will come from one activity or another—
or maybe both.*

ECCLESIASTES 11:6 NLT

We rarely get to the end of the day and feel like we have accomplished everything. What matters is that you have done something. The advice of Scripture is to decide that a few minutes late is better than absent. Let's acknowledge our collective fatigue, and know that we can only do our best.

Reflect on today and realize that waiting for a burst of creativity, or a break in the weather, is not the only thing you need to get on with work. Ask God to help you attack your projects, and see what happens.

God, I am tired and don't know if I was very productive today. Help me to stop waiting for the right time to get things done and instead work diligently toward the things that matter.

What are you waiting for? What do you need to start moving on?

Search Me

Search me, God, and know my heart;
test me and know my anxious thoughts.

PSALM 139:23 NIV

This may be the boldest prayer in all of Scripture. Think about it. Do you really want to ask God to search out every corner of your heart—to put your mind to a test that will reveal all your hidden anxieties? A predictable knee-jerk reaction would be a resounding, "No!" but what if we did ask, what if he did search?

Once God has exposed it all, there's nothing to hide. We may be afraid of discovering hidden flaws, but why? Once they're flushed out of hiding, we can deal with them. He can deal with them. What freedom awaits the sincere speaker of this prayer.

Okay, Lord. Search me. Show me what I've hidden, forgotten, and buried. Show me what has grown in the places I've neglected. Expose the lurking anxieties too vague to name, that they lose their hold on me completely. Lay bare unspoken jealousies and shame, so together we can confront them—and send them away. Search me, God, and set me free.

God, I invite your searching gaze into my heart.
Examine me through and through;
find out everything that may be hidden within me.
Put me to the test and sift through all my anxious cares.

PSALM 139:23 TPT

God sees even what we imagine, hears what we think but do not say. How deeply he must love us to forgive our every thought.

We may be tempted to hide the worst of it: the jealousy, anger, and fear, but then we would miss out on experiencing the depth of his love as he sends it all away. Let him in. Let him overwhelm it all with grace.

Come closer, Father. Is there anything tucked away in my heart that's keeping me from you? I want to show you everything so you can forgive it all, change it all, replace it all with love.

Are you ready to invite this experience? Sit with the Lord in however you are feeling about him sifting through your heart.

So It Will

> "I will give them one heart,
> and put a new spirit within them.
> And I will take the heart of stone out of their flesh
> and give them a heart of flesh."
>
> EZEKIEL 11:19 NASB

It's an incredible, beautiful, impossible picture: everyone with one heart. Every person on this earth believing, valuing, loving, and working for the same thing. We'd see an end to hunger, to war, and to oppression. None of those things would exist if the whole world had hearts that beat for God. No one could go hungry, because no one could bear to allow it. With nothing to fight about and no one to battle against, all fighting would have to cease.

All bearing the heart of God, all containing his Spirit, this world would be overwhelmed by beauty. There would be no end to grace. There would be no containing joy.

Father God, please do it. Remove my cold, hard heart and replace it with yours. What sound, the synchronous beating? What beauty, the glowing faces of those who are of your flesh. It sounds like heaven, God, and I'm ready for it to come.

> *"I will give them singleness of heart*
> *and put a new spirit within them.*
> *I will take away their stony, stubborn heart*
> *and give them a tender, responsive heart."*

EZEKIEL 11:19 NLT

I will. This isn't a fantasy. It's a promise. There will be a day where we all see eye to eye, and every eye is on the Savior. There will be a day when the Holy Spirit is the spirit that lives in every human soul.

There will be an end to selfishness, stubbornness, and cruelty. He said it will happen, and so it will.

God, I believe you. I believe you will change our hearts, renew our spirits, and unite us in purpose and in love. Your will be done, God, and may it be soon.

What promise of God's do you most eagerly await to see fulfilled?

Nothing Better

I know that there is nothing better for people than to be happy and to do good while they live. That each of them may eat and drink, and find satisfaction in all their toil—this is the gift of God.

ECCLESIASTES 3:12-13 NIV

It cannot be put more clearly. There is nothing better than to be happy in your life. Your life is made up of now. Each moment you live, each breath you take, it's right this very second.

To find happiness in your life is to find the best thing. And to find satisfaction in your effort is to find the gift of God. Treasure your life. Be satisfied with where you are. Satisfaction is living each day as if it were the dream.

God, I want to be content with where I am in life. Even more than that, I want to be happy. Thank you that you still care about my dreams, and thank you that life is a journey and process of shaping and re-shaping those dreams. Thank you for every moment, including right now.

I know that everything God does will endure forever;
nothing can be added to it and nothing taken from it.
God does it so that people will fear him.

ECCLESIASTES 3:14, NIV

Pretending we are someone else, or somewhere else, begins early in childhood and more subtly continues as we age. We still allow imagination to transport us to other places, and other circumstances.

Somehow it is easier for us to embrace the wonder of "what if" than the reality of "what is." Know who you are and where you are today, and embrace it all with faith.

Father, as I look back on some of my childhood dreams, I realize that it was nice to dream and it made me feel happy. But today is my reality and I pray that you would help me to see my life as a gift. Stir joy in my heart once again.

What dreams are you still holding on to? Enjoy the process of getting to those dreams and remember that God wants your happiness.

Precious Pursuit

Surely goodness and mercy shall follow me all the days of my life;
and I will dwell in the house of the LORD forever.

PSALM 23:6 NKJV

What is it about being followed by a puppy, or toddler, or pretty much anything adorable that makes us feel so special? When something precious pursues us, we feel precious. When something lovable wants to be near us, we feel lovable.

What a refreshing, uplifting image this is in Psalm 23, being followed by goodness and mercy. If goodness is staying close to us, we must be good. With mercy so near, we need only turn around to receive it. We must indeed be special for the Lord to send such welcome blessings to watch over us.

Father God, to feel your goodness and mercy at my back makes me feel safe, cherished, and special. Thank you, God, for your relentless pursuit of me, and for giving me grace on the many days I try to outrun it. Help me slow down so I am overtaken by your goodness and bombarded with your mercy and love.

Surely your goodness and love will follow me
all the days of my life,
and I will dwell in the house of the Lord forever.

PSALM 23:6 NIV

Where that girl comes, trouble follows. It's an old expression, but one that has held its meaning over time. When we leave a place, we leave something behind.

As children of God, our legacy can be goodness and love. What a goal, to be the kind of person who makes a deposit of love, and leaves a trail of goodness, everywhere we go. And why shouldn't it be when our home is with the Lord?

Yes, God, I want to leave a wake of goodness behind me, a legacy of truth. Like a delicate signature scent, let my presence leave sweet reminders of you behind. Because you are my home, the atmosphere around me is peaceful, generous, and good. Even after I'm gone, let these remain wherever I have been.

What qualities would people say you bring to a room? What is left behind when you depart?

Little Foxes

Catch for us the foxes, the little foxes that ruin the vineyards—
for our vineyards are in blossom.

SONG OF SOLOMON 2:15 NRSV

Foxes are known for their cunning. They're sneaky little things, hunting their prey on the sly. They're known for their ability to camouflage themselves, hiding as they circle, and then suddenly pouncing on their intended target.

Our enemy is a cunning one, and he uses our sin and temptations in the same sly way. They're camouflaged in the corners of our minds where we don't even notice until it's often too late. We see it when we're already caught, and our sin is shaking us to the point where we're ready to give up and give in.

God, give me an alert mind today, so I can be aware of the little things that try to creep in and destroy my relationship with you and with others. Let me catch the foxes before they cause harm.

My beloved is mine and I am his;
he pastures his flock among the lilies.

SONG OF SOLOMON 2:16 NRSV

God wants us to be like vineyards that are in bloom. This lush and beautiful field is where true relationships can develop, but we always need to be on guard for the foxes. It can be hard to know when a little fox has snuck into your heart.

Sometimes we are caught off guard and realize that we have let something unwanted come into our lives. Look for the ways that sin might be hiding in your heart, and give it over to God so he can prevent the unnecessary shaking in your life.

God, search my heart and give me wisdom and strength to get rid of the annoying little foxes that might be running amuck—I only want your goodness in my heart so I can truly bloom.

Can you identify the foxes in your situations? Ask for God's wisdom to discern what is from him and what is not.

Generous Heart

"Give, and it will be given to you. They will pour into your lap a good measure—pressed down, shaken together, and running over. For by your standard of measure it will be measured to you in return."

LUKE 6:38 NASB

I didn't want to go, but I forced myself and it ended up being an amazing night! It's so true, isn't it, and so often? When we deny our personal feelings and take one for the team, we are blessed by the experience in ways we wouldn't have imagined. A wife who reluctantly attends a work function for her husband meets a delightful new friend. A beleaguered mother ignores her fatigue and volunteers in her child's classroom, and receives a thank you gift of homemade bath salts.

God sees when our desire to help, to give, to serve outweighs our desire to rest, to hang onto what we have, and to be served. He so loves a generous heart, and especially when our generosity costs us something. He loves to give back even more than we let go.

Generous God, each time I give generously, you pour your blessings back on me. You replace what I gave and more, and you also grant me joy. You bring new people, new blessings, new gifts into my life each time I'm willing to give a piece of it away. Thank you for your generous heart.

"Give, and you will receive. You will be given much. Pressed down, shaken together, and running over, it will spill into your lap. The way you give to others is the way God will give to you."

LUKE 6:38 NCV

Some days, we just don't want to hear this. I'm generous enough. I do enough. It's human, and the Lord understands. He doesn't become angry with us or withhold his love. But we do miss out on some joy, and on the unexpected gifts that accompany our willingness to give.

On the days it's hard to go, go anyway. On the days you feel like there's nothing left to give, give anyway. And in so doing, be blessed.

Father God, even though I have seen your blessings a million times, I still have days where I just want to keep what's mine—my time, my resources. Thank you for reminding me it is you who gives them, and you who always replaces anything I willingly give in your name. And with the renewed supply, you add to it joy, friendship, and other beautiful gifts.

Spend some time recalling the many blessings you have received through giving. Thank the Lord for his incredible generosity toward you, and for giving you a generous heart.

Fierce Love

Place me like a seal over your heart, like a seal on your arm;
for love is as strong as death, its jealousy unyielding as the grave.
It burns like blazing fire, like a mighty flame.

SONG OF SOLOMON 8:6 NIV

God's love is not weak. When we think of love in a romantic
way, it can seem like a delicate concept. Yet love is the thing
that holds people together through storms; it is the force that
compels us to act impulsively or irrationally. It drives almost
all our decisions and behaviors.

Love is as strong and real as death, and God is the author
of this powerful emotion. As you consider his love this
morning, think about the power of love, and let your faith be
strengthened because of this power.

God, I am grateful for your love that gives me so much purpose.
Help me to live today in the strength of your love, and to let the
power of love emanate from me to others.

Many waters cannot quench love; rivers cannot sweep it away.
If one were to give all the wealth of one's house for love,
it would be utterly scorned.

SONG OF SOLOMON 8:6 NIV

There is, quite literally, nothing that can compare to love.
Humans have been trying to explain love from the beginning
of creation, yet it doesn't seem as though words are enough.
When we see true love in action, it illuminates God, because
he is love.

When you see love that changes lives, situations, and
relationships for the better, you know that is God's power. We
can't get enough of love, and love won't go away. Embrace it,
accept it, and give it without limit.

God, let me be a person who loves fiercely. Let me give all that I can
because I know you have given me everything out of your great love
for me. Allow my heart to be full of this love tonight, and let me be
ready to give without limits tomorrow.

Have you experienced God's love today? Be ready to give it
away tomorrow.

Keep Still

> The LORD will fight for you,
> and you shall hold your peace.
>
> EXODUS 14:14 NKJV

What do you carry into battle? In a literal sense, you bring a weapon and a shield. Battling an illness, you might come armed with medications and a treatment plan. Facing a tough conversation, you hold onto your convictions and your well-rehearsed point of view. How often, in any battle do you consider bringing peace?

"And you shall hold your peace." What a beautiful picture this is, letting God do the fighting while we fill our arms with peace. Imagine heading into every confrontation behind the Lord. He devises the plan of attack, he determines the outcome, and because you trust him, because you know he is good and that he fights for you, you hold onto peace.

Lord God, with you as my sword and shield, my arms are free. Whatever enemy I face, I trust you to lead the fight. Peace is the sword I carry, disarming fear. Peace is also the shield that covers me, protecting me from doubt. Victory is ours and after victory, even more peace.

The LORD will fight for you,
and you have only to keep still.

EXODUS 14:14, NRSV

Shhh. Just keep still. One of the first lessons you learn about hide and seek is the value of stillness. The "enemy" may be only inches from you, but if you don't move, if you don't make a sound, they may leave without realizing you are even there.

Silence can keep you safe. When we trust the Lord to fight for us, one of the best things we can do is be still and let him fight. Resist the urge to run past him, swinging your sword. Keep still, hold your peace, and watch him win.

Oh Father, I don't always get this one right, do I? I ask for your help, I say I'm going to trust you, and then the moment things don't seem to be happening fast enough, or going my way, I jump up and give away my position. Help me to keep still. I know that you are God, and I trust you with my life.

Are you comfortable with keeping still, holding your peace, and trusting the Lord to fight your battles, or do you tend to run into the fray? Call on the Holy Spirit to increase your trust.

Rejoice

Rejoice in the Lord always. I will say it again: Rejoice!

PHILIPPIANS 4:4 NIV

Have you ever just decided to be happy? Maybe you didn't really want to be where you were, or be doing what you were doing, but you knew that if you just embraced it, you could find a way to enjoy it? We can't always control our situations, and emotions sneak up on us sometimes, but attitude is a choice. Choose joy!

What might this look like? Praise music—and a bit of dancing like no one's watching—while you clean. Meditating on the Lord's beauty while you wait. Remembering his blessings on your daily commute. You'll still be cleaning, waiting, commuting, but if you choose it, the joy of the Lord can join you there.

I confess it, Lord. My first thought was that this can't be done. I can't always feel joyful. Then, once again, you helped me see through your wise and joyful eyes. I may not feel amazing, but I can still rejoice. I can raise my voice, move my feet, and recall all the ways you bring joy to life. Before I know it, my feelings just may join the song.

Rejoice in the Lord always; again I will say, rejoice.

PHILIPPIANS 4:4 ESV

What of the happy days, where joy comes as easily as breath? Do you remember to invite the Lord to the celebration?

As you revel, as you glory and glee, do you remember the author of joy? A wonderful situation can take our eyes off the One who made it possible. Caught up in the moment, we can forget its Maker. Rejoice in the Lord; he's waiting to dance with you.

Oh, Father, sometimes the best moments are the ones I forget to thank you for. I'm wrapped up in the happiness of the people I love, the fun and the laughter, and I fail to notice you there, smiling, the one who made it happen. I owe all my best memories to you, along with all my thanks and praise. Each time I rejoice, God, let my first thought be of you.

Your Father wants you to be able to rejoice always. Which of today's perspectives felt more "for you"?

Appreciate the Faithful

I am praying that you will put into action the generosity that comes from your faith as you understand and experience all the good things we have in Christ. Your love has given me much joy and comfort, my brother, for your kindness has often refreshed the hearts of God's people.

PHILEMON 1:6-7 NLT

If you could write a letter to someone who has been a loyal, faithful, servant of Christ, would it sound a lot like what Paul has written to Philemon? Encouraging people with your words is a good habit to get into.

If you think about a time when you have been extremely generous or kind, you will know that it feels right to be appreciated. Take note today of people who have demonstrated kindness, and remember to show your appreciation.

Jesus, thank you for your loyal servants that are all around. Their generosity and kindness is what keeps your church encouraged and refreshed. Refresh those people who are selflessly doing your work, and remind me to appreciate them as often as I can.

*That is why I am boldly asking a favor of you. I could demand it in
the name of Christ because it is the right thing for you to do.
But because of our love, I prefer simply to ask you.
Consider this as a request from me—Paul, an old man
and now also a prisoner for the sake of Christ Jesus.*

PHILEMON 1:8-9 NLT

Trust between friends is a wonderful thing. Paul could have
placed an obligation on Philemon to help him out, but instead
he knew that as a faithful friend, all he needed to do was ask.

Do you have friends that you can trust like this? Everybody
needs that kind and generous person in their life who
they can trust will help them out when they need it. More
importantly, are you someone that a friend could ask to help
them in time of need?

*Jesus, thank you for the generosity of friends in my life. I pray that
you would increase my love for others so I can also be someone
who is relied upon to do the right thing. Help me to be a person who
is trusted to take care of others.*

Will you respond generously to a request from a friend?

Letting Him Drive

> LORD, I know that people's lives are not their own;
> it is not for them to direct their steps.
>
> JEREMIAH 10:23 NIV

When you surrendered your life to Christ, how much thought did you put into the fact that you were surrendering your life? Jesus, Take the Wheel is a great song, but most of us have a hard time actually removing our hands and letting him drive. It sounds scary—and it would be, if we didn't have such an awesome, faithful God.

We can trust him! With every step we take in faith, we can believe we are moving toward meaning, truth, and light. His plan is perfect, and unlike anyone else we will ever meet, he cannot, will not, steer us wrong.

God, I trust you. I have faith in the plans you have for me, and despite my grasping fingers, I do want you to drive. Every place you lead me is just where I belong, and each time you draw me onward, I know the way will be rewarding and the destination sweet. You will never steer me wrong; I trust you with my life.

> *I know, O LORD, that the way of human beings*
> *is not in their control,*
> *that mortals as they walk cannot direct their steps.*

JEREMIAH 10:23 NRSV

When we follow the Lord, we don't need to know where we are going. We don't have to worry about leading someone else in the wrong direction. When we have trusted him with our journeys, we are free to simply live.

Even if we wander off the path—and we will wander—his marvelous light will show us the way back. What a relief this is, knowing the one we follow knows exactly where we need to go, and will do everything in his awesome power to get us there.

Father, I feel so free when I follow you. I don't need the map; I just need to keep you in my sight. Speeding up and slowing down in rhythm with you, I trust the journey because I trust my leader. I pray that it will be obvious to anyone following me that you are the one true guide.

How much comfort do you take —or resistance do you feel— knowing it is God who directs your steps?

Spiritual Growth

You have been believers so long now that you ought to be teaching others. Instead, you need someone to teach you again the basic things about God's word. You are like babies who need milk and cannot eat solid food.

HEBREWS 5:12 NLT

It would be frustrating to go to school and never learn a thing. The point of learning is to gain understanding so we can be better skilled and prepared for what is ahead.

In the same way, our goal is to become mature in Christ. Maturity brings a sureness to your faith and steady trust that Christ is working through you. You might not reach this goal today, but you are on your way.

God, thank you that you allow me to grow in you each day. Help me to be a little more mature in you today than I was yesterday.

Someone who lives on milk is still an infant and doesn't know how to do what is right. Solid food is for those who are mature, who through training have the skill to recognize the difference between right and wrong.

HEBREWS 5:13–14 NLT

Not too long after our bones finish growing, we realize the real growth is just getting started. We start to experience relationships, working, and responsibilities. In each of these things, we need Godly wisdom—the ability to discern what is right and wrong in our decision making.

No matter what our age today, most of us are still working on wisdom. When we are growing in Christ, it's a process that never really ends. Scripture says this is the way he made you, to grow in your humanity, becoming physically and spiritually mature.

Jesus, I ask that you will help me to grow in wisdom each day as I am stretched and challenged.

Reflect on your growth tonight. Where is God stretching and challenging you?

Good Work

God is not unjust; he will not overlook your work and the love that you showed for his sake in serving the saints, as you still do.

HEBREWS 6:10 NRSV

When we accept the gift of Christ's salvation, we can be assured that we will live for eternity with our Father in heaven. There is nothing that we can do by our actions alone that ensures a place for us. But that doesn't mean the buck stops there.

Though not a requirement for admittance through the pearly gates, a life lived doing good deeds is something every Christ follower should seek to attain.

Thank you, Jesus, for showing me how to live a life a love and humility. Help others to see my good works and to recognize that my life has been marked by you.

We want each one of you to show the same diligence so as to realize the full assurance of hope to the very end, so that you may not become sluggish, but imitators of those who through faith and patience inherit the promises.

HEBREWS 6:11-12 NRSV

You may not have thought today was much different from the last, and perhaps you don't see the good deeds that you have done as being particularly spiritual. Remember that God created you as an image-bearer, that just by choosing to follow Jesus you are being like him.

Be encouraged that you are a shining example of his love and that others will see how a life with Christ is a beautiful one.

Jesus, I choose to believe in your light and your love, and I choose to follow you. There are people I saw today, and there will be people I see tomorrow; I ask that I will continue to influence them with the truth of a life in Christ.

What is different about your life? Can others see that you love Jesus by the choices you are making?

Money Love

*Keep your lives free from the love of money,
and be content with what you have; for he has said,
"I will never leave you or forsake you."*

HEBREWS 13:5 NRSV

Sometimes money feels like water in our hands. It slips right through our fingers and is gone as soon as it's acquired.

As Christians, we know that we should trust God with our every need. But do we really? Are we confident that no matter what circumstances come our way, God is going to take care of our finances? Or do we become consumed with worry that we will not have enough?

Holy Spirit, I invite you into my financial life today. I know that you are involved in all parts of life and that you know the wisest way about everything. Please guide me in wisdom with money; let me not fall into the trap of spending more than I need to.

We can say with confidence, "The Lord is my helper;
I will not be afraid. What can anyone do to me?"

HEBREWS 13:6 NRSV

Right after God tells us not to love money, he reminds us that he'll never leave or forsake us. He knew that we would worry about our finances. He knew that fear would come far more easily than contentment.

Remember that no matter how little or how much money you have, God is control. He is more than able to provide for all your needs and he will never forsake you.

Jesus, teach me contentment. I have a lot of things that I feel like I need right now, and I need perspective to know that a lot of these things are just a matter of wanting. Help me to prioritize generosity over consuming.

What are you spending your money on? Are you content with what you have?

In His Example

The reward for humility and fear of the LORD
is riches and honor and life.

PROVERBS 22:4 ESV

If someone offered to give you a new car if you would simply wash theirs, how long would it take you to grab your bucket and sponge? A reward so much greater than the sacrifice is hard to resist. And yet we do.

All God asks of us in exchange for an abundant, rewarding life is that we give him the respect he deserves. He wants our humble, sincere acknowledgement that his ways are better. He wants our trust. As we place our faith in him, life grows richer in every way. We acknowledge our smallness, and he makes us greater. We willingly offer him all we have, and he gives us more than we ever wanted.

God, what you offer is so much greater than what you ask. For humility, you offer honor. And yet I cling to pride. For respect you offer riches, abundance, and life, and yet I stubbornly insist on my own way. Help me, God, to remember who you are. You are God, the Almighty. You deserve all my love and respect, and in return, though I don't deserve it at all, you give me all of yours.

Laying your life down in tender surrender before the Lord
will bring life, prosperity, and honor as your reward.

PROVERBS 22:4 TPT

Perhaps the reason humility is so hard to achieve is that we so desire its promised reward of honor. Perhaps the reason it's so hard to give up control is that we so desire the prosperous, abundant life we are told is waiting.

Focused on the prize, we lose our footing on the path. Doesn't this prove our smallness, our utter need for him? We simply cannot do this without the Lord. The glory and riches we crave are only found in him, in his example. Humbling, isn't it? And the humbling sets us on our way.

Precious Jesus, only in you can I find the perfection, the blessings, and the glory I strive for. I want, I reach, and I grab. And then I am reminded of you, who wanted only to see me saved; who reached only those who needed healing; who grabbed only onto the Father's will. And I am humbled. Thank you, God, for your incredible humility. One step at a time, may I follow your example straight to my reward.

What prize have you been too focused on lately? Can you allow God to step in and help you reach your goal?

This Is the Way

Your ears shall hear a word behind you, saying,
"This is the way, walk in it."

ISAIAH 30:21 NKJV

Decisions, decisions. It seems a week never goes by without our needing to make at least one important choice. Whether job related, relationship motivated, or something as seemingly innocent as how to spend a free Friday, wouldn't it be nice to have an arrow pointing us in the right direction—especially if we are in danger of making a wrong turn?

According to the Word, we have exactly that. When we truly desire to walk the path God sets us on, and when we earnestly seek his voice, he promises to lead us in the right direction. Stay on his path today.

God, I need your help with some important decisions today. Let my ears hear your voice to guide me in the right direction.

Whenever you turn to the right hand
or whenever you turn to the left.

Isaiah 30:21 NKJV

Consider the decisions you have had to make today. What decisions will you need to make tomorrow? Whether you choose the right or the left, know that God is able to guide you into his best for the situation.

You might not get it right every time but his ever-present Spirit is right there, ready to put you back on the path each time you wander off.

Holy Spirit, thank you that you are the guiding voice behind me. Help me to become more aware of what you are speaking to me.

What guidance do you need right now?

Not Just Fair

*Every valley shall be lifted up, and every mountain
and hill be made low; the uneven ground shall become level,
and the rough places a plain.*

ISAIAH 40:4 NRSV

Imagine an arena where everyone—in every seat—had the same, unobstructed, close-up view of the stage or field. Imagine a hotel in which every single room had an identical, gorgeous view of the ocean—of both the rising and the setting sun. Imagine everything not just equal and fair, but extraordinary and wonderful. Imagine!

One day we won't have to imagine it. One day, this will be true. All will be well; all will be easy. No climbing, no stumbling, no struggle. No straining to see. Not just fair, but glorious, one day we will all gaze upon the King.

Father, how I love imagining this. The beauty, the glory, the sound—and I with a front row seat. Everyone, everywhere with a front row seat. You are so much more than fair, God; you are generous, extravagant, and gloriously good.

*Every valley shall be lifted up, and every mountain
and hill be made low; the uneven ground shall become level,
and the rough places a plain.*

ISAIAH 40:4 ESV

There will be days this promise can't come soon enough—
days it may be hard to cling to. Pain, grief and loss can leave
us feeling lost, circling a mountain ever higher, the summit
remaining out of reach.

Keep climbing. Climb with the hope of one who knows the
path will become smooth, flat, and easy. He has said it is so.

*I believe you, God. The struggle ends. I believe you enough to keep
struggling. I know every step I take in faith will be rewarded with
blessings. I know every stumble, switchback, and trip through the
valley is carrying me nearer to you. Your promise gives me hope,
and your hope fuels my steps. All will be right; all will be well.
As far as any eye can see, every path will end at you.*

Which part of the climb do you relate to right now?

Look Up

Lift up your eyes on high and see who has created these stars,
the One who leads forth their host by number,
He calls them all by name.

ISAIAH 40:26 NASB

If you have ever had the chance to be in a remote location on a clear night, you will know what it is like to look up into the sky and marvel at the magnificent display of stars. It is such a breathtaking view—one that reminds us of the greatness of our God.

Do you feel insignificant in God's great world today? Remember that God has a perfect plan for this world, and you complete the plan. Lift up your eyes and know that God knows your name and that you are not missing from his plan.

God, you are so great. When I think of everything you created, I am amazed that you care about a plan for my life. Thank you that I can trust that you are in control.

Because of the greatness of His might
and the strength of His power,
not one of them is missing.

ISAIAH 40:26 NASB

Many times, in the Bible, humanity is compared to the stars. We are reminded of how many people God has created. Yet, God says that he both leads and calls them by name.

If the stars appear magnificent, then how much more magnificent is the One who created them? We worship a God who is able to remember each of us by name, and to know that not one of us is missing.

God, I am blessed that you know my name. As I go to sleep tonight, I am reminded of the wonderful life that you have planned for me. Even when things get hard, I know that you lead and call me into your light.

Can you look back on your life and recognize God's hand in significant moments? Thank this great and almighty God for his specific care for your life.

Let Him

*It's time to be made new by every revelation
that's been given to you.*

EPHESIANS 4:23 TPT

An injured animal will sometimes reject your help.
Experience or instinct may have taught them to fear you, so
you must approach them gently, with open hands. Though
we have no reason to fear the Lord, he knows life can leave us
skittish, like a bird with a damaged wing or a deer caught in
barbed wire. And so, he comes gently.

He won't insist we accept his help; we must allow it. He can
take every broken, damaged, wounded attitude, every ugly,
sinful thought, and make them new—if we will let him. With
your permission, the Spirit offers wholeness where you are
fragmented, confidence in place of your fear, and gentleness
where the world has made you fierce. If you will let him, the
Spirit will make you new.

*Holy Spirit, help me accept the gift of newness you offer. As you
reveal more and more of your goodness, more and more of your
intentions toward me, let me be made new. Where I fear, give me
faith. Where I doubt, give me confidence. Where I would cower,
give me the strength to rise. God, wherever I would resist you, with
your help, I will let you make me new.*

Let the Spirit renew your thoughts and attitudes.

Ephesians 4:23 NLT

Is there anything on this earth more difficult to control than the mind? If we could control our anxious thoughts, if we could prevent selfish desires from taking hold, how much easier it would be to stay in God's will.

As with so many things in God's kingdom, the way to this blessed control is surrender. We must give him the thoughts as they arise, hand over the attitudes the moment they show themselves, and let him turn them into something lovely, good, and new.

God, send your ever-helpful Spirit to renew my mind. I need my unworthy thoughts replaced with revelations of your worthiness, remembrances of your beauty. I need fear sent away by confidence and faith. I am too weak, God, my mind is too small. Holy Spirit, replace it with the mind of Christ, and give me strength.

Spend some time baring your mind before the Lord, inviting the Holy Spirit to renew every thought and attitude that is keeping you from experiencing more of the bountiful, blessed life he wants you to have.

New Paths

"I am about to do something new.
See, I have already begun! Do you not see it?"

ISAIAH 43:19 NLT

The clean slate of a new day is filled with an air of expectation.
It's like deep down inside, there is something built into our
heart and mind that longs to start afresh.

This morning is that chance for you to start again. You may
have had a bad day yesterday or felt like you didn't complete
what you needed to, but today is a new day. Whether you
are a goal setter or someone who approaches the day with
a "whatever may come" attitude, you have God's mercy and
grace to help you achieve it.

God, thank you for letting me start new today and every day.
I pray for the faith to see what you have already begun.

> *"I will make a pathway through the wilderness.*
> *I will create rivers in the dry wasteland."*
>
> ISAIAH 43:19 NLT

This day, and every one that follows, is yours. It is yours to choose who and how to love, to serve, and even to be.

The choice you made in reading this page represents the choice to take this journey in the company of your heavenly Father. This is how you give him space to create pathways and rivers in those dry areas of your life. That is a beautiful place to start.

God, thank you for remaining faithful to me today. Help me to make space for you to create paths and rivers in areas that I feel tired and dry.

What new thing would you like to do? What pathways do you need God to clear?

Never Too Late

Behold, the LORD's hand is not so short that it cannot save.

ISAIAH 59:1 NASB

When Jesus hung on the cross, there were two thieves hanging beside him. One of those thieves, as he hung in his final moments of life, asked Jesus for grace and a second chance. That thief—minutes before death—was given forgiveness and eternal life.

The very same day he entered paradise as a forgiven and clean man. In light of his story, how can we ever say that it's too late to turn it all around?

Give me a fresh start today, God. I need to remember that your mercy and forgiveness awaits me every single morning. I trust in that forgiveness today and ask for a renewed sense of purpose.

Nor is His ear so dull that it cannot hear.

ISAIAH 59:1 NASB

Do you have regrets in your life that you wish you could take back? Things that you aren't proud of? You lay awake at night thinking about mistakes you've made and you wonder if you've gone too far to ever get back.

If you feel like it's too late to change something in your life for the better, remember the story of the thief on the cross. There is always hope in Jesus. The God we serve is the God of second chances. That might sound cliché, but it couldn't be truer. His love has no end and his grace knows no boundary. It is never too late for you to follow him with your life.

God, thank you for reminding me that your love is always ready to save me from worry, fear, or self-doubt. Help me to rest tonight in the knowledge that you are willing and ready to rescue me.

What do you need saving from this evening? Ask God to help you and trust that he will listen.

We Have Time

Be careful how you live. Don't live like fools, but like those who are wise. Make the most of every opportunity in these evil days. Don't act thoughtlessly, but understand what the Lord wants you to do.

EPHESIANS 5:15–17 NLT

Time is one of those things we never seem to have enough of. Many days we race against the clock to get everything done. We seem to lack the time we need for even the most important things—things like being in God's Word, spending intentional time with loved ones, or volunteering to help those in need.

Take a good hard look at your day today and think about how you can spend your time most wisely—in a way that will make the most of the moments and opportunities you have.

Lord, I take this opportunity now to prioritize time with you. I pray that you would help me create more and more space for these times.

Be careful how you walk, not as unwise men but as wise, making the most of your time, because the days are evil. So then do not be foolish, but understand what the will of the Lord is.

EPHESIANS 5:15-17 NASB

At the end of the day, there is one reality we must remember: we have time for what we make time for. It's easy to feel busy, but what are we truly busying ourselves with? Are we finding time to spend browsing social media or watching re-runs of our favorite TV shows? Are we finding time to take a long shower or sleep for a few extra minutes in the morning?

Things we choose to make time for aren't always wrong, but if we feel pressed for time and are unable to spend time with the Lord, we may need to rethink where our time goes.

Heavenly Father, I thank you for yet another opportunity to think about you and my faith. I want to honor you in giving this time to you and pray that you would bless me by speaking into my life so I am restored and renewed by these times.

How are you spending most of your time in the evenings? Could your priorities use a reshuffle?

Struggle to Trust

Trust in the LORD with all your heart,
And lean not on your own understanding;
In all your ways acknowledge Him,
And He shall direct your paths.

PROVERBS 3:5-6 NKJV

There can be seasons where things don't work out in your favor and life seems harder than normal. It could be related to relationships, work, sports, or even family dynamics. When things are tough in these areas, it tends to greatly affect our feelings, our mindset, and even our trust in God. We might feel like we're in the desert all alone.

The good news is that God knows just where we are. We are not lost. Many times when we are walking through difficult situations, the Lord has allowed us to experience those difficulties to test what is in our hearts. He is refining and maturing us.

God, I know you are trying to teach me something. I want to be willing to learn. Please give me strength.

Trust the LORD with all your heart,
and don't depend on your own understanding.
Remember the LORD in all you do,
and he will give you success.

PROVERBS 3:5-6 NCV

The next time you find yourself in one of these seasons, don't stop trusting God! Go to him immediately and ask him what he wants to teach you. Though it may feel like he is far away, he's actually close by, molding and shaping you like a potter does with clay.

When you make yourself vulnerable to God, he will reveal the things he is working on, and assure you that there is purpose to your season in the desert. Trust in him and he will carry you through!

God, I admit I don't like being in the desert. But I want to grow and mature in my relationship with you, so teach me while I'm here.

Are you struggling to trust God in this season?

True Religion

*Pure and undefiled religion in the sight of our God
and Father is this: to visit orphans and widows in their distress,
and to keep oneself unstained by the world.*

JAMES 1:27 NASB

Many people today ask what religion can do for them.
How can it alleviate their fears, save them from death, and
improve their quality of life? Christianity has never been
about what we can get from it.

True religion— the kind that is acceptable to God—is found
in giving ourselves to those who need the most. It's not about
our comfort, our happiness, or even our ticket to heaven. It's
about reflecting the glory of Christ on the earth.

*Jesus, I want to reflect your glory today. Give me the opportunity to
give to those in need in any form that it might come. Give me the
boldness to respond, and keep me from ignorance.*

Religion that is pure and undefiled before God the Father is this:
to visit orphans and widows in their affliction,
and to keep oneself unstained from the world.

JAMES 1:27 ESV

The tender Father heart of God is far more interested in developing your love and Christ-like character than he is in keeping you comfortable. His compassion and intense love for mankind will not be satisfied with comfortable, cushioned Christianity.

If you want to bring praise to God, intentionally seek out situations where you can put into practice your undefiled religion. Make it your mission to meet needs, to love, and to bring life.

God, I am glad to have been more aware of the needs around me today. I know that everyday there will be an opportunity, so I pray for wisdom with how to respond to the call of helping others.

Where and when can you best respond to the needs of others around you?

Real Value

*"Where your treasure is,
there your heart will be also."*

MATTHEW 6:21 NIV

Status, titles, popularity, and expensive houses are some common things valued by society. It's difficult not to value these ourselves. But what has true value?

God wants us to focus on valuing things that are of him—things like love, generosity, righteousness, and honesty. These bring lasting value because they add to the kingdom of heaven. Titles and popularity are temporary; they can be taken away in a single day. Think about the things you value today.

God, I know there are things that I have been valuing too greatly. Help me to reevaluate the actual worth of what I am pursuing.

*"Wherever your treasure is,
there the desires of your heart will also be."*

MATTHEW 6:21 NLT

If you happen to be popular, or can afford that expensive house, that's fine, but the moment you find yourself being motivated by, and becoming focused on, those things, you have given it too much value. You can't place equal value on homes and righteousness; it just doesn't work that way.

God is not impressed by status. He is, however, very impressed by the love he sees in your heart, the honest words you speak, and the generosity you display. Be aware of what you find valuable because that is what your heart will spend the most time going after.

Father, help me to place the right value on the right things. I want to chase after real treasure.

What do you think is valuable in life?

Yes Faith

Abram believed the Lord. And the Lord accepted Abram's faith,
and that faith made him right with God.

GENESIS 15:6 NCV

Have you ever stepped out and said yes to something crazy for God? You followed him into the middle of the ocean and trusted him to keep you afloat. Stepping out in faith isn't easy. In fact, it's messy. It's a lot of wondering what you're doing, and why you're doing it. It's a lot of closing your eyes and begging God to remind you of all the things he placed on your heart when he originally gave you the vision.

When you stand in the truth that you have obeyed, it doesn't really matter how everything looks or feels. What matters is that you were obedient. You believed what God was telling you.

God, I say yes to you this morning! Yes to your Word, yes to your calling, yes to your truth.

Abram believed the Lord,
and he credited it to him as righteousness.

GENESIS 15:6 NIV

Stepping out in faith is about boldly facing your harshest
critics and telling them you're not sure if everything will work
out. It's being at peace in total chaos. It's putting yourself
out there and wondering if you'll live up to expectation. It's
wondering if you have anything to offer after all.

There is peace in obedience—peace that even when you're
criticized, laughed at, and misunderstood, the God of the
universe is pleased. And everything else fades away in light
of that awesome reality. If God is asking you to do something
that terrifies you, step out in faith. Obey him. Believe him. It
will be worth it.

*Lord God, you are awesome. I believe in your plan for my life and
for how my life fits into the bigger picture. Tonight, I choose to trust
in this plan for my life, and I pray that you would give me the
courage to take this hope into the days to come.*

How is God testing your faith? Are you willing to say yes?

Not Beyond Repair

He heals the brokenhearted
and bandages their wounds.

PSALM 147:3 NLT

Sometimes when we look closely at ourselves, all we see is a broken and shattered remnant of what we once were. Sin, tragedy, rejection, or heartbreak can leave us feeling terrible. We wonder how we can pick up the pieces and be made whole again.

In our brokenness, it's easy to feel hopeless. We try so many methods to fill the void. We may look to relationships, things, or drugs to fix us. They can make us feel better temporarily, but eventually we realize that despite all our efforts, we still feel broken and incomplete.

Jesus, I don't know how you do it, but I thank you for loving me in all of my brokenness. I ask you to make me whole today.

He heals the brokenhearted
and binds up their wounds.

God is faithful. He doesn't leave us alone in our brokenness, instead, he meets us in our ugliness, takes our broken pieces, and tenderly puts us back together again. Why? Because he loves us too much to leave us in the state we are in. He wants us to experience healing and restoration.

In him we find wholeness that the best doctor or medicine can't provide. He is the only one that can heal our pain completely. His love is so deep it can even remove scars.

Father, I need you tonight. Only you can heal the inner parts of me that feel like they are beyond repair.

Trust God in your brokenness today.

Point of Worry

"Can all your worries add a single moment to your life?"

MATTHEW 6:27 NLT

It's easy to worry about the future. How am I going to do on my review? Am I going to get that promotion? What will she say when I confront her? How am I going to pay down my debt? These are a few examples that can send our minds racing.

What is the point of worry? Has worry ever helped anyone feel better? Has it ever solved the problem? No. Each day has enough problems of its own. It is better to take each day one step at a time and let God lead us through it. The things that are for tomorrow will still be there tomorrow, and that's where they should stay for now. Then, when the time comes, we can ask God for help.

God, I take rest and comfort in knowing that you are for me and you are more than enough. Let those thoughts eliminate the worry that tries to creep into my mind today.

"Can any one of you by worrying add a single hour to your life?"
MATTHEW 6:27 NIV

Everything you walk through with God is not going to be easy, but worry does not have to be part of it. If you seek God during tough times, you can have confidence that he has heard you, and he will work out his good and perfect will.

We often rehash things and stir up all kinds of new worry. Don't go there. Let God take care of it, and allow yourself to let it go. Everything is not always going to land in your favor, and everyone isn't always going to be thrilled with you. You can try your best, but the real work belongs to God. Let him do it.

Father, tonight I place all my concerns in your hands and let them go. Thank you for taking them from me.

Where are your most common areas of worry, and how can you let God carry you through them?

Storytelling

Jesus constantly used these illustrations when speaking to the crowds. In fact, because the prophets said that he would use so many, he never spoke to them without at least one illustration. For it had been prophesied, "I will talk in parables; I will explain mysteries hidden since the beginning of time."

MATTHEW 13:34-35 TLB

We enjoy listening to stories because they help us to relate with a concept and personalize an idea. We hear a lofty explanation and struggle to understand, but a story illustrates the same thought and we become connected to it.

Jesus was a storyteller. While he walked the earth, he told people many stories in order to teach them something. Jesus used parables and imagery instead of just spitting it out so that people would meditate, speculate, study, and absorb the words to better understand them. The parables that Jesus told weren't just simple stories; their symbolisms revealed secrets of the kingdom of heaven and made its glory digestible for the common man.

Thank you, Jesus, for your stories. Open my eyes to see the creativity and truth in them.

All these things Jesus spoke to the multitude in parables;
and without a parable He did not speak to them,
that it might be fulfilled which was spoken by the prophet, saying:
"I will open My mouth in parables;
I will utter things kept secret from the foundation of the world."

MATTHEW 13:34-35 NKJV

When people who don't know God hear the Gospel, it can be confusing because their eyes have not been opened by the Holy Spirit. When you share with them your own story of God's work in your life, their hearts and minds may be more easily opened.

Take a few moments to think about who you could share your God stories with this week.

Heavenly Father, I thank you that you have given me my own story. Help me to tell my story, in honesty and creativity, so that people's hearts and minds can be opened to the power of your grace in my life.

What is your story of God's work in your life?

The Struggle

Let your roots grow down into him and draw up nourishment from him. See that you go on growing in the Lord, and become strong and vigorous in the truth you were taught. Let your lives overflow with joy and thanksgiving for all he has done.

COLOSSIANS 2:7 TLB

In the weeks leading up to Thanksgiving, the theme of gratitude becomes all but inescapable. This can be wonderful, reminding us of all the good in our lives, but it can also be painful. What if we're in a season where thankfulness eludes us? What if counting our blessings seems to take no time at all?

If this is you, you are not alone. Pore over his Word, and let his love and truth pour over you. The struggle will end. The blessings will come. All will be well.

Lord, today help me to be full of gratitude even if I'm finding it hard to be thankful. You are always good and faithful.

*Having been firmly rooted and now being built up in Him
and established in your faith, just as you were instructed,
and overflowing with gratitude.*

COLOSSIANS 2:7 NASB

There will always be times when struggle seems more
prevalent than blessing, when gratitude seems like an
impossible requirement, and faith, once so familiar, has
gone into hiding.

Release your heart from any guilt bubbling up inside, and
sink your roots into Jesus. Let gratitude and faith overflow
from one into the other, and may all your roots intertwine in
the rich, fertile soil of God's love and truth.

*Thank you, God, that I can depend on you for a heart of gratitude.
It doesn't always come naturally, but it is possible to dwell on
the many blessings I have and create an underlying attitude of
thankfulness.*

Begin speaking out all the things you are grateful for.

Appetite

"No one can serve two masters; for a slave will either hate the one and love the other, or be devoted to the one and despise the other. You cannot serve God and wealth."

MATTHEW 6:24 NRSV

Appetite is a funny thing. Our bodies have the ability to communicate hunger to our brains, and our brains then cause us to seek out a solution to the problem. When we are genuinely hungry, we look for food that will fill our stomachs and quiet our hunger.

Our souls have appetites also, but we so easily fill our time and energy with the world's entertainment. We fill ourselves up with things that will never be able to satisfy and leave little room for the only one who can.

Lord, when I get hungry today, remind me also to hunger for you. Help me to fill that hunger with goodness and not evil, so I am spiritually fit and healthy.

> *"No one can serve two masters. The person will hate one master and love the other, or will follow one master and refuse to follow the other. You cannot serve both God and worldly riches."*
>
> MATTHEW 6:24, NCV

There is a throne in your heart upon which only one master can sit—and you must choose wisely who will take residence there.

Will you allow your life to be ruled by the pursuit of things which will never last, or will you accept nothing less than eternal stock for your life's investment?

Lord God, be the master of my life. I don't want to be ruled by this world and the things that so easily trap me. Teach me to resist the temptations that easily distract me from your ways. Let me walk in your light and only serve you.

Are you battling between two masters? Ask God to help you to love him first.

Declared Holy

He brought out his people with rejoicing,
his chosen ones with shouts of joy.

PSALM 105:43 NIV

Have you ever felt captive to the dark thoughts inside your head? Do you sometimes feel trapped by the poor choices you've made? Has life been overwhelming you with all you've endured?

Rejoice, my friend, because you no longer need to feel imprisoned by it all. The Bible tells us that we are set free from what would enslave us. God has set aside his chosen ones, and that includes you!

Oh God, the joy I feel because of you is indescribable. I'm so thankful you have set me free from all that burdened me.

He brought his people out with joy,
his chosen ones with singing.

PSALM 105:43 ESV

God has brought us out of bondage and into joy. He chose to rescue us and as he does, he sings over us!

Release your feelings of guilt—and your burdens—and instead be glad. There is great joy in being able to relieve yourself of the heaviness you've been carrying around. And you can do so because our God and Savior has wiped your slate clean. It's time to party—you are free!

Father, I pray I'd continue to shake off the chains of sin and remember you came to release me from all that would keep me captive and set me free into joy.

Do you feel God's joy over you as he leads you out of bondage?

Warm Welcome

Accept one another, then,
just as Christ accepted you,
in order to bring praise to God.

ROMANS 15:7 NIV

Have you ever met someone and immediately felt a connection? Maybe you were drawn to their personality and a friendship was born. Have you ever met someone you struggled to connect with? Maybe the way they dressed, acted, talked, or chose their career was completely foreign to you.

We all have our natural friendships. We don't have to be best friends with everyone we meet because the truth of it is, we won't. But what if, despite our differences, we still accepted all those we come in contact with?

Jesus, thank you for accepting me. Let me have the same spirit of acceptance for everyone that you do. Prompt me to lay aside personal preferences, so I can show love without bias.

Accept one another,
just as Christ also accepted us
to the glory of God.

ROMANS 15:7 NASB

As Christians, our main goal is to bring praise to God. By accepting others with the same measure of absolute acceptance that Christ extends to us, we honor God and bring him praise.

Let's strive to accept those around us and to genuinely welcome them with open arms in spite of our differences. Think of someone you need to show acceptance to and make a point of doing so this week.

Lord, show me the times when I haven't been very accepting of others. I might be comfortable with my own friends and family, but I know there are people who sit on the outside and need to be invited in. Give me the wisdom to know when to do this.

Who is sitting on the outside of your circle? Can you invite them in sometimes?

New Opportunities

You know that when your faith is tested,
your endurance has a chance to grow.

JAMES 1:3 NLT

It's kind of hard having trouble be an opportunity for joy, isn't it? In fact, it's our instinct to feel just the opposite. And yet we are asked to view it that way despite those instincts.

That's because, when times of trouble come our way, we become stronger in the long run. We are stretched in new ways, learning and growing as we go. Growing endurance is something to rejoice over!

God, it's hard to look at times of trouble in a positive light. Help me to trust you with what you are doing in my life.

The testing of your faith produces endurance.

JAMES 1:3 NASB

If we always stayed just the way we are today, we'd never experience personal growth. But when we look at tough times as an opportunity to change for the better, we can begin to feel thankful for those times.

Try to delight in your rough patches, relying on the Lord to get you through it all.

Help me to find joy in the midst of suffering, and to know that as I grow emotionally, I am turning into the person you have created me to be.

What testing are you going through now that is producing endurance?

Source of Happiness

Come, everyone!
Clap your hands!
Shout to God with joyful praise!

PSALM 47:1 NLT

When you're feeling euphoric, doesn't it make you want to sing with gladness? Your feet start tapping along, and soon your whole body is getting into the feeling. David felt the same way all those years ago as we wrote what we now know as the Psalms.

Take a look at his words. Don't they feel like they could have been written in a modern-day song? Spend some time this morning shouting to God with joyful praise!

Father, I've never known exhilaration like the feeling that comes from knowing your love. I praise you this morning because you are so good.

Clap your hands, all peoples!
Shout to God with loud songs of joy!

PSALM 47:1 ESV

Knowing the true joy that comes from a loving relationship with God isn't something new. People have been clapping their hands with glee for thousands of years. And yet the joy of the Lord feels just as fresh and new every time we experience it as if it were happening for the first time.

So go ahead and sing if you're feeling the joy of the Lord. He's a good Father—and worthy of your praise tonight!

God, thank you for the incredible gift of your overwhelming joy.
I want to sing your praises all the days of my life.

Sing a new song of joy to the Lord tonight.

No Condemnation

Straightening up, Jesus said to her, "Woman, where are they? Did no one condemn you?" She said, "No one, Lord." And Jesus said, "I do not condemn you either. Go. From now on sin no more."

JOHN 8:10-11 NASB

Most of us know the story of the woman caught in adultery. One of the intriguing moments was when Jesus was questioned about whether or not the woman should be stoned. His response is to stoop down and start writing in the dirt. Jesus' action of stooping in the dirt literally defines one interpretation of the word grace.

As others stood casting judgement, Jesus removed himself from the accusers, stooping low and occupying himself elsewhere. It spoke volumes about his lack of participation in the crowd's judgement. Because of Jesus' distraction, the eyes of the onlookers were drawn off the woman, perhaps lifting a portion of her shame. With their attention focused on Jesus, he said the words that saved the woman's life: "Let him who has never sinned cast the first stone." One by one, the accusers walked away.

Forgive me, Lord, in my judgement. Thank you that you freely tell me to go and sin no more.

Jesus straightened up and said to her, "Woman, where are they?
Has no one condemned you?" She said, "No one, sir."
And Jesus said, "Neither do I condemn you.
Go your way, and from now on do not sin again."

JOHN 8:10-11 NRSV

Jesus was the only one qualified to stone the adulterous woman. This is a beautiful foreshadowing of the redemption he later brought to all sinners.

Beloved, Jesus is the only one qualified to condemn you, and he chose to condemn himself instead. You are free and clean because of the grace of Jesus Christ.

Lord, this picture of your grace brings me to tears. I am humbled by your graciousness toward someone who was being accused so harshly. Thank you that you show the same grace toward me. Forgive me in this moment and wash me with your love.

What do you need forgiveness for? Bring it to Jesus who is full of compassion for you.

Quiet Strength

The meek shall inherit the land
and delight themselves in abundant peace.

PSALM 37:11 NIV

Our culture follows the motto "If you've got it, flaunt it!" Riches, beauty, cute kids, desirable status, and beautiful vacations are continually posted online. Real-time updates of everyone else's amazing lives parade around in our mind, causing unrest and discontentment. The Bible talks a lot about meekness; it is not surprising that this is a word we don't hear or understand in our culture.

Meekness means quiet strength. It is humility that models the humility of our Savior. God says the meek are those who will have what everyone really desires—delight and abundant peace!

God, help me to find delight in you, and to quit the comparison game. I want that quiet strength that is found in humility.

The meek shall inherit the land
and delight themselves in abundant peace.

PSALM 37:11 ESV

Do we really think that what we see on social media is the entirety of someone's life? Look more closely and you will see they face the same struggles you do. We are human after all.

True blessing is having the joy of the Lord: a spiritual prosperity incomparable to earthly riches. Take some time tonight, that you might have spent scrolling social media, and give it to the Lord. Ask him to reveal areas of your life that are breeding discontentment and pride, and instead seek to model meekness and humility.

Lord, I repent of discontentment that I have allowed to rob me of your peace. Help me to demonstrate gratitude for my life, just the way it is.

What's the best way for you to practice meekness?

Pure Water

> *I want more than anything*
> *to be in the courtyards of the LORD's Temple.*
> *My whole being wants*
> *to be with the living God.*
>
> PSALM 84:2 NCV

Have you ever noticed that the more consistently you drink water, the more your body thirsts for it? And the less you drink water, the less you consciously desire it. Though you still need water to live, you become satisfied with small amounts of it disguised in other foods and drinks. But for a body that has become accustomed to pure water on a daily basis, only straight water will quench its thirst.

The same principle applies to God's presence in our lives. The more we enter his presence, the more we long to stay there. The more we sit at his feet and listen to what he has to say, the more we need his Word to continue living.

Lord, let my thirst for you return. I can never get enough of your presence, but often I don't find myself feeling like I need you and that's because I haven't been seeking you. I pray as I start the day that you would fill me so I will continue to desire you more.

My soul longs, yes, even faints
*For the courts of the L*ORD*;*
My heart and my flesh cry out for the living God.

PSALM 84:2 NKJV

If we allow ourselves to become satisfied with candy-coated truth and second-hand revelation, we will slowly begin to lose our hunger for the pure, untainted presence of the living God.

Does your entire being long to be with God? Press into Jesus until you can no longer be satisfied with anything less than the purest form of his presence. Cultivate your hunger and your fascination with him until you literally crave him. Spend your life feasting on his truth, knowing his character, and adoring his heart.

God, I am glad to be reminded of my desire to be with you. I enjoy spending time with you; I enjoy talking about my day with you. As I spend more of these times with you, let my desire increase for your presence all over my life.

What does it look like for you to be in the courtyards of the Lord's temple? Spend some time there tonight.

Pursue God

A joyful heart is good medicine,
but a crushed spirit dries up the bones.

PROVERBS 17:22 ESV

We all have a medicine cabinet at home. It's the spot you go to for the bumps and bruises, the aches and pains that life brings our way. Bloody knee? Slap a Band-Aid on it. Feeling a headache coming on? There's a pill for that. Tummy troubles? There's a cure for that too.

But there's a medicine that's even better than any over-the-counter pharmaceutical you could take. And it's available at any time—you'll never run out! Ask God for a joyful heart today and feel it soothe your aches and pains away.

Lord, there's no better medicine for my soul than turning to you.
I want to sing with joy because of your great love.

A happy heart is like good medicine,
but a broken spirit drains your strength.

PROVERBS 17:22 NCV

The joy that comes from a deep and real relationship with the Lord is like medicine to your very soul. There's no better cure for the aches and pains that sorrow can bring you like turning your face to him and soaking in his love for you.

You can rejoice in knowing God is for you. He wants you to know elation like you've never known before! Tonight, before you go to bed, smile. Start the process of having a happy heart.

God, I'm so glad you make yourself so available to the ones who seek you out. Help me to have a happy heart.

Even if it seems crazy, smile at your life right now.

Giving Thanks

*Swing wide, you gates of righteousness, and let me pass through,
and I will enter into your presence to worship only you!
I have found the gateway to God,
the pathway to his presence for all his lovers.*

PSALM 118:19-20 TPT

What happens in our souls when we say thank you to God? When we consecrate a passing second by breathing gratitude into it? What happens to our very being when we acknowledge the weight and glory of even the most insignificant gift?

With each moment of paused reflection, each thank-filled statement, we are set free. Set free from negativity. Set free from dark thoughts of death, pain, suffering, and ugliness. We enter his gates with thanksgiving. We enter his holy place. We walk directly through the door he created.

Father, thank you for all that you have done in this earth, in my family, and in my life. I am grateful for you bringing me through difficult times and joyful times. I choose to thank you in the middle of this crazy life, because I owe it all to you.

Open to me the gates of righteousness;
I shall enter through them, I shall give thanks to the LORD.
This is the gate of the LORD;
The righteous will enter through it.

PSALM 118:19-20 NASB

To walk in thanksgiving is to walk right into God's presence. This season of thanksgiving has a way of taking our hearts and righting them. It opens our eyes to wonder and splendor in casual moments. It puts things into perspective and restores triumph to the defeated soul.

Practice saying thank you today—knowing that through your thankfulness, you will usher yourself into the presence of God.

I am so glad, Jesus, that being thankful gets me a ticket into your presence. Let my life be marked with thankfulness and a gladness that spills out into the way that I think, speak, and act. I have found the gateway to you and I revel in being near you.

What are you thankful for tonight? How has God brought these things into your life?

Longing

Restore to me the joy of your salvation
and grant me a willing spirit, to sustain me.

PSALM 51:12 NIV

Picture a mountain of calorie-free chocolate cake, served up to you at the end of a delicious dinner. Or maybe you prefer salty over sweet, and a big bowl of salsa with chips is what beckons you. Isn't your mouth just salivating at the thought of it?

Imagine indulging at any time, knowing that it's good for you and doesn't come with any repercussions. You know what's even better than any of that? The sweet taste of the joy that comes from the Lord.

Lord, I want to taste the sweetness of the joy that comes from knowing you. As each day passes, I crave more of you!

Restore to me the joy of your salvation,
and make me willing to obey you.

PSALM 51:12 NLT

The joy of the Lord is better than the most delicious meal you could ever imagine. It fills us up to overflowing and pours hope and peace over others as they come into contact with you.

Just like the imaginary treats at the table, you can dive in to God's joy any time without worry. It tastes great and it's good for you (it's like an advertiser's dream come true!). The best part is that you'll never run out of the great joy that the Holy Spirit brings, and you'll continue to crave more with every passing moment.

God, I dive into your joy this evening. I thank you for the sweetness that it brings to my life.

Have you tasted the sweetness of the joy of the Lord?

Perfect

His divine power has granted to us everything pertaining to life and godliness, through the true knowledge of Him who called us by His own glory and excellence.

2 PETER 1:3 NASB

Each of us is keenly aware of our own weaknesses. We know all our flaws too well and we make eliminating them our goal. But no matter how much effort we put out, we can never, and will never, achieve perfection.

Despite most of us realizing that we will never be perfect, we still put unreasonable pressure on ourselves. Whether in a task, in our character, or in our walk with Christ, we easily become frustrated when we reach for perfection and can't grasp it. If we allow perfectionism to drive our performance, then we will quench our own potential and inhibit our effectiveness.

Lord, thank you that this life is not about my perfection, but about yours. I will do my best to imitate your glory and excellence, but I know that this only comes by your grace. Help me to experience this today.

By his divine power, God has given us everything we need for living
a godly life. We have received all this by coming to know him,
the one who called us to himself by means of his marvelous glory
and excellence.

2 PETER 1:3 NLT

God gives you the freedom to not be perfect. In fact, his power is all the more perfect when displayed in your weakness because when you aren't the main point, Jesus is. When you mess up, God has to take over and the result of that action is always perfection.

Think about what it means to be made perfect through Jesus. Can you truly accept your perfection tonight in light of what he has done for you?

God, I wasn't perfect today. I'm pretty sure I'm not perfect any day. But I can rest tonight, knowing that your power is made perfect in my weakness. Forgive my sins. I thank you for a fresh start tomorrow.

Where can you see God's perfection shining through your imperfection?

Satisfied

Because your love is better than life,
my lips will glorify you.
I will praise you as long as I live,
and in your name I will lift up my hands.
I will be fully satisfied as with the richest of foods;
with singing lips my mouth will praise you.

PSALM 63:3-5 NIV

There are times in our lives when we really need answers or a breakthrough, and sometimes we just want to be blessed. Our loving Father says to simply ask.

God wants to give us good gifts. He knows what is best for us. His love is better than life itself, and he knows exactly how to satisfy us.

Lord, there are many things that I need and many things I want. I ask you for them now because I know that you are a loving Father who wants to answer me today.

Because your love is better than life,
I will praise you.
I will praise you as long as I live.
I will lift up my hands in prayer to your name.
I will be content as if I had eaten the best foods.
My lips will sing, and my mouth will praise you.

PSALM 63:3-5 NCV

You might not want to ask God for things because you feel they are too much, or they're too specific. God is able to handle your requests—he won't give you things that will bring you harm or that you will use for selfish gain.

The truth is that God wants us to ask him for everything. He is delighted when we trust in him for the smallest and the largest of things. Trust him for whatever it is that you need tonight.

God, I trust you for the small requests and the large ones tonight. I know you will provide everything I need at the right time and in the right measure.

Can you be fully satisfied with all the Lord has given you?

Starting Over

Praise the LORD!
Oh, give thanks to the LORD, for He is good!
For His mercy endures forever.

PSALM 106:1 NKJV

Have you ever wished you could have a do-over? It would be so great to turn back the clock, reverse a decision, and do it differently. There is wisdom in looking back, but we can't change what was done in the past.

When we embrace God's mercy that is new every morning, there does not need to be any carryover of yesterday's mistakes. Our part in the transaction may require repentance of sin or forgiving someone, perhaps even ourselves. Bathed in his mercies, we can begin each day squeaky clean!

Lord, I am so grateful that your love and your mercies never end. You extend them to me brand new every morning. Great is your faithfulness!

Praise the Lord!
Oh give thanks to the Lord,
for he is good,
for his steadfast love endures forever!

PSALM 106:1 ESV

There are some things we can do over, like tweak the recipe or rip the seam, but most often, the important big decisions can't be changed… except when it comes to spiritual things.

God tells us that we can start over every morning because his mercies will be there. Whatever went awry the day before, whatever mess we made from poor choices, we can begin the next day with a completely clean slate! Praise the Lord for that tonight!

Father, thank you for a clean slate. I am so grateful for your mercy that allows me to start over each day.

Look forward to a new day with new mercy tomorrow.

Found Delightful

Let those who delight in my righteousness
shout for joy and be glad
and say evermore,
"Great is the LORD,
who delights in the welfare of his servant!"

PSALM 35:27 ESV

Despite this season of thanksgiving, it can be a struggle to find delight. If the holiday spirit isn't quite abundant, take delight in God's righteousness. Shout for joy and be glad! And hold fast to the promise of his delight in you. His delight isn't circumstantial.

Thank God for past triumphs and current struggles that lead to a future of strength. You are delightful to God. Believe that today.

God, you see all of me and still find me delightful. Thank you.

Give great joy to those who came to my defense.
Let them continually say,
"Great is the LORD,
who delights in blessing his servant with peace!"

PSALM 35:27 NLT

Regardless of your situation today, God finds you delightful. It isn't a patronizing delight, like an adult chuckling while a toddler throws a temper tantrum; rather, he sees right past whatever emotion we are expressing to the depths of who he knows us to be.

It's humbling to think that God finds us delightful, even when we are acting immaturely, or we struggle with the same sin over and over again. He delights in us and offers us peace from the striving.

Father, I am humbled to be found delightful by you. Thank you for being so patient with me and for seeing past my actions right into my potential.

Take a moment to rest in God's delight over you today.

Worthy

"You are worthy, O Lord,
To receive glory and honor and power;
For You created all things,
And by Your will they exist and were created."

REVELATION 4:11 NKJV

Worship is our natural response to the goodness of God. It's not simply an emotional reaction—worship is also the act of offering back to God the glory that he rightly deserves.

When we stop to think about God's power, majesty, and creativity, we cannot help but glorify him because he is so worthy of the highest form of honor.

Creator God, I want to look for you in everything, so I can give
praise back to you for all you've done.

"Worthy are you, our Lord and God,
to receive glory and honor and power,
for you created all things,
and by your will they existed and were created."

REVELATION 4:11 ESV

Imagine being able to say that you created everything. Stop and think about that for little while. Our God created the entire world—by his will. There is no one else worthy of receiving all glory, honor, and power.

By glorifying God in our daily lives, those around us will take notice and some will ultimately be led to join us in praising him.

God, help me to praise you in the way that you are worthy of. Help me to respond to you with honor, appreciation, and worship.

Thank God today for all that he has created.

Stillness

"Be still, and know that I am God;
I will be exalted among the nations,
I will be exalted in the earth!"

PSALM 46:10 NKJV

Dusk settles on a chilly winter night. A gray fog hovers and snow begins to fall: cold, blustering snow…the kind that sticks. The snow keeps coming until you can barely see one hundred feet in front of you. In the woods, it's quiet; all you can hear is the gentle wind, and all you can see is snow and trees. A pure white blanket of snow restores the earth, and as it falls, it restores you.

Sometimes we have to get outside of the noise and chaos of our own four walls. We have to step out into the snow, or the sun, or the breeze. We have to get alone, get silent, and clear the clutter from our minds and hearts as we stand in God's natural sanctuary.

Lord, give me this moment to be still and know that you are God.

"Be still, and know that I am God.
I will be exalted among the nations,
I will be exalted in the earth!"

PSALM 46:10 ESV

There is so much power in the stillness of knowing God as you stand serene in the world he created.

The busyness of your life will always be there, but never forget to take the moments you can, to stop and know your God. In those moments, you will find refreshment and strength to take on whatever will come next.

God, it is so right to have this time to be still. Thank you for the quietness and stillness of the night. Sometimes I dread having to go to bed, but tonight, let me lay in the peace and quiet and hand my thoughts and hopes over to you.

What thoughts come to you while you are waiting in the stillness? Can you see, feel, or hear God in the quiet?

Sacrifice of Thanksgiving

Offer to God a sacrifice of thanksgiving
Call upon Me in the day of trouble;
I shall rescue you, and you will honor Me.

PSALM 50:14-15 NASB

The Israelites in the Old Testament had a complicated list of rituals and sacrifices to follow. Among the five special offerings, one was the peace offering, or the sacrifice of thanksgiving. God asked that an animal without defect be offered to him from a heart that was full of gratitude for his grace.

It's not always easy to be thankful. In times of great difficulty when everything in the natural screams "I don't like this!" gratitude comes at great sacrifice. It is a denial of the natural response, dying to one's own preference, and in submission saying, "God, your way is best and I thank you."

Lord, today I want to say thanks for being my God. As I call out to you, I know you will be my deliverer and get all the glory in the process!

> *"Give an offering to show thanks to God.*
> *Give God Most High what you have promised.*
> *Call to me in times of trouble.*
> *I will save you, and you will honor me."*

PSALM 50:14–15 NCV

When Jesus came, old requirements were replaced by the new so that our worship could be an expression of our hearts directly through our lips. No need for complicated rituals and sacrifices—just a thankful heart.

Having a grateful heart gives us the privilege of calling on God in our day of trouble and the assurance of his deliverance.

God, thank you for the grace you show me each day. I offer my sacrifice of thanksgiving today and every day, especially when it's difficult to have a heart of gratitude.

Can you offer God your sacrifice of praise tonight?

Illusion of Control

Submit therefore to God.
Resist the devil and he will flee from you.

JAMES 4:7 NASB

Submit to God and resist the devil. How is it that such straightforward advice seems so difficult to follow? Might it be because our culture seems to so often suggest the exact opposite? In movies or shows, a character living by this advice is presented as a novelty, or an oddity, and typically succumbs to the pressure to be normal or fit in.

Until we get this right and submit to the one who wants only peace, goodness and joy for us, we are under the authority of the one who wants to destroy us. Like a frightened cockroach, he will run for his life once we expose him to the light of God's truth, but not before. Until we stand with God and tell the devil no, he's going to hang around.

God, I regret each time I've chosen dark over light, or what is easy over what is right. I can't believe I ever thought fitting in mattered more than standing proudly next to you. Help me, Jesus, to resist the enemy's lure. Help me resist him and send him scurrying far from me. I don't want to be "normal," God, until I am in heaven—where normal is to spend all my time worshipping you.

Give yourselves completely to God.
Stand against the devil, and the devil will run from you.

JAMES 4:7 NCV

What stops us from giving ourselves completely to God? We fear not having control, even though deep down we know we don't have it anyway. We are deceived into thinking things will be better if we make all our own decisions and fight all our own battles. We are controlled by impulse, entitlement, and a million other of the enemy's tricks.

The devil does all he can to hold us back, because he knows he cannot stand against the Lord. Once we belong completely to God, the devil has no choice but to set us free and run away.

Spirit of God, please help me. Pry open these fingers, clinging so pitifully to the illusion of control. Unclench these fists, holding so tightly to the idea I'm entitled to my "freedom", which is really just another of the enemy's traps. Stretch open my hands, Holy Spirit, and help me lift them heavenward. I hand over my life to you, God. all I am is yours and because of this, I am finally free.

Where are you weak? Whether the struggle is over screen time or a temptation that could ruin your life, ask the Lord to stand with you as you say "No!"

Ways to Remember

I will always remind you about these things—even though you already know them and are standing firm in the truth you have been taught. And it is only right that I should keep on reminding you as long as I live.

2 PETER 1:12-13 NLT

It is so important to continue to stand in the truth of the gospel of Jesus. These days, there are so many other ideas that are competing to tell us what is best for us. We read about health trends, ways to improve our mental agility, time management strategies—anything for self-betterment.

None of these are inherently wrong, but they can distract you from a focus on the truth found in God's Word. This is why you need to find ways to remind yourself of the truth: reminders that are set for the rest of your life. Be encouraged that you are being reminded of God's truth every day.

God, I know that your truth should be above what the world finds important. Thank you for the big and small things that you will present me with today to remind me of your great love and my salvation.

Our Lord Jesus Christ has shown me that I must soon leave this earthly life, so I will work hard to make sure you always remember these things after I am gone.

2 PETER 1:14-15 NLT

It is as important to remind others of Christ's love as it is to be reminded of it yourself. Each generation of Christians that have gone before us have left their mark on the world because they shared Jesus through their actions and deeds.

In the same way, you are able to pass on Christ's love through what you say and do. This isn't to be experienced as a burden but as a joy.

God, let me be more aware of the impact of my faith on those generations to come. I am encouraged that you work through me so others will know of your love. Keep me motivated to pass on the blessing that was handed to me.

How can you see your faith being passed down through generations?

All for Nothing

I do not nullify the grace of God;
for if justification comes through the law,
then Christ died for nothing.

GALATIANS 2:21 NRSV

Imagine spending months preparing your house to go on the market. You've repainted every room, remodeled the kitchen, repaved the driveway, and now it's time to sell the house. At the first open house, you get a full price cash offer. The only catch is that the buyer plans to tear the house down. Suddenly those months of work seem all for nothing.

Anyone who believes they can get to heaven just by working hard or being a good person, is also implying Jesus' brutal death was all for nothing. Without accepting his gift of grace, we toil needlessly, and worse, we relegate Jesus' ultimate sacrifice and glorious resurrection to the status of a magic trick. Instead, let us run to the arms of grace with all our might and tell our Lord his death was not all for nothing because his death was for us.

God, forgive me for trying to earn my place in heaven. I know full well I can never do enough to deserve it, and I can't bear the thought of rejecting the glorious miracle of grace. Your death was not all for nothing. It was for me, and I will thank you every day of my life for accomplishing what I never could.

I do not treat the grace of God as meaningless.
For if keeping the law could make us right with God,
then there was no need for Christ to die.

GALATIANS 2:21 NLT

If you've ever worked hard to choose the perfect gift and only to have your efforts met with ingratitude, you know how hurtful it can be. Despite the care you took in its selection, and the joy it gave you to give it, it seemed to mean little or nothing to the recipient.

Considering how hurt we can be over the rejection of a something trivial like a child's toy or printed scarf, Jesus' sorrow must be unimaginable when a person he loves refuses the grace offered by his death and resurrection.

Jesus, though I know I can never thank you too much, I feel I still don't try nearly enough. I could tell you every day how blown away I am by the depth of your love, how utterly awed I am that you considered me worth dying to save, and I'd still owe you a million songs of praise. May that song be ever on my lips, God, that you may know how deep my gratitude is.

How often do you consider what Christ did for you? Search your heart and ask if it is often enough.

God's Interpretation

We have the prophetic word more fully confirmed, to which you will do well to pay attention as to a lamp shining in a dark place, until the day dawns and the morning star rises in your hearts, knowing this first of all, that no prophecy of Scripture comes from someone's own interpretation.

2 PETER 1:19-20 ESV

When the people of God tried to interpret the prophecies from Scripture, they didn't have full understanding. When we read the words of these prophesies today, they seem to make a lot more sense in light of Christ's life, death and resurrection.

The best way to interpret Scripture is to come from the knowledge that what is written is from God. He knew what he intended, and he meant for it to be written that way. Trust God's words and marvel at the plan that he has made from the beginning.

God, thank you for your Scripture that was read thousands of years ago and finally came true. Help me to pay attention to your Word, knowing that it can be a lamp to light my path.

No prophecy was ever produced by the will of man, but men spoke from God as they were carried along by the Holy Spirit.

2 PETER 1:21 ESV

We have all forms of foretelling in our day, from horoscopes to psychics. The search to know the future is a quest that humans will never conquer because the future is not for us to know.

God guides us into understanding what is to come by telling us some things in Scripture. These are the prophecies that the Holy Spirit put in the heart of people to write down, and they are words that you can trust because they are from God.

Jesus, help me to stay away from the temptation of trying to interpret prophecy or trying to determine exactly what the future will be like. Give me greater understanding and insight into the prophetic word that is in Scripture.

What promises can you find in Scripture about the future?

Comparable

> *Keep me from looking at worthless things.*
> *Let me live by your word.*
>
> PSALM 119:37 NCV

Is there anyone out there who doesn't need this prayer? It's much easier to see in others than in ourselves; we see young people spending hours on mind-numbing television and snapping and sending endless photos of themselves and think, What a waste of time! But what us? How many of our distractions and entertainments are truly worthwhile?

Before you slip into a shame cycle, remember there is no condemnation in Christ. Verses like this one are meant to help us have the most meaningful, God-honoring lives we possibly can. Our Lord has so much to offer us, so much to teach and show us, and so many ways for us to grow in love, beauty, and grace! We need only keep our eyes on him.

Holy Spirit, help me keep my eyes on the Lord! Show me irresistible beauty, uncontainable love, and unearned grace. As I am tempted to settle for lesser things, let me constantly question whether they are worthy of my time. God, you are so precious that none of the worldly things I distract or entertain myself with can compare.

Help me turn my eyes away from illusions
so that I pursue only that which is true;
drench my soul with life as I walk in your paths.

What a life one could live, pursuing only that which is true! Just think of it, the richness of seeing only true art, experiencing real love, and living in authentic service. It's almost overwhelming.

We've conditioned ourselves to believe we need down time, and current culture offers no shortage of ways to numb the mind. But what if that's an illusion—a lie—orchestrated to keep us from knowing the incredible blessing of a life drenched glorious truth?

God, open my eyes! Take away my taste for lesser things, for numbness and substitution. Immersed in your beauty and truth, let all illusions melt away. Illuminate your path with blinding light, until it's all I can see, then overwhelm me with a desire to pursue only excellence, compassion, and love.

What lesser thing, or illusion, has captured too much of your attention? Ask the Lord to change the way you see it, and to show you something better.

Differing Times

Do not forget this one thing, dear friends:
With the Lord a day is like a thousand years,
and a thousand years are like a day.

2 PETER 3:8 NIV

Time is an interesting human phenomenon. Even though it is constant, one minute can seem different depending on the context. If you are running on a treadmill at a really fast speed at the highest incline, one minute feels excruciating. If you are talking on the phone to one of your closest friends, that minute goes insanely fast.

God isn't fooled by time; he knows how to work in and outside of it. If you are feeling like it is taking a long time for God to bring some of his promises to fruition, remind yourself that his timing is right.

God, it seems like I have been waiting a really long time to see your promises come true. Give me patience, knowing that you have it all under control. Remind me of the promises that you have already fulfilled, and fill me with joy for the day ahead.

The Lord is not slow in keeping his promise,
as some understand slowness.
Instead he is patient with you,
not wanting anyone to perish,
but everyone to come to repentance.

2 PETER 3:9 NIV

Have you felt like your day has been rushed along by all the activities and need to get things done? We are so used to rushing through life that we find waiting hard. God is not slow. He is patient because he is waiting for us.

Jesus will return when the timing is right, but his heart is all about his love for those who still need his revelation to reach them. Respect God's need to do things in his timing and continue to wait expectedly for his return.

God, thank you for your great love that compels you to wait for those who you love. Thank you that you seek out the lost and celebrate when they are found. Help me to be part of furthering your kingdom by bringing those lost sheep to you.

Who do you know that needs to come to repentance? Pray for their salvation.

All Come True

Mary responded, "I am the Lord's servant.
May everything you have said about me come true."
And then the angel left her.

LUKE 1:38 NLT

Given the extraordinary news that she, an unwed teenager, will bear the Son of God, Mary unhesitatingly agrees. I am the Lord's servant. Can you imagine? No questions, no doubts, and no fears, just humble acceptance. Look at what she says next: "May everything you have said about me come true." What beautiful faith, what trust!

What do you suppose the Lord has spoken over you and your life? Given his abiding love for you, it can only be something wonderful. Despite our limited understanding of his ways, we can trust—with the certainty of Mary—that anything the Lord speaks over our lives is the only truth we need to fulfill.

Father God, may everything you have spoken over me come true.
Empower and embolden me to explore every desire you have placed
in my heart, and to develop and use every talent you have given
me for the glory of your kingdom. Help me to believe the things you
have said about me, to embrace the hope you see in me, and to see
it all come true.

Then Mary said, "Here am I, the servant of the Lord;
let it be with me according to your word."
Then the angel departed from her.

LUKE 1:38 NRSV

What do you suppose Mary relied on when she heard the whispers? From whom did she gather strength when met with disapproving stares? Bringing this news to Joseph, and her parents, where did she get the courage to trust they would believe the unbelievable truth?

The source of Mary's hope is the source of ours too, and the well of her courage the same one we visit. The Lord gives us strength. He is our hope. Let it be with each of us according to his Word.

God, here I am, your servant. I reject the fear of the unknown, of public opinion, and of change. I embrace whatever you have for planned me, knowing there is nothing better. You are my hope, and the well of my strength. My courage is from my faith in you, and I surrender my life to your perfect plan.

How is God your source of hope?

Petitions

*"Now, our God, hear the prayers and petitions of your servant.
For your sake, LORD, look with favor on your desolate sanctuary.
Give ear, our God, and hear; open your eyes and see the desolation
of the city that bears your Name. We do not make requests of you
because we are righteous, but because of your great mercy."*

DANIEL 9:17-18 NIV

Are you waiting for a breakthrough in your circumstances?
Maybe you have been praying for an unbelieving family
member, a strained relationship, an answer to your financial
stress, or clarity for a big decision ahead.

Fasting doesn't often top the list of what to do when you
really need that breakthrough, and it's not that hard to
guess why it isn't a popular option. It takes self-control and
determination to pray and petition God for an answer, but it
will be worth it.

*Lord God, I turn my face toward you today and I again ask for
a breakthrough in my circumstances. Help me to think about
you during my day and to continue to pray for your strength and
endurance. If I need to fast, bring that conviction to my heart.*

> "LORD, listen. LORD, forgive! LORD, hear and act!
> For your sake, my God, do not delay,
> because your city and your people bear your Name."
>
> DANIEL 9:19 NIV

Consider what the Bible says about fasting and notice how it goes hand in hand with prayer.

There is a certain humility that accompanies fasting; it requires sobriety of heart, reflection, and focus. It brings your impulses into submission and gives you confidence in your self-control.

More importantly, it seems to let the Lord know that you mean business—that you are ready to receive his revelation and guidance.

God, I know that you might be calling me to petition you in some way. If it's not food, then give me something to give up so my heart can really press in toward what you want for my life.

Can you commit to make fasting and deep petition a spiritual discipline in your life? You may just get the answers you were looking for, and perhaps even ones that you were not.

Guard My Tongue

Let no evil talk come out of your mouths,
but only what is useful for building up, as there is need,
so that your words may give grace to those who hear.

EPHESIANS 4:29 NRSV

Wait. I didn't mean that. It's happened to all of us. The moment the words left our lips, we knew. We may have meant it in the moment, but we didn't really mean it. Frustration, confusion, and anger can release words that are not a true reflection of our hearts. May God grant us, and those hurt by our careless words, his grace.

For so many of us, there is no body part harder to control than the tongue, especially when it appears to work faster than the mind. How do we ensure our angry, unkind thoughts never become words? We pray. The moment we feel slighted, hurt, or otherwise tempted to speak on impulse, we call on the Lord, and give him control of our speech.

God, guard my tongue. Stay close, protecting my thoughts from becoming words I can't reclaim. Turn my anger to compassion, and my frustration to peace. As I remember who I am in you, I'll find the grace to either stay silent or speak love.

Let no corrupt word proceed out of your mouth, but what is good for necessary edification, that it may impart grace to the hearers.

EPHESIANS 4:29 NKJV

Our words need protection from far more than just anger, don't they? Words of criticism, self-promotion, and impulse also fight to be spoken.

In order to speak only life, we must belong to the giver of life. To utter only love, we must live in love. If we truly and fully give him our hearts, he'll fill them with his goodness, which will spill out in our speech. Our words won't need protection when we overflow with grace.

God, take over my heart, please. Replace my critical eye with appreciation for differences. Extract my need for attention and approval and put in its place a desire to build up others. Seize my impulses and make them captives of your grace. When I speak spontaneously, let it be to impart love, goodness, and peace.

In what circumstance are you most likely to speak without thinking, or to say what doesn't need saying? Invite the Lord to nudge you into grace instead.

Lasting Love

Do not love the world or anything in the world.
If anyone loves the world, love for the Father is not in them.

1 JOHN 2:15 NIV

It's so easy to fall prey to the wants and desires of the world. There's the latest this, and the coolest that, and we have a hunger to own it all. We see a neighbor with a shiny new car, and suddenly ours seems old and unappealing. A friend shows up for coffee with a high end new phone, and we instantly want a better one, too.

There's nothing inherently wrong with new things, and we're not sinning simply by making an acquisition. It's more about the priority we give our purchases than the purchases themselves. It's about our hearts.

God, let me love you with my whole heart and put you above anything else in this world.

Everything in the world—
the lust of the flesh,
the lust of the eyes,
and the pride of life—
comes not from the Father
but from the world.

1 John 2:15-16 NIV

Are you coveting all that the world has to offer, or is the ache in your heart a yearning for Jesus' presence?

Pray for protection from the desires of the world.

It's hard, God, to put you first in such a busy and demanding world. Sometimes I just want to do it the world's way. I pray that you would forgive me for missing the mark and help me to set my eyes on you this evening, so I wake up with you on my mind.

What are you putting first in your life?

Wonderful Aroma

Perfume and incense bring joy to the heart,
and the pleasantness of a friend
springs from their heartfelt advice.

PROVERBS 27:9 NIV

What is your absolute favorite fragrance? From foods to flowers to expertly blended perfumes, our sense of smell can trigger powerful emotions and memories. Simmering red sauce takes us to Grandma's lap, cut grass brings back a perfect summer afternoon, while sandalwood, jasmine and rose transport us to the memory of a magical night.

As with all our senses, our sense of smell is a gift from the Lord. It can keep us safe, and it can bring us joy—through both memory and the sheer pleasure of a wonderful aroma. As you pay attention to the smells around you, take note of the feelings they arouse. Turn your mind to the Lord, maker of all your senses, and thank him for this unique and precious gift.

God, your creativity and intricacy never cease to amaze me. How can something as simple as the smell of cinnamon evoke such feelings of happiness and warmth? Maker of my senses, author of my joy, thank you for your wonderful gifts.

The heartfelt counsel of a friend
is as sweet as perfume and incense.

PROVERBS 27:9 NLT

As delightful as any fragrance is to our noses, so to our hearts are friends who counts us as treasure. Their compassion brings warmth and security, while their wisdom invites peace.

To be around people who love us by choice, and willingly tether their hearts to ours, is a gift as sweet as the senses can enjoy.

God, how sweet is your gift of friendship! These people who choose to love me, unbound by history and blood, are treasures. As precious as any sight I might behold, song I might hear, or fragrance I may smell, the compassion and warm acceptance of a friend is priceless and rare.
Help me to treat my friends with the love and gratitude they deserve, God, and to be a treasure in their lives as well.

Spend some time tonight contemplating the most important relationships in your life. Thank the Lord for loving you through them.

Don't Lose It

Watch out that you do not lose what we have worked for,
but that you may be rewarded fully.

2 JOHN 1:8 NIV

Imagine gathering all your hard-earned wages for a week's work, putting it in your back pocket and then losing it all on your way home. It would be so frustrating to have nothing to show for all your efforts; it would be a waste.

There is an urgency to the gospel that the apostles wanted us to catch on to. The preservation of the truth, the demonstration of Christ's love, and the spreading of the Word are paramount to seeing his kingdom advance. Be part of this good work so we can experience the reward of seeing people saved.

Jesus, I want to see your love spread to as many people as it can get to. Help me to not let go of the truth that is in my heart. Give me a chance to spread your love today.

Anyone who runs ahead and does not continue in the teaching of Christ does not have God; whoever continues in the teaching has both the Father and the Son.

2 JOHN 1:9 NIV

There are a lot of people who proclaim to know the truth about the world, but it is crucial that we know the gospel of Jesus Christ. Jesus revealed who God is, and he said there is no other way to the Father.

If you want to know God, you have to stick close to knowing Jesus and being diligent with remembering and putting into practice all that he said and did. Anything less than Christ is not the Father at all. Cling to the truth and let it all be about Jesus.

God, I never want to run ahead with teaching that doesn't encompass the work of Jesus. Continue to reveal yourself to me so I know the Father more and more.

Have you been tempted to follow teachings that don't mention Christ? Make sure to examine what you are hearing for the truth and presence of Jesus.

A Kind Word

*Encourage one another and build one another up,
just as you are doing.*

1 THESSALONIANS 5:11 ESV

One of the most precious things about Christian friendship is the spiritual gift of encouragement. When we are on the receiving end, these lovely people always have a kind word. They see the good in us, and in everyone, and have an inspired, beautifully-timed way of expressing their belief in and fondness for us. It never feels patronizing or gratuitous; the sincere words of an encourager give life.

As an encourager, you may find good thoughts about others come to you constantly, and to share them is as natural as breathing. When people respond to our encouragement with pleasant surprise and sincere gratitude, it's affirming. Keep sharing your good thoughts, friend, because you never know who needs to hear your words, or who needs to know they are seen. Speaking life into someone is a beautiful gift.

Lord God, thank you for the gift of encouragement. I know how amazing I feel when I'm with someone to whom you've given an extra measure. The things they say—the things they see—give me strength and keep me going. God, I humbly ask for the gift of speaking life and spreading love. I want to be shown the beauty of your children and tell them what I see.

Encourage each other and give each other strength,
just as you are doing now.

1 Thessalonians 5:11 NCV

After gathering with other people, are you usually uplifted, feeling strong and loving, or are you out of sorts, feeling somewhat empty? If your social time is building you up, you know the Spirit of God is present, giving words of encouragement to say and to receive. Gossip, complaining and venting never seem to make their way into the conversation when he is around. Praise God for his loving presence.

As for the draining encounters, pray things change. Can you be the one to shift the tide, breathing welcome life into the conversation? Might others respond so well to your encouragement they too, begin to be a blessing?

Father, make me sensitive to your Spirit when I gather with others. Let me sense, share, and appreciate the people I am with when your light and love are all around us. In conversations that go dark, give me wisdom. Make me an encourager, contagious with your warmth.

Prayerfully assess your relationships. Where are you naturally encouraged and encouraging, and where do you need the help of the Holy Spirit to spread light instead of darkness?

One of Many

God saw their works, that they turned from their evil way;
and God relented from the disaster that He had said
He would bring upon them, and He did not do it.
But it displeased Jonah exceedingly, and he became angry.

JONAH 3:10–4:1 NKJV

Even if we think of ourselves as highly flexible, when plans are established, most of us prefer to see things unfold as scheduled. Some of us get downright fussy in the wake of unexpected change. Such a man was Jonah.

After much resistance, Jonah informed the people of Nineveh that God planned to destroy them for their wickedness in forty days' time. However, they repented—and so the Lord relented. Jonah was furious, but why? Was he jealous, wanting God's mercy only for Israel? Embarrassed his prophecy was not fulfilled? Or was he just put out, having come all that way for nothing—a nothing which, to Nineveh, was life over death?

It's easy to recognize Jonah's selfishness, God, but do I respond better when you disrupt my plans? Have I not felt envy, embarrassment, and entitlement as well? Do I not behave as if my comfort were your sole concern? Forgive me, God, for questioning your perfect wisdom. In honor of Nineveh, let me remember I am but one of many souls, all of whom you love.

When God saw what the people did, that they stopped doing evil,
he changed his mind and did not do what he had warned.
He did not punish them.
But this made Jonah very unhappy, and he became angry.

JONAH 3:10-4:1 NCV

Answer honestly: have you ever been a little disappointed to see someone get off easily? Even though it didn't affect you directly, was your sense of retribution ever offended by mercy?

Matthew 20 has a story of field workers, all of whom got the same wage, regardless of how many hours they worked. Again, it's not fair—but it's good, actually very good news for us. Were God concerned with being fair, none of us would be on our way to heaven. We don't deserve it. But mercifully, God isn't fair.

Oh, God, what concern is it of mine if, on the last day, you decide to forgive everyone everything? It is your will that none should perish, God, so let me do my part here on earth to share that amazing news. You may not be fair, but you are incredibly, unreasonably good. Thank you, God, for the unfair gift of mercy.

How comfortable or uncomfortable are you with this view of God? Share your heart with him. He loves to help you work things through.

Promised Peace

"In that day I will make a covenant for them with the beasts of the field, the birds in the sky and the creatures that move along the ground. Bow and sword and battle I will abolish from the land, so that all may lie down in safety."

HOSEA 2:18 NIV

We strive for peace in our countries, cities, workplaces, and homes. It is sad that humans have made so many weapons for the sake of protecting themselves from each other. We want to be safe and yet we fight for our own sense of justice.

What a great day it will be when God can fulfill his promise of bringing true justice and peace to the earth. If you are worried about the strife of today, look expectantly toward the time when all of humanity will once again be at peace. This is his promise to us.

Jesus, it is hard to imagine a world without war and heartbreak, yet I long for that day. Help me to bring a small portion of this peace into my sphere of influence today.

"I will betroth you to me forever; I will betroth you in righteousness and justice, in love and compassion. I will betroth you in faithfulness, and you will acknowledge the LORD."

HOSEA 2:19-20 NIV

Unlike some of the human vows we make, God's promise is forever. When he returns to complete his kingdom on earth, we will experience true righteousness, justice, and the fullness of love. While we are still waiting, God has work for us to do.

God wants to work through you so people can see his heart that is geared toward justice, peace, and love. Were you able to represent some of these things today? Let God speak to you tonight about how you can make a difference in your part of the world.

God, I am passionate about justice and peace. Thank you for creating within me a heart that cares about this world and what happens in it. Give me ideas and energy to contribute toward goodwill on earth.

What actions could you take that can represent God's justice, love, and peace to the world?

Cousin of Hope

If we hope for what we do not see,
we wait for it with patience.

ROMANS 8:25 NRSV

Whether a docile family pet who tolerates endless tugs on his tail and rides on his back, or a teacher who never raises her voice and can answer the same question over and over without frustration, true patience is a marvel, isn't it? While a precious few are born with a seemingly endless supply, the rest of us must pray for this rare and precious commodity.

Listed among the fruits of the Spirit, patience is not something God expects us to possess abundantly on our own, but a gift he gives to those who seek it. It is the product of peace, and the cousin of hope. From a heart at rest and a belief in the coming rightness of all things, patience is born.

Father God, please help me grow in patience. You gave me a little already and it was just enough to make me recognize my need for more. Humbly, aware of my limits, I ask your Spirit to grant me peace. Give me hope, God, that all I don't yet see is coming, and make me patient as I wait.

If we hope for what we do not see,
with perseverance we wait eagerly for it.

ROMANS 8:25 NASB

What better model of patience could we ask for than the Lord?

Think of the questions, complaints, and confessions he hears from us, day after day after day. And still, he welcomes us. He waits for us: eagerly, expectantly, and patiently. His kindness never runs out, nor does his supply of second chances.

God, your patience knows no limit. I can question you daily, come to you over and over with the same pet sins to forgive, and you oblige. Lovingly, gently, you listen, respond, and grant your grace. Continue to be patient with me, God, as I work on extending my own. You are my example, so I know I'll get this right.

What aspect of God's patience most amazes you? Which shortcoming of your own patience would you most like his grace for, and help with?

Getting Anywhere

Jesus said to him, "I am the way, the truth, and the life.
No one comes to the Father except through Me."

JOHN 14:6 NKJV

Anyone who uses a smartphone or car navigation system to plan their driving routes has probably wondered how they ever got anywhere before this? Real-time updates on construction, accidents and other factors affecting travel-time constantly alert you to the best way to get where you are going.

Those who follow Christ can wonder the same thing: how did we ever get anywhere before the Lord showed us the way? How did we make decisions before he pointed us to the truth? How did we even get through the day, before Jesus infused meaning into our lives? When we were lost, deceived, and empty, he found us, chose us, and lead us safely home.

Oh Jesus, how did I manage before you took up residence in my heart? I was lost, deceived, and empty, and I didn't even know it. I couldn't see the barriers, delays, and dead ends ahead of me. I wrongly believed I knew the best way—that I was living the best life. Thank you, God, for your infallible truth, for being my way, and for this beautiful life.

Jesus said to him, "I am the way, and the truth, and the life;
no one comes to the Father but through Me."

JOHN 14:6 NASB

Jesus is the Lord of opportunity. Because of his sacrifice, we are free to make our way to the Father. Because of his grace, we are free to come continually before him to confess our sins, present our requests, and offer our praise. Because of his love, we are free to love others and to invite them to share in his blessings. The world will try to convince us God is but one of many ways. The enemy will try to confuse us with lies and lead us to death.

Let's be clear; God is the way. He speaks and is the truth. In him, we have eternal life.

God, the life you offer is one of endless, timeless opportunity. Instead of making my way through the world, you invite me to come to the Father. Instead of pursuing false hope, perishable things, and empty praise, you open the door to the hope of resurrection, the miracle of grace.

Mediate on each concept of Jesus as way, truth, and life, individually. Where have you most felt his impact? Where do you need to pray for more of his influence?

Spiritual Prophecy

"I will pour out my spirit on all flesh; your sons and your daughters shall prophesy, your old men shall dream dreams, and your young men shall see visions."

JOEL 2:28 NRSV

Before Jesus came to earth, God revealed himself through the prophets who spoke his words to his people. God always planned for there to be a time when he would speak directly to his children, through the Holy Spirit.

We are part of the other side of this prophesy. We have received the Holy Spirit and God is able to speak through us. He will even give us dreams and visions. Have you asked God for these, believing that he can and will speak to you?

Holy Spirit, thank you that your presence is for everyone who believes in the name of Jesus. Help me to hear your voice in my day today, and let me respond with belief that you are speaking.

"Even on the male and female slaves,
in those days, I will pour out my spirit."

JOEL 2:29 NRSV

God's Spirit was always intended for everyone. Even though God had chosen Israel as a nation to speak through, his plan has always been for all of humanity. When Jesus came to earth, he showed that his mercy and grace was for all people.

We now know that there is no separation for those who are in Christ Jesus. God is speaking through you and he is speaking through others. Have you been listening?

Holy Spirit, thank you that you do not show favoritism toward any kind of person. I know that you are able to speak through others. At times, I am skeptical about your voice, so please give me the ability to recognize your voice when you speak.

What is the Holy Spirit saying to you tonight?

Everything for God

*The answer is, if you eat or drink, or if you do anything,
do it all for the glory of God.*

1 CORINTHIANS 10:31 NCV

Are you busy? Most of us answer in the affirmative. We pack our schedules with commitments, obligations, necessities, rewards, and—hopefully—rest. Like a master juggler, we toss in one more ball, then one more ball, until one of them drops. Scrambling to retrieve it, we also risk those still aloft. These are ideal opportunities to check in and ask why you are juggling so much.

One reason is simple: pride. We enjoy the applause. We bask in the limelight as people marvel at all we accomplish. When our attention turns to the praise we are seeking, the balls begin to drop. Another reason we juggle, though, is to live a God-honoring life. We want to give, serve, experience community, steward our responsibilities, and care for ourselves—for him. We know it is pleasing to God when we make meaningful use of our time. When our motive is to do everything for God, he helps us juggle.

God, I know I try to do too much. I do it to please you and bring you glory, but I also do it for myself. I want my life to bring you glory, God, and I can't do that when I am focused on myself.

Whether you eat or drink, or whatever you do,
do everything for the glory of God.

1 CORINTHIANS 10:31 NRSV

What is more important: following custom or showing respect? Most often than not, they go hand in hand but occasionally, as in this verse, we are asked to make a choice. Here, Paul is helping the church in Corinth decide when it is okay to eat and drink certain things. His advice is to do what brings glory to God.

Is it more loving to toast or to abstain? Which will best honor the Lord? May this Christmas season be filled with choices that please our God and draw others into his light.

Father, I wish all decisions were simple. Please allow your Holy Spirit to help me discern. If it will compromise my integrity, and confuse others about your statutes, may I decline. If it will show us both as welcoming, gracious, and filled with love, may I wholeheartedly partake. May every gift I buy, event I attend, and glass I raise this Christmas season shine a spotlight on your love and grace.

Do you find yourself conflicted about things surrounding the Christmas season in a struggle between worldliness and your faith? Invite the Holy Spirit to speak truth to you, so your heart will be at peace.

Formation

The LORD is the one who shaped the mountains,
stirs up the winds, and reveals his thoughts to mankind.

AMOS 4:13 NLT

We often talk about the power and love of God, and indeed these qualities shape our understanding of him. When we read and experience all that he has created, we also perceive him as an intelligent and creative God. To form the splendor of the mountains and crafted the wind to shape waves on the ocean are just some of his many visual testimonies of brilliant creativity.

God has put that creativity in your heart and mind—you are his image-bearer. Whatever you may be doing today be encouraged to tap into this resource of imagination.

God, I don't always see myself as a creative person or a person who has time to be creative. Open my eyes to see all the different forms of creativity and help me to use it throughout my day.

He turns the light of dawn into darkness and treads on the heights
of the earth. The Lord God of Heaven's Armies is his name!

AMOS 4:13 NLT

As the light gives way to darkness tonight, think of the
Creator of the universe who thought up the whole system of
the sun and moon, day and night. It is incredible to think of
all that God has imagined for earth, and yet his creativity did
not stop there.

God is also the Creator of the known universe and everything
in the heavens. Let his greatness overwhelm your mind
and heart, knowing with certainty that he is in control of
everything.

Heavenly Father, you have created such a wonderful world and I
am thankful for all the creation that I have been able to appreciate
today. Help me to see your beauty all around me as I go into
tomorrow. May I be reminded of your greatness.

How did you notice God's creativity today?

Surrounding Love

"I am with you always, even to the end of the age."

MATTHEW 28:20 NASB

God is here. Right now, he is with you. Can you sense his presence? Even when you don't feel him, he never leaves you. What can compare to the moments when you do feel him, when every sense confirms he is here? When his love surrounds you, and his power runs through you, only then are you fully and gloriously alive.

How did we become worthy of such a blessing? We can't deserve it, or earn it, and yet he chooses to remain. Out of love for us, he leaves his presence with us. We can't offend him, hurt him, or dishonor him in such a way that will cause him to depart from us. May this inspire us to live lives that are respectful, honoring and aware.

God, how can I adequately thank you for your nearness? The moments I can feel you are the most powerful of my life, and to know you are there even when I can't feel you fills me with peace. I pray that the gift of your presence will create in me a heart that strives, always, to be worthy of it.

"I am with you always, even to the end of the age."

MATTHEW 28:20 NKJV

Reflecting on the less-than-exemplary moments of our lives, we can spiral into shame when we remember the was with us even then. Sister, this is not his plan. Those feelings are not of him. He seeks to uplift, not condemn.

God reminds us of his presence, so we can live in his grace. With him so near, forgiveness is but a breath away. He is with us for support, encouragement, and, yes, conviction—but conviction that leads to repentance, not guilt and shame. When we sense him witnessing our sin, we can turn into the waiting arms of grace.

Oh Jesus, there are things I wish you hadn't seen. There are words I'd love you not to have heard, and moments I'd prefer to rewind and live differently. And yet, knowing you were right there— and that you stayed anyway—fills me with a holy conviction. Surprised, I find myself grateful for your witness as I swim in your grace. This grace fills me with hope, God, for which I gladly surrender my shame.

Tonight, be still before the Lord and invite him to make his presence fully felt in you. Swim in his grace, soar in his power, and rest in his love.

Comfort Food

This is my comfort in my affliction,
that your promise gives me life.

PSALM 119:50 ESV

What is your favorite comfort food? Mashed potatoes and gravy? Chicken soup? Ice cream? What is it about a particular meal that gives you feelings of safety or relief? Is it the food itself, or the memories attached to it?

Better than the ultimate comfort food are the Lord's soft and strong arms. His embrace is warm and secure. He has loved, comforted and carried you through a lifetime of memories. Even the comfort we get from our go-to dishes is really from him. It is he who gave us the senses to appreciate the tastes, textures, and temperatures that bring us pleasure, relief, and peace.

Father God, I feel almost silly for turning to comfort food when your arms are so near. The fleeting relief I get from a bowl of ice cream can't possibly compare to the lasting comfort of knowing you hold my life in your hands and count it precious. Thank you for giving me tiny glimpses of your warmth, security, and permanence. thank you all the more for being the true source of all the comfort I'll ever need.

My comfort in my suffering is this:
your promise preserves my life.

PSALM 119:50 NIV

God provides many sources of comfort. Wise words from our mothers are words he gives them, delivered with a tenderness born of his own. It is he who gives our fathers the gentleness and strength to hold us just how we need to be held. God himself inspires the compassion and generosity of a friend who meets us in our need. The words of the Bible, vast in their capacity to comfort and instruct, are words he breathed into being.

Beyond the comfort he generously bestows, God also gives us life-preserving promises. What better example is there than his offer of eternal life through his saving grace?

God, your comfort is everywhere! I never lack for sources of consolation. Thank you for the people you send to love me, the wisdom embedded in your Word, and the constant comfort of communion with you. Your promises, provision, and peace are perfect, Father.

What are three places you turn for comfort? Can you see the Lord's hand in each one?

Yet I Rejoice

Even though the fig trees have no blossoms, and there are no grapes on the vines; even though the olive crop fails, and the fields lie empty and barren; even though the flocks die in the fields, and the cattle barns are empty, yet I will rejoice in the LORD! I will be joyful in the God of my salvation!

HABAKKUK 3:17-18 NLT

Life is full of disappointments, and sometimes there are seasons when nothing goes your way. You may have an illness that you are still battling, you might have lost a job, or seen your children go through some hard times. You could replace this Scripture with your own words of sorrow. The difference between you and those who do not have Jesus, is that you have an internal peace and joy that goes beyond your circumstances.

You may be unwell, but you can still be grateful, you may have gone through hardships, but you still believe in God's provision. You may have lost much, but know that your treasure is in heaven. There is a lot to rejoice in the Lord for. May your life today be a witness of the hope of Christ within you.

Jesus, thank you so much for the salvation that you freely gave to me. I choose today to be joyful in the God of my salvation.

The Sovereign LORD is my strength!
He makes me as surefooted as a deer,
able to tread upon the heights.

HABAKKUK 3:19 NLT

A deer is a beautifully swift animal, able to navigate the toughest of terrains. This is our testament as his children—that even when things get steep and tricky, he makes our feet swift and nimble, giving us strength and surety as we walk through the hardships into the successful heights of the mountaintops.

Whether you are trying to navigate those difficult times, or have reached a mountaintop, praise the God who gives you strength and skill.

God, thank you so much for being my strength and giving my feet a sure place to land every time I need your help. I praise you for helping me through and bringing me to mountaintops.

Are you trying to walk through some difficult and intense times right now, or are you able to testify to the strength that God has given you to reach the other side?

Thank the Lord

Let us be thankful, because we have a kingdom that cannot be shaken. We should worship God in a way that pleases him with respect and fear,

HEBREWS 12:28 NCV

Thank the Lord. As preparations for another Christmas reach their peak, pause. No matter how many moments you have already taken to stop and remember why we feast, exchange gifts, and gather, take another one now. We are commemorating God's decision to be born as an infant and live the human experience for himself. Already perfect, he was moved by a desire to have even more empathy for us.

Imagine how his love grew for mothers as he was held in Mary's arms. Imagine the depth of his compassion for those who are persecuted after his family fled to Egypt. As he fasted, think of how his heart broke for the hungry. All-powerful, almighty, and entirely worthy, he humbled himself for us. Thank the Lord.

God, My words are so inadequate, my praise so small. Focused on the color, light, and warmth of the season, , I can lose sight of what you gave up there in heaven for me to have all these blessings on earth. Thank you, Lord! Thank you.

Since we are receiving a kingdom that cannot be shaken, let us be thankful, and so worship God acceptably with reverence and awe.

HEBREWS 12:28 NIV

Of all the gifts of the season, what can compare to the kingdom of heaven? Instead of a stocking stuffer, God is giving us a divine inheritance. In this easily-shaken, never-satisfied world, we are receiving the priceless gift of a steadfast, satiating kingdom.

Let us be thankful indeed, and let us worship him with all the reverence, awe, and love he deserves.

God, as much as I delight in receiving a thoughtfully chosen gift, your gifts are so much better! I carry your kingdom in my heart, Lord. therefore, I am unshakeable. Incomparably, you bless my life with confidence in your promises, joy in your presence, gratitude for all that you are, and a hope that cannot be taken from me.

Pause tonight and ask the Lord to fill your heart with a fresh reverence for the Christmas season and its eternal relevance.

Double Gift

This message about Jesus Christ has revealed his plan for you Gentiles, a plan kept secret from the beginning of time. But now as the prophets foretold and as the eternal God has commanded, this message is made known to all Gentiles everywhere, so that they too might believe and obey him.

ROMANS 16:25-26 NLT

It seems there's a fun-loving soul in every family who enjoys hiding a gift within a gift. They'll hide a gift card tucked inside a pair of socks or some cash where you wouldn't expect it. If the recipient goes too quickly, failing to examine and appreciate each gift, they could miss one of great value.

Hidden in Romans 16, amidst a lengthy series of greetings, is one of the most marvelous revelations in all of Scripture. We were always part of God's plan! Though the entire Old Testament is about his abiding love for Israel, his chosen people, the beautiful truth of the New Testament is this: we are all chosen, since the beginning of time!

Father God, I am so amazed by your love, and by the intricacy of your plan! As deep as your love for Israel, as powerful as your connection to Moses, as eternal as your covenant with Abraham, so too is your desire for me. Thank you for choosing me, loving me, and planning all along to call me yours.

The message about Christ is the secret that was hidden for long ages past but is now made known. It has been made clear through the writings of the prophets. And by the command of the eternal God it is made known to all nations that they might believe and obey.

ROMANS 16:25-26 NCV

Why do you suppose the Lord kept his plan a secret? Consider another type of gift-giver: the secret giver. At Grandma's, as she hugs you goodbye, she slips a bill inside your hand while holding a finger to her lips to keep the exchange clandestine. How special you feel! How singled out!

Years later, you realize all the grandkids got these secret gifts. If everyone got one, why the secret? She simply wanted you to feel special and chosen, and to know you were uniquely loved.

Oh God, far beyond even a Grandmother's love, you adore us! want us each to know how much we matter, so even though you planned it all along, you let us discover your salvation, your grace, and your boundless, beautiful love for ourselves. May we honor you this Christmas by loving each of our people—and you, precious Lord—individually, openly, and completely.

Do you know someone whose love language is giving gifts? Be sure to acknowledge how loved and seen you feel by their gifts this year, and let your Father know too.

No Ordinary Miracle

"Today in the town of David a Savior has been born to you;
he is the Messiah, the Lord."

LUKE 2:11 NIV

Consider for a moment that the Father sent the Son into the world exactly as we enter it: vulnerable, helpless, and small. Not wanting to miss a moment of what it means to be human, to feel as we feel, the Lord empathetically arrived the hard way. He started out tiny, knowing nothing except the sound of his mother's voice and the warmth of her body.

May our remembrance of Jesus' youth and vulnerability soften our hearts toward little ones, giving us more patience for their questions and more delight in their silliness. May our awareness of the loneliness, rejection, and loss he endured open our hearts to the wounded, inviting them into healing and light. May our understanding of patience with which he awaited his purpose increase our hope as we wait for ours.

God, I'm so touched by the picture of your humanity, and so moved by your helplessness and fragility on those first days of your life. Inspire me, Jesus, to reach out to the helpless and fragile. Thank you for your humanity, Lord; I pray my awareness of it increases mine.

"There is born to you this day in the city of David a Savior, who is Christ the Lord."

LUKE 2:11 NKJV

Local news shows will often do a short feature on Christmas babies: those sweet, little ones born on the day we honor our Lord's birth. Born on any other day, no particular fanfare would accompany their entrance. Yet, because we have made Christ's birthday such an important day on the calendar, these babies get some special attention.

Now picture the scene long ago, as shepherds followed a glorious light and the instructions of the angels to the birthplace of the original Christmas baby. Imagine their delight as they gazed upon what would be an ordinary miracle on any other day but knowing in their hearts there was nothing ordinary about this child and sensing the world would never be the same.

Jesus, through the ordinary miracle of birth, you came to save the ordinary and the exceptional alike. Already having left heaven, you who are most exceptional became ordinary too. May I never take your sacrifice for granted, Lord. There was nothing ordinary about it.

Ponder the image of Jesus as a tiny, helpless baby. Imagine the astounding joy of holding him in your arms.

Just Go

He said, "Come." And when Peter had come down out of the boat,
he walked on the water to go to Jesus.

MATTHEW 14:29 NKJV

Peter walked on the water. Simply because he obeyed Jesus,
Peter did something otherwise impossible. The verse doesn't
say Jesus turned the water to ice, or that he made a bridge, or
that Peter levitated. It says Peter walked on the water.

Why do we limit ourselves, and the Lord? That impossible
thing he's calling you to, the one you can't stop thinking
about? Go. When you know it is from Lord, then you also you
know the Lord is with you. Fix your eyes on him, place your
faith in him, and go. Don't get bogged down worrying about
timing or other practicalities, just go.

I'm coming, Jesus! Wherever you call me, I'm coming. I won't
wait for you to make it convenient; I won't resist until you make
it comfortable. Your voice—your presence—is enough for me. Your
invitation is all the courage, possibility, and belief I need.

He said, "Come." So Peter got out of the boat, started walking on the water, and came toward Jesus.

MATTHEW 14:29 NRSV

Do you remember what happens in the verses after this one? Peter takes his eyes off Jesus. He looks at the waves, absorbs the impossibility of what is happening, and he panics. His faith shaken, he begins to sink and cries out, "Save me, Lord!" Peter no longer able to stand on the sea, Jesus gives him his hand.

"Why did you doubt me?" Jesus asks. And in this question, Peter hears the subtext. You were doing it! You were almost there. Why did you allow your fear to keep you from getting to me? Indeed, why do we?

God, with all my attention on you, fear is forgotten. I see love, possibilities, and you. Only when I shift my gaze away from you does doubt creep in. When I start questioning everything, I immediately start sinking. Jesus, take my chin, hold my gaze, and remind me anything is possible. Show me where I am. Show me I'm already doing it. I'm almost there.

Where is Jesus inviting you to join him? Ask the Holy Spirit for the courage to just go.

Your Names

> "A child has been born to us; God has given a son to us. He will
> be responsible for leading the people. His name will be Wonderful
> Counselor, Powerful God, Father Who Lives Forever, Prince of Peace."

ISAIAH 9:6 NCV

Reading the powerful words of the prophet Isaiah, written
so many generations before the night in Bethlehem that we
honor tonight, the magnificence and intricacy God's plan is
on full display. The patience, the passion, and the beautiful,
redeeming purpose of it all are simply breathtaking. Through
the foretelling of Christ's birth, along with so much more of
his amazing life, God reminds us all his promises are true.

However, wherever, and with whomever you gather to
celebrate and honor him, leave room for awe. Invite the
Wonderful Counselor to advise you, the Powerful God to help
and strengthen you, the Father Who Lives Forever to give you a
glimpse of eternity, and the Prince of Peace to still your heart.

*Awesome God, in all your names and in all three persons, you
are holy. I worship the Father who planned the world, the Son
who came to save it, and the Spirit who lives in me and helps me
comprehend it all. Thank you, God, for all you are and all you
have done.*

> *"Unto us a Child is born, unto us a Son is given;*
> *and the government will be upon His shoulder.*
> *And His name will be called Wonderful, Counselor,*
> *Mighty God, Everlasting Father, Prince of Peace."*
>
> ISAIAH 9:6 NKJV

As we consider each of the names of Jesus that were revealed to Isaiah, ask God to reveal more of himself to you.

Wonderful. The Lord performed many miracles and wonders, things the world has never seen. Counselor. His wisdom was infallible, leading always to love and reconciliation. Mighty God. Able to wither trees and quiet a raging sea, Jesus' voice contained all the power of heaven. Everlasting Father. Through his resurrection, Jesus reigns forever with—and as— our God. Prince of Peace. Through his Spirit, our hearts can rest, now and forever, on the truth of his love for us.

Jesus, how I love your names! all the names you go by, and all the incredible things you have done and continue to do, are cause for praise. I especially want to honor your sacrifice in leaving heaven, becoming human, and all that followed. As helpless babe and as Mighty God, you have my heart.

Meditate on Isaiah's words. Which name of Christ speaks most to you tonight?

Hurled into the Sea

"You hurled me into the depths, into the very heart of the seas, and the currents swirled about me; all your waves and breakers swept over me. I said, 'I have been banished from your sight; yet I will look again toward your holy temple.'"

JONAH 2:3-4 NIV

It doesn't matter whether you feel like you are drowning because you have intentionally walked away from God or whether circumstances have simply overwhelmed you. Expressing how you feel about being distant from God or grace is important.

If you feel like this today, tell God. In the same way that you express your sorrow, be intentional about directing your words and heart toward God. Look toward his holy temple, not away from it. God is near and will answer your cries.

God, at times I do feel like I am drowning. I feel stressed or anxious about everything that I have to get done today. Although I may feel distant from you, I choose to look toward you and trust you for answers.

"The engulfing waters threatened me, the deep surrounded me; seaweed was wrapped around my head. To the roots of the mountains I sank down; the earth beneath barred me in forever. But you, LORD my God, brought my life up from the pit."

JONAH 2:5-6 NIV

You can probably remember times in your life where you felt like you hit rock bottom. Perhaps today has been one of those days you didn't feel like you could sink any lower. We all have those days, or those seasons, in our lives and they can feel lonely, desperate, and discouraging.

Think of Jonah tonight and how he must have felt. There are people throughout history and there are people right now who have been in the deepest of pits—you are not alone. Let your life be a testimony that God does indeed bring you out of the pit. Rejoice in the fact that God will always rescue his children.

God, as I reflect tonight on those low points in my life, I know that you were with me, hearing my cries for help. Thank you for providing a way out and being my strength and source of life while I was going through it. May I always testify to your mercy and help.

Do you remember the moments when God has lifted you from those pits of life? Rejoice and praise him for those times.

As I Wait

It is not yet time for the message to come true, but that time is coming soon; the message will come true. It may seem like a long time, but be patient and wait for it, because it will surely come; it will not be delayed.

HABAKKUK 2:3 NCV

God's timing is perfect. We know this, and we believe it, don't we? We embrace this truth wholeheartedly—right up to the point where it conflicts with our own timing. Then we doubt. We question. We wonder. What's he doing? What's taking so long? Eventually, we see the wisdom and we are grateful. A missed opportunity leads to a better one. A missed traffic light avoids an accident.

Although the Lord loves a dramatic moment, he also enjoys subtlety. He invites us, as we are waiting, to slow down and look around. Little shots of humor, bits of beauty, and glimpses of grace are everywhere, keeping us company as we wait.

Precious God, your timing is always better than mine. I know this, though sometimes I forget. Thank you for proving, in ways both big and small, that you, the Father of time, know exactly what you are doing, and when you will do it.

Still the vision awaits its appointed time; it hastens to the end—
it will not lie. If it seems slow, wait for it; it will surely come;
it will not delay.

HABAKKUK 2:3 ESV

Does staring at the clock make waiting better? Waiting is a part of life, but we aren't called to stop everything we ought to be doing while we wait. Let us be sure to live while we wait for the Lord to fulfill his promises, both to us and the world. Read books, run races, play in waves, make babies, and bake bread.

The minutes will pass sixty seconds at a time whether we are watching on the clock or not. The Lord will make sure everything happens in just the right time, so we may as well leave the timing up to him and focus on living.

I believe you, God, and I trust your timing. Help me remember to live as I wait. Show me the beauty of the minutes themselves, lest I get caught up in counting them as they pass. Distract me, God, with beauty, with love, and with meaning, while I wait.

Is there an area where surrendering to the Lord's wisdom and perfect timing would bring peace to your life?

Lawmaker and Judge

There is only one true Lawgiver and Judge,
the One who has the power to save and destroy—
so who do you think you are to judge your neighbor?

JAMES 4:12 TPT

Let's take a moment and read that question again. Any time it's asked, it's a sign we've probably overstepped. There will always be people—in every religion, every country, and every culture—who disapprove of others. Let's do all we can to make sure we are not those people.

We know the Judge. We know he is merciful, gracious, and loving. We know that repentance moves him to forgiveness; remorse to compassion. We know he wants his heavenly home filled to overflowing with the redeemed, so who are we to block the entrance?

Father, forgive me for thinking that I know what is in someone's heart, and what is between you and them. Forgive me for thinking the grace given me is only available to me. Who do I think I am? Remind me, God, that I am yours, and that you decided it would be so. As someone who has benefitted by your awesome mercy, may I never wish it withheld from anyone you call your child.

> *God is the only Lawmaker and Judge.*
> *He is the only One who can save and destroy.*
> *So it is not right for you to judge your neighbor.*

JAMES 4:12 NCV

We may, at times, feel ourselves sinking in the quicksand of public opinion. Whether we've been misunderstood, or the chastisement from the masses is completely deserved, may we remember how very little it matters what others think of us. Just as we should not judge others, others should not judge us. If they do, they are acting in error, and we should brush their words and opinions aside.

Only God defines who we are and decides where we are going.

Father God, I pray for you to help me withstand and ignore the judgements of others. I pray their words will not sway, change, or hurt me, because only your decision stands. Only your opinion matters. If I need conviction, I trust it to come from you. Only you know my heart, God, and only you can change it. I trust it to your keeping. and submit it to your judgement.

Do you battle more with judging, or being judged? Invite the Spirit to speak to your heart regarding both.

Amen

Blessed be the LORD forever.
Amen and Amen.

PSALM 89:52 NRSV

As you say goodbye to another calendar year, it's a wonderful time to reflect on all the ways the Lord has met you during the past 365 days. How many times have you benefitted from his grace, been delivered by his healing, or been awed by his displays of beauty and glory? What sadness and struggles did you walk through together? What surprises and delights?

How have you grown and changed? What new things has he shown you about himself, within his Word? What more have you learned about purpose? What dreams do you have for the next year? What hopeful anticipation is stirring your heart? Pour it all out to him, in honor and praise.

Father God, I love looking back and seeing your incredible faithfulness. What a year it's been, filled with growth and with grace. All my praise is for you, God, as I recall the thousands of ways you are beautiful. Thank you for teaching me, for leading me, and for loving me.

Blessed be the LORD forever!
Amen and Amen.

PSALM 89:52 NASB

Are you familiar with the meaning of the word, amen? It's more than just a punctuation mark at the end of a prayer or something that means, "I'm done now." Amen is best translated as "so be it," or "let it be so."

When we say amen, we are saying we believe him, we trust him, and we surrender to his will. What a wonderful way to end a year, and begin another, with a humble, hopeful amen!

Precious God, looking back on this year, I recall prayers answered just as I petitioned, and others answered in a way that was immeasurably better. Thank you for providing what I needed over what I thought I wanted. I can also think of answers I am still waiting for. This fills me with such excitement and hope. I can't wait to see how you respond. I trust your wisdom, God, and I rely on your perfect timing.

When you reflect on your year, notice the ways your relationship with the Lord has deepened? Where has he shown himself most faithful? Where did you most benefit from his grace? May God bless you beyond all measure in the year to come. Amen.